AF529713

ENTREPRENEURIAL TRAINING
Theory and Practice

ENTREPRENEURIAL TRAINING
Theory and Practice

Edited by
S. Kaliyamoorthy
K. Chandrasekar

KANISHKA PUBLISHERS, DISTRIBUTORS
NEW DELHI-110 002

KANISHKA PUBLISHERS, DISTRIBUTORS
4697/5-21 A, Ansari Road, Daryaganj
New Delhi-110 002
Phones : 2327 0497, 2328 8285
Fax : 011-2328 8285
e-mail: kanishka_publishing@yahoo.co.in

First Published 2007

© Editors

ISBN 978-81-7391-989-3

PRINTED IN INDIA

Published by Madan Sachdeva for Kanishka Publishers, Distributors, 4697/5-21A, Ansari Road, Daryaganj, New Delhi-110 002, Typeset by Sunshine Graphics, Delhi, and Printed at Nice Printing Press, Delhi.

Preface

Alagappa University is the First University in the nation to establish EDCs at all its affiliated colleges. With the launching of the EDCs at Alagappa University by the Hon'ble Education Minister of State of Tamil Nadu, Entrepreneurship Development Cells have been established in 23 colleges affiliated to the University. Two Nodal officers are appointed from each college to coordinate the activities of EDCs. The Entrepreneurship and Management Development Cell of Alagappa Institute of Management and Centre for Entrepreneurship Development (CED), Madurai jointly hosted a Training of Trainers programme to all the Nodal officers from the affiliated colleges, to train them with regard to organizing of Entrepreneurship Awareness Camps at their colleges.

Alagappa Institute of Management has not thought of stopping with that initiative alone, but also to endeavour into the field of researching the trend and changes that has occurred in the Entrepreneurial training and seeks to arrive at some concrete solutions to face the challenges in entrepreneurial training. It is with this scope in mind that the foundation for the seminar on 'Trends and Challenges in Entrepreneurial Training' was laid down at the Institute.

The main aim behind this Seminar was to bring out the problems existing in the present EDPs, to highlight the changes in Entrepreneurial Training Methods, to bring out the strategies to provide value-based services to the potential Entrepreneurs, to forecast the future trends in Entrepreneurship, and to collect the views of experts on the Entrepreneurial Training.

The world is challenged with innumerable impediments characterized as social backwardness, unemployment, poor standard of living and fair competition. It is high time for everyone to fight against these evils. Entrepreneurship development uniquely strives towards achieving excellence in all the above mentioned areas.

This has created a special significance on building entrepreneurial culture in the young minds to make the future peaceful. To achieve this development, what is required are the efficient Entrepreneurial training programmes, which will be useful in creating a positive impact. Today, there have emerged plenty of institutions to impart these training. But, in this changing environment, it is essential to analyse the effectiveness of these programmes towards it goal-fulfillment. This Seminar is proposed to be organised to highlight the problems in conducting such training programmes and to evolve new techniques in performing the programmes to the need.

The Seminar was focused to those who are involved in the field of Entrepreneurship Promotion and Training. Persons from Academia like Faculty and Research Scholars, Industry, and Institutions for Entrepreneurship, found the Seminar of great utility to them. Opportunities were open to the potential Entrepreneurs and Young entrepreneurs.

The main highlight of the programme was that Experts from various established Institutions like Entrepreneurship Development of Institute of India (EDII), Science and Technology Entrepreneurs Park (STEP-TREC), Small Industries Service Institute (SISI), etc., on entrepreneurship put across their views on the topics of discussion during the Seminar. Experts from Industry gave value addition to the Seminar.

Research Papers on the Theme of **"Changing Needs in Entrepreneurial Training"**, based on the objectives of the Seminar were discussed at length during the Seminar and has contributed several feasible outcomes on the theme, to be implemented towards the objectives of the seminar. This text provides a collection of the best papers selected through blind review of several experts from among the 112 papers received for the programme. It is felt that the text would provide immense valuable inputs to the professors of various universities, researchers and to those Institutions involved in the process of training the Entrepreneurs, considered to be the noblest act contributing to the economic development of the nation.

Editors

Contents

PART—II
Challenges and Opportunities in Entrepreneurial Training

PART—III

Performance Evaluation of Entrepreneurial Training Institutions

List of Contributors

Dr. S. Kaliyamoorthy, Professor and Director, Alagappa Institute of Management, Alagappa University, Karaikudi.

Mr. K. Chandrasekar, Lecturer, Department of Educational Management, National Institute of Technical Teachers' Training and Research (NITTTR), Chennai.

Mr. S. Prem Kumar, Senior Lecturer in Management Studies, Kumaraguru College of Technology, Coimbatore.

Mr. G. Nallavan, Asst. Professor, Department of Electrical Engineering, Panimalar Engineering College, Chennai.

Dr. S. David Amirtha Rajan, PG Head, Department of Commerce, The American College, Madurai.

Dr. Mrs. P. Gnana Soundari, Reader in Economics, Lady Doak College, Madurai.

Prof. M.D. Manoharan, Principal/Director, Department of MBA.

Mr. K.R. Srinivasan, Lecturer in MBA Sourashtra College, Madurai.

Dr. Ayub Khan Dawood, Reader, P.G. Department of Commerce, Quaide Milleth College, Medavakkam, Chennai.

Mr. Mu. Subrahmanian, Senior Lecturer, SRM School of Management, SRM Institute of Science and Technology, Deemed University, Chennai.

Dr. M. Jeyarathnam, Professor, KLN Engineering College, Madurai.

Dr. T. Ramasamy, Department of Management Studies, Government Arts College, Paramakudi.

Ms. K. Leelavathy, Lecturer in Commerce, D.R.B.C.C.C. Hindu College, Chennai.

Ms. S. Subadra, Lecturer in Commerce, Trinity College for Women, Namakkal.

Mr. V. Ramesh Kumar and Mr. M. Vinod, Lecturer, Sri Muthukumaran Institute of Technology, Chennai.

Mr. P. S. Nagarajan, Lecturer, National Institute of Management Studies, Chennai.

Mr. E. Josam Titus, Mr. S.R. John Jebaraj and Mr. M. Sivagnanasundarm, Faculty, Management Studies,Mepco Schlenk Engineering College, Sivakasi.

Mr. G. Muruganantham, Lecturer, Management Studies, Sri Muthukumaran Institute of Technology, Chennai.

Mr. M. Viswanathan and Mr. P.T. Vijaya Raja Kumar, Research Associates, Alagappa Institute of Management, Alagappa University, Karaikudi.

Dr. M. Abul Hasan Sathali, Quaide Milleth College, Medavakkam, Chennai.

Prof. A.C. Anbudevi , Lecturer, Economics Department, Sourashtra College, Madurai.

Dr. G. Jayabal, Reader in Management, Alagappa University, Karaikudi.

Mr. G. Prabakaran, Senior Lecturer, PMP Arts and Science College, Dharmapuri.

Dr. V. Saikumari, Senior Lecturer, Department of Management Studies, Sathyabama Institute of Science and Technology, Chennai.

Mr. S.A.Vijayaraj, Senior Lecturer, Department of Management Studies, Jeppiaar Engineering College, Chennai.

Prof. A.M. Suresh, Head of Department–MBA, Post Graduate Department of Management Studies, Dayananda Sagar College of Management and Information Technology, Bangalore.

Ms. M.A. Vijaya, Lecturer, Department of Management Studies, GRD Institute of Management, Dr. GR. Damodaran College of Science, Coimbatore.

Dr. Mrs. K. Indumathi, Professor, Department of Psychology, PSG College of Arts and Science, Coimbatore.

Mrs. H. Rashmi and Ms. Subraja, Lecturer, MSNM Besant Institute of Post Graduate Studies, Mangalore .

Dr. P. Natarajan, Reader, Department of International Business and Commerce Alagappa University, Karaikudi.

Mrs. K. Thirumamagal, Ph.D. Scholar, Department of International Business and Commerce, Alagappa University, Karaikudi.

Mrs. T. Kalpana, Lecturer in Commerce, Government Arts College for Women, Sivagangai.

Dr. C. Natarajan, Lecturer in Commerce, Directorate of Distance Education, Annamalai University, Annamalai Nagar.

Mr. S. Asok Kumar, Lecturer in Management Studies, VMRF Deemed University, Ariyanoor, Salem.

B. Rajasekaran, Lecturer (SG) and Head, Department of Commerce and Computer Applications, Park's College, Tirupur.

Dr. A. Sakunthalai, Assistant Professor, Coastal Saline Research Centre, Tamil Nadu Agriculture University, Ramanathapuram.

Mr. K. Ramakrishnan, Teaching Assistant Coastal Saline Research Centre, Tamil Nadu Agricultural University, Ramanathapuram.

Prof. C. T. Sam Luther, Head, Department of Management Studies, Nesamony Memorial Christian College, Marthandam.

Dr. M. Ezhilarasan, Reader, Thiagarajar College of Arts, Madurai.

Mrs. M. Selvalakshmi, Thiagarajar School of Management, Thirupparankundram, Madurai.

Mr. R. Ayyamperumal, Lecturer in Management Studies, VHNSN College, Virudhunagar.

1
Entrepreneurial Training–An Overview

Mr. K. Chandrasekar and Dr. S. Kaliyamoorthy

"The important thing is not being afraid to take a chance. Remember, the greatest failure is to not try. Once you find something you love to do, be the best at doing it." – Debbi Fields, founder of Mrs. Fields Cookies

'Are Entrepreneurs Born or Made?'

The answer for the question is based on the grooming of the entrepreneurs. Certainly, most of us would accept that entrepreneurs are being made, since no one comes forward to start his enterprise on his own. Though we might have come across a few born-entrepreneurs we cannot conclude that these entrepreneurs have inbuilt skills of entrepreneurship in them due to birth. The so-called born-entrepreneurs are often believed to have acquired their entrepreneurial skills through their education or else through other means of training. Hence, both the born-entrepreneurs and the made-entrepreneurs have made the training of entrepreneurs as an essential need in the life of entrepreneurs. Adequate training and development has become the necessity for a qualified individual to think about the establishment of his enterprise.

The world is challenged with innumerable impediments characterized as social backwardness, unemployment, poor standard of living and fair competition. It is high time for everyone to fight against these evils. Entrepreneurship development uniquely strives towards achieving excellence in all the above mentioned areas.

This has created a special significance on building entrepreneurial culture in the young minds to make the future peaceful. To achieve this development, what is required are the efficient Entrepreneurial training programmes, which will be useful in creating a positive impact. Today, there have emerged plenty of institutions to impart these training. But, in this changing environment, it is essential to analyse the effectiveness of these programmes towards it goal-fulfillment.

Let us go through the words of the Prime person of our Nation in this regard.

"I would like to share two observations relevant to today's people. When you look at small children, they are always smiling. When they start going to primary school and carry a big bag on their shoulders, the smile reduces. When they reach the secondary school, the smile further reduces. During higher secondary course, the smile virtually vanishes. When they enter college, they become more serious and after completing the college they are in a state of big worry. Simultaneously, during this period, the concerns of what is in store next linking financial situations and the competitiveness involved in entering into the specific field dominates the mind of the children and parents. This is the situation which we all have to overcome. Can we make an education system, which will retain the smile on the faces of our children right through the period of their education till they take up a job as they start attending the school? Is it possible? This can come if we make the education system creative throughout and provide full employment opportunity to all the youth based on their aptitude. This creativity can come by reducing the theoretical burden in the primary level, progressively increasing the theory in the secondary and finally leading to higher level teaching and create self-reliance among individuals to undertake entrepreneurship and be an employment generator rather than employment seeker." – ***President of India, Dr. A.P.J. Abdul Kalam***

Today the world and nation are seeing an expeditious change from the era of seeking employment to the noble environment of providing employment. But, the one crucial issue remaining unanswered is the above question, for which still reasoning are going on among various experts. Of course, one important view to be remembered is that, most of the emerging entrepreneurs are totally new to the field and have not experienced these skills earlier in their childhood. There is also a contention that the entrepreneurs are reared from their childhood itself to achieve something big, which leads them to start an enterprise. But that may be a meagre portion of a pie, wherein the remaining consisting of the different entrepreneurial skills is contributed by what is popularly known as Entrepreneurial Training Programmes.

As stated by all, India is a developing country, which strives its mighty to achieve economic self-reliance in all fields, by way of efficient utilization of its available resources. To be proudly affirmed, India has chosen the right strategy to achieve its economic excellence, i.e., through Entrepreneurship. This is well marked by the nearly 800 Institutions established all over the nation by the government, NGOs, and Corporates with the foremost intention to create the next generation Entrepreneurs and to train them adequately.

Entrepreneurship Development Training Programmes are organized at different places by the various Institutions, all through the calendar days, with an ulterior motive to cover up larger target segment. Thus Entrepreneurship Development Programmes (EDPs) are conducted with the aim to identify, select, train and motivate potential entrepreneurs so that they can become job creators instead of job seekers, and to utilise developed human resources in the right direction for generating self-employment and employment opportunities for others.

Good entrepreneur can create a healthy economy of a country. Entrepreneurship development is a very important catalyst in context of the rapid growth of small and medium industries in a country. The efficient performance of this sub-sector is dependent on effective utilization of man, machine and materials and human factor plays more important role as compared to machine and tools. Hence continuous effort for entrepreneurship development in the Small and Medium Enterprise (SME) sector is essential for effective utilization of the human resources. For creation of new SME and for operating these enterprises successfully, development of entrepreneurship is a recognized pre requisite and this target can be achieved only through systematic training programme.

The objective of entrepreneurship development training programme is to develop entrepreneurial traits of entrepreneurs for motivating and enabling them to create new industries in the country and enhancing capabilities to manage their enterprise efficiently. The broad objectives of the EDP are as follows:

- To create entrepreneurial awareness to the young generation and motivate them to establish small and medium enterprises.
- To trained up the prospective new and young entrepreneurs to maintain and run their enterprises successfully.
- To enabling the entrepreneurs about the global production and market strategy in context of market economy.
- To encourage the entrepreneurs to establish pollution free SMEs.

For setting up an industrial enterprise, the essential quality required of an individual is entrepreneurship. This quality can be developed through training to enhance capability of an individual to acquire knowledge and skill for identifying and selecting their own projects. They will also be able to prepare project proposals for their enterprises. The training programme will improve personal traits, enhance competencies and managerial capabilities of entrepreneurs enabling them to invite, maintain and run an enterprise/business successfully.

The hidden side of these EDPs is that whether they are able to cater to the right needs of the right segment. The resulting answer to this issue is critical to be noted. It has been found by analysis that the success rate of EDPs in our country is only around 24 per cent, which has been proved through various studies conducted by different institutions in various places. Why is it so? What are the reasons behind it? What can be done to improve it? Trying to find out the answers to the above questions will give a clear picture of the present trend of EDPs and the challenges to be faced by them in the future.

This has necessitated many institutions and organizations to look for strategic options to improve the value addition of the Training programmes. It is a well known fact that the world has turned out to be competitive in all aspects. Hence the Entrepreneurship Development Institutions has also to face the challenges ahead of them in providing efficient training to the future generation entrepreneurs, which will cater to their needs and serve their purpose. It is with this main objective, that many of the Entrepreneurship Development Institutions in the nation have began to organize variety of programmes like Seminars, Workshops, Conferences and the like, for the Trainers, Faculty, and also to the potential and existing Entrepreneurs.

Proclaimed to be the most economically sound nation among the Developing countries, and the one of the richest Asian Countries, India's present ideology is to develop its strong industrial base joining together the hands of the entrepreneurs in the country. Entrepreneurs have been playing a significant role in the development of the country, not only now, but from the beginning of the 18th century itself. Though the theoretical concept of entrepreneurship has seen its emergence only during the 19th century, India boasts itself to have seen many leading entrepreneurs, which is clear from the history of the nation. It was the role of Indian traders, who are otherwise also known as entrepreneurs, which speaks in the Indian history of freedom, as the British were attracted towards India due to their flourishing business.

Ever since from then, many successful small and big entrepreneurs have taken up their initiative to contribute towards the economic development of the country. Today, we Indians can be proud to have some of the worlds leading entrepreneurs like Shri Narayanamurthy, Shri Azim Premji, Tatas, Ambanis, Sundaram Iyengar, etc.

This has created a special significance on building entrepreneurial culture in the young minds to make the future peaceful. To achieve this development, what is required are the efficient Entrepreneurial Training Programmes, which will be useful in creating a positive impact. In this changing environment, it is essential to analyse the effectiveness of these programmes towards it goal-fulfillment. Programmes are organised to highlight the problems in conducting such training programmes and to evolve new techniques in performing the programmes to the need.

Let us hope to see India as a Super Power by 2020, as dreamed by our Honourable President Dr. A.P.J. Abdul Kalam. Excellence in Action comes with the practicing of excellent strategies through excellent thinking.

PART I

The Pedagogy for Entrepreneurial Training

2

Changes Ahead of Using New Pedagogical Tools for EDP

Mr. K. Chandrasekar and Dr. S. Kaliyamoorthy

Introduction

It can be said that liberalization, privatization and globalization, has opened up our economy through all corners. But the disappointing view is that, they have not encouraged to reduce the rate of unemployment in the nation. Of course, the dangerous evil threatening our economy is 'unemployment' and 'under-employment'. Measures on war-footing basis are being adapted by the nation to curtail the effects of those evils, and to prevent spreading through the generations. Among them, one notable method is by organizing Entrepreneurship Development Programme (EDP), which is targeted to promote self-employment among the qualified masses.

The philosophy of Entrepreneurship Development Programme (EDP) is based on the assumption that entrepreneurs are not only born, but can also be identified, trained and thus created. EDPs are meant to cover all types of training programmes which are imparted to the individuals, with the aim to make the trainees to acquire the necessary skills required to start-up and sustain any enterprise. Therefore, any kind of programmes, such as awareness programmes, promotional programmes and training classes are included under the meaning of EDP.

EDP–As Practiced Today

Our nation recognized the practice of organizing EDPs, late in the 1970's, after the popular Kakinada experiment by David McClelland on entrepreneurial motivation. EDPs in India gained momentum only during 1990s, when there was a staunch need for eliminating unemployment. Thus EDPs are conducted with the aim to identify, select, train and motivate potential entrepreneurs so that they can become job creators instead of job seekers, and to utilise developed human resources in the right direction for generating self-employment and employment opportunities for others.

EDPs in our nation are categorized as Awareness Training Programmes, Entrepreneurial Training Programmes and Industrial Training Programmes.

- Awareness programmes, are organized to create awareness and to explain the merits in going for entrepreneurship, which targets the freshly qualified individuals.
- Entrepreneurial training programmes are meant to train and motivate potential entrepreneurs to make them utilise their skills towards create and establish new enterprises.
- Industrial training programmes target the existing entrepreneurs to provide industry specific training, to assist the entrepreneurs to improve in the areas of product development and technology developments.

In all these categories of EDPs, information is given through various media about the programme and the participants or the trainees are selected based on their application made. Schedule is prepared for various sessions for the programme and all other preliminary works are done.

During the programme, inputs are given on different areas relating to establishment of new enterprise. Various resource persons are invited to deal with their specific expertise to the participants. The EDP gives information regarding financial sources, government norms and regulations, legal rules, and about the incentives or subsidies for entrepreneurs.

Need of the Hour

It has been found by analysis that the success rate of EDPs in our country is only around 24 per cent, which has been proved through various studies conducted by different institutions in various places. Why is it so? What are the reasons behind it? What can be done to improve it? Trying to find out the answers to the above questions will give a clear picture of the present trend of EDPs and the challenges to be faced by them in the future.

Table–2.1
Performance of EDPs

Description	*Number*	*Percentage*
Study Coverage		
1. EDPs covered	145	25
2. EDP Trainees covered	1295	30
3. Trainees Interviewed	865	66.8
Performance Level of EDPs		
1. No. of Units set-up by the EDP trainees	277	21.4
2. Trainees actively under process	78	6
3. Trainees blocked under process	129	9.9
4. Trainees who gave-up	381	29.4
5. Non-traceable trainees	146	11.3
6. Start-ups among non-available trainees	59	4.6
7. Non-start-ups among non-available trainees	225	17.4
8. Actual start-ups rate	336	25.9
9. Expected final start-ups rate	414	31.9

Source: Dinesh N. Awasthi, *Evaluation of EDPs*, Sage Publications, 2003.

Today, almost every Entrepreneur Development Institutions organize EDPs around the year for different participants. These EDPs do not suffice the complete need of the potential entrepreneurs, to make them to establish their new enterprise.

EDPs are just another form of training, replicating the usual lecture classes in any educational institutions. A schedule is prepared for the days of the training programme, and different resource persons are fixed for each session. The resource persons just try to inculcate the various information relating to the establishment of a new enterprise, by the traditional way of lecturing and using some visual aids. Table 2.1 depicts the poor performance level of the EDPs in our country, which is revealed through a study conducted by the EDII, Ahmedabad, during 1998-2002. The study was focused on about 600 EDPs organized all over the country.

Some resource persons do rarely utilize the techniques of involving the participants in few analytical exercises such as management games, role plays and case discussion. But the ultimate failure in this segment is that, only few or a part of the participants are made to involve in this exercises. This may be due to reasons of time and facility inadequacy, unwillingness of the participants, redundant methods, etc.

Hence there is a strong-felt need for some new and strategically applicable methods of training, which brings out the real inner-quotient of the potential entrepreneurs. EDPs should be such that it explores the entrepreneur's inner hidden skills and abilities, and not try to inculcate or impart the skills required to become the entrepreneurs.

Strategic Process – New Pedagogical Tools

To meet out changing trends in EDPs, experts and institutions are trying to come out with new tools to equip the entrepreneurs of today with highly competitive skills. Some of these tools have been discussed in the forthcoming paragraphs.

Case Studies

Though, this has been a widely practiced and accepted tool in every development training programmes, in the case of EDPs, it has seen a very little interference as an effective tool. Case studies, in some EDPs are meant for a group which will analyse and discuss the case in the programme, wherein other participants listen to that calmly. This is not the right way. When there is a case study analysis to be done, the subject matter of the case should be provided to all the participants or to all the groups, beforehand and they should be requested to analyse the case indepth. When the participants re-assemble for the next session, they should be asked to give their individuals views and the discussion should be promoted for the different views putforth. It is simply said that, when there is a case analysis, there will not be any final solution. This method tries to bring out or understand the analytical ability and problem solving skills of the entrepreneurs.

Group Exercises

Group exercises are meant to make the trainees to work together among groups. This tool gives an opportunity to expose the team-building ability, leadership skills, cooperation and trust-building abilities of the entrepreneurs. Under this tool, the trainees will be partitioned into various groups, which contain people of different skills and talents.

Simulation Exercises

The entrepreneurs are required to act accordingly in the simulated situation. Most generally, a future business environment is developed artificially, to explore the possibilities of the entrepreneur's actions in such a situation. This makes the entrepreneurs to understand the various environments prevailing around him and the strategy to be followed in tackling the different problems.

Short-term Project

In the case of potential entrepreneurs, they are yet to develop their enterprise. Hence they can be given an opportunity to study the problem prevailing in the environment. Under this tool, the participant, i.e. the entrepreneurs, go out to various types of units and learn what and how it is carrying out its different functions. The participants may be required to submit a report of the different analysis done by them, to understand clearly about their enterprise building skills.

Model Building

Entrepreneurs often fail due to non-complying of advancement in technology. Entrepreneurs do possess the skill to develop new products or technology for their enterprise. Through model building exercise, the entrepreneurs will gain momentum in equipping their product development skills. This tool requires the entrepreneurs to come out with prototype models of few innovative products.

Brainstorming

Brainstorming is a strategic tool which can be used to evolve different useful alternatives to solve any kind of problem. In brainstorming the entrepreneurs are provided with a platform to expose their problem solving skills and to learn the decision-making process. Entrepreneurs, when they decide upon to start their own enterprise, are faced with different criticalities such as to select the best project idea, chose the ownership forms, and the like. For these problems, brainstorming stands as a single point solution to the entrepreneurs.

Field Exercises

Establishing an enterprise requires several preliminary actions to be carried out, such as, market survey, environmental analysis, feasibility studies and the like. In order to initiate the entrepreneur's capabilities, during the EDPs, they may be sent on field exercises, to conduct survey about the different factors that are required to promote new enterprises.

Online EDPs

Today, due to rapid technological advancements in telecommunications and information technology, it is made easier than ever to reach a wider target population. The dearth in the success rate of EDPs can be also accounted to the non-accessibility of these programmes to those who really are in need of it. This obstacle can be overcome with the usage of IT and telecommunications networks, which makes it possible to have Online EDPs conducted across the country.

In line with the Satellite classrooms introduced by many Universities in India, Entrepreneurship Institutions can also make it possible to conduct EDPs through Satellite channels, with the help of Video Conferencing and Internet facilities. These EDPs will be of immense utility to those potential entrepreneurs, who want to attend the EDPs, but have inability due to time and place.

In the Online EDPs, facilities should be provided for interactions with the Experts, to enable immediate information on different areas of Entrepreneurship for the participants, who view the EDPs at the remote end. Online EDPs have the added advantage of being recorded and viewed at time of convenience. Online EDPs are seen as another revolution in the field of entrepreneurial promotion, which has the viability to widen conceptually and geographically.

Changes Ahead

The ever increasing problem of unemployment in our Nation has made the Institutions and Government to look ahead for a change in the trend, which caters both the needs of the Individuals and the Nation. This search has resulted with the rendering of the importance of Entrepreneurship among the masses.

The 700 worth mentioning Institutions have taken up the noble cause of promoting entrepreneurship in the country. These institutions, shall try to adapt the new strategic methods, described above in the EDPs, which is sure to increase the success rate. Adaptation of the methods is in line with the conceptual grid as described by Randolph in his work, as shown in Table 1.2.

Table-1.2
Conceptual Grid of Learning Styles and Pedagogical Techniques

Concrete Experience

Active Experimentation (left) / *Reflective Observation* (right)

III. Active– applied	*II. Reflective – applied*
Changes in skills and attitudes Role plays Management simulation Processing discussion T-groups/encounter groups Learning diaries Field projects Management of learning groups Counselling	Changes in application Motives Applied lecture Limited discussions Cases Role plays Problem-oriented exams Programmed instruction with emphasis on skills
IV. Active–theoretical	*I. Reflective – theoretical*
Changes in understanding Focused learning groups Argumentative discussions Experiments/Research Suggested readings Analysis papers Workshops Content-oriented exams	Change in knowledge Theory lectures Required readings Handouts Programmed instruction with emphasis on concepts Theory papers

Abstract Conceptualisation

Source: Randolph and Posner, *Designing Meaningful Learning Situations in Management,* 1999.

It is highly important to have a continuous relationship with the participants who have taken the EDP. After the EDP, there should be continuous follow-ups to monitor the upcoming of the entrepreneurs, at every stage of the enterprise development. EDPs should also be an instrument to provide help to secure the required financial assistance for the needy entrepreneurs.

Conclusion

Resources are plenty at our disposal, but the rate of utilisation is negligible. The People and the Government are bringing their focus towards the optimum utilisation, leading to self-development and ultimate economic development. EDPs are a handy tool available for the Institutions, which serve for the noble cause of generating the Owners of the Tomorrow's World.

Thus EDPs should be viewed as a real 'Enterprise Building Exercise', rather than a training programme.

REFERENCES

Baumol, W. (1990). Entrepreneurship: Productive, unproductive and destructive. *Journal of Political Economy*, 98:5, 893-921.

Bygrave, W. and Hofer, C. (1991). Theorizing about entrepreneurship. *Entrepreneurship: Theory and Practice*, 16:2.

Gupta, C.B. and Srinivasan, N.P. (1998). *Entrepreneurship Development in India*, Sultan Chand & Sons, New Delhi.

Low, M. and MacMillan, I. (1988). Entrepreneurship: Past research and future challenges. *Journal of Management*, 14:2.

Russell, R.D. (1996). The emergence of entrepreneurship in Eastern Europe: A Self-organizing Perspective. *International Journal of Commerce and Management*, 6:1&2.

Schumpeter, J. (1934). *The Theory of Economic Development*. Cambridge, MA.: Harvard.

Zahra, S. and Schulte, W. (1994). International entrepreneurship: Beyond myth and folklore. *International Journal of Commerce and Management*, 4:1&2.

http://economics.about.com/od/globalizationtrade/

http:/www.ssi.nic.in/

http://www.laghu-udyog.com/

3

Cognitive Approach for Evolving Entrepreneurial Training Model

Dr. S. Kaliyamoorthy, Mr. S. Prem Kumar and Mr. G. Nallavan

Introduction

A key question in entrepreneurship research has long been "Why do some persons choose to become entrepreneurs while others do not?" Initial efforts to answer this question focused largely on the personal characteristics of entrepreneurs (Shaver & Scott, 1991). The basic premise underlying such research was simple: Entrepreneurs are different from other persons with respect to certain traits, and it is these differences that lead them to say "Yes" when opportunity arrives. Informal observation suggests that entrepreneurs are different from most other people in terms of their personal traits.

For instance, it has been—and still is—widely assumed that entrepreneurs are far above average in their willingness to take risks, their desire to excel (*i.e.,* their achievement motivation), their personal optimism, and in their powerful preference for shaping their own destiny (Hatten, 1997). But researchers could not identify clear-cut differences between entrepreneurs and other persons with respect to what seemed to be the most relevant dimensions of personality (Robert, 1997). This resulted many researchers gradually concluded that finding clear-cut differences between entrepreneurs and other persons was a difficult task (Yukl, 1994).

Some persons choose to become entrepreneurs not because they possess specific traits, but rather because they tend to think about many situations—including ones involving risk and opportunity—somewhat differently than other persons. Such a cognitive perspective has recently risen to the fore (some would say "to dominance") in psychology and other behavioural sciences, and has added greatly to the understanding of many important topics, including how we reason, form judgments, and reach decisions (Barsalou, 1996). Such knowledge can prove invaluable in understanding many aspects of entrepreneurship. This fact motivated the authors to think on entrepreneurial cognitions and work on evolving an entrepreneurial training model using cognitive approach.

Conceptual Framework

In order to be successful, all entrepreneurs must possess some sort of entrepreneurial motivation and spirit. However, high-technology entrepreneurs usually depend on the transfer of knowledge learned or created at other existing organizations. Entrepreneurial knowledge is typically transferred by the personal acquisition of the knowledge from the source organization. To acquire knowledge, an individual must have been exposed to the source of knowledge. Different knowledge development systems create different sets of capabilities which collectively build different types of competences. Different types of knowledge development systems and competences create different types of entrepreneurs (Wright, 1997).

But the basic question underlying is, do entrepreneurs really differ from other persons with respect to certain aspects of cognition? A small but growing body of research suggests that they do (Baron, in press). For instance, a recent study by Palich and Bagby (1995) found that while entrepreneurs and non-entrepreneurs did not differ in overall risk-taking propensity, they did differ in terms of how they thought about business situations: entrepreneurs tended to categorize such situations as having more strengths, opportunities, and potential for gain than did non-entrepreneurs.

Kahneman and Lovallo (1994) argued that entrepreneurs tend to adopt an "inside view," one that focuses on the current situation and reflects their personal involvement in it rather than an "outside view," one that compares the current situation dispassionately to the results obtained in past, related situations. Acquiring different competences that are essential for entrepreneurship is essential to be successful entrepreneurs. The premise that the acquisition and formation of various competencies by people may be attributed to the processes and experiences they go through in life, such as schooling and training. Business knowledge and skills is one of these competencies.

Business Skills Cognition can be viewed in five broad business dimensions, namely, Business Growth and Diversification (BGD), Risk Aversion and Financing (RAF), Business Promotion and Marketing (BPM), Business Documentation (BD) and Pricing, Organization and Supervision (POS). These dimensions ensure that all the major aspects of business behaviour and practice are exhaustively covered for completeness (Bosire, 2003).

There is a greater need for definitional development so as to understand how entrepreneurs think and make decisions. The term 'entrepreneurial cognitions' consists of two different terms. For arriving the combined meaning of these two terms, the domain of each term is considered and defined separately.

Entrepreneurship

Entrepreneurship is the process of opportunity recognition and implementation. It often begins with a vision or idea for a product or process coupled with a passion or zeal to make that idea a reality. Hence, entrepreneurship is fundamentally less about technical skills than about people and their passions and it is a lot more about inner drive than outward trappings and appearances (Johnsrud, 1991).

The point is that entrepreneurship is usually about very determined people, people who make their own circumstances and break and succeed. If entrepreneurship is fundamentally about people and ideas, then the question arises is, 'what is business?'. Johnsrud (1997) simply states that a business is an organization that has customers. To stay in business, an entrepreneur has to match that idea or dream with what a customer thinks he or she wants, and again this requires understanding people.

One way of conceptualizing entrepreneurship is to consider it to be an intersection or nexus of individuals or teams, opportunities, and modes of organizing (Busenitz, *et al.*, 2003). Entrepreneurship can be viewed in its essence to be individuals or teams, creating works, such as products and services, for other persons in a market place (Mitchell, 2002). In other words, entrepreneurship is about individuals who create opportunities where others do not, and who attempt to exploit those opportunities through various modes of organizing, without regard to resources currently controlled (Stevenson & Jarillo, 1990).

Cognitions

Cognition and cognitive psychology concern themselves with the study of individual perceptions, memory, and thinking (Estes, 1975). Cognitions have been defined as all processes by which sensory input is transformed, reduced, elaborated, stored, recovered, and used (Neisser, 1967). As psychology scholars began to recognize the limitations of the earlier behaviourist approach (Skinner, 1953), cognitive psychology emerged to help explain the mental processes that occur within individuals as they interact with other people and the environment around them. Social cognition theory considers that individuals exist within a total situation or configuration of forces described by two pairs of factors: one being cognition and motivation, and the other being the person in the situation (emphasis in original) (Fiske & Taylor, 1984). Social cognition theory, for example, introduces the idea of knowledge structures: mental models (cognitions) that are ordered in such a way as to optimize personal effectiveness within given situations.

Thus, where entrepreneurship consists of individuals and teams creating works for other persons within a market environment, the concepts developed in cognitive psychology are increasingly being found to be useful tools to help probe entrepreneurial-related phenomena.

Entrepreneurial Cognitions

Based on the definitions of entrepreneurship and cognitions, entrepreneurial cognitions is defined as follows: entrepreneurial cognitions are the knowledge structures that people use to make assessments, judgments, or decisions involving opportunity evaluation, venture creation, and growth.

In other words, research in entrepreneurial cognition is about understanding how entrepreneurs use simplifying mental models to piece together previously unconnected information that helps them to identify and invent new products or services, and to assemble the necessary resources to start and grow businesses (Mitchell, *et al.*, 2002).

Training

Dale S. Beach (1980) defines training as 'the organized procedure by which people learn knowledge and/or skill for a definite purpose'.

It refers to the teaching and learning activities carried on for the primary purpose of helping the people to acquire and apply the knowledge, skills, abilities and attitudes needed for accomplishing a particular task (Subba Rao, 1999). Defining clearly the ways and means by which the knowledge and skills are transferred effectively to the people is absolutely essential. It is, indeed, a significant as well as a difficult task. A model expresses the structure/process of a complicated system. Hence, an entrepreneurial training model means an organized structure/process which shows the sequence of activities to be carried on for imparting the knowledge and skills adequately to the aspiring entrepreneurs.

Relevance of Cognitive Approach in Entrepreneurship

The possibility of making a multidisciplinary view of the entrepreneur (MacMillan & Katz, 1992) in an effort to synthesize and give insight into the function of this fundamental worker in the job of wealth creation by the use of information processing and entrepreneurial cognition is to be empirically checked as there still does not appear to be a satisfactory answer to the question: Why are some people and not others able to discover and exploit particular entrepreneurial opportunities?

It has been asserted that two broad categories of factors influence the probability that particular people will discover particular opportunities: (1) the possession of the information necessary to identify an opportunity, and (2) the cognitive properties necessary to exploit it (Shane & Venkataraman, 2000). According to these criteria, then, research that contributes to a better understanding of information processing and entrepreneurial cognition has an important role to play in the development of the entrepreneurship literature.

Within the multidisciplinary tradition of entrepreneurship research, theory that attempts to explain the relationship between the entrepreneur and new venture formation origins from several fields: economics, personality psychology, and strategy. Each of these approaches makes its contribution, but each also has it shortcomings. While economic theories have been useful in helping to identify what entrepreneurship is and when it occurs, they have been less beneficial in helping to explain the more micro questions of how and why. Researchers contributing to the existing entrepreneurship literature have been unable to report a unique set of personality traits that characterize the entrepreneur (Shaver, 1995).

Until Herron (1990) demonstrated that entrepreneurial skill and skill propensity are related to new venture performance, the persistent attempts of researchers in the new venture performance stream to link the attributes of the entrepreneurial individual to performance (MacMillan & Day, 1987) met with little success. Thus, actual practice within the entrepreneurship community has differed from much of the research reported to date, and therefore, new approaches that explain the contribution of the entrepreneur to new venture formation continue to be needed. The cognitive perspective provides some useful lenses which helps in exploring entrepreneur-related phenomena and addressing some of the meaningful issues in which the researchers have been largely ineffective in probing.

Until the cognition view emerged, it was somewhat ironic that entrepreneurship researchers could not clearly identify systematic (theoretical) reasons for the uniqueness of entrepreneurs, while those who were immersed within the entrepreneurship world knew that these people were somehow distinct. The assertions of the cognitive view of entrepreneurship represent a refreshing change: the articulation of a theoretically rigorous and empirically testable approach that does systematically explain the role of the individual in the entrepreneurial process (Mitchell, 2002).

Specifically, the entrepreneurial cognitions view offers to help us understand how entrepreneurs think and "why" they do some of the things they do, and in doing so, to provide a theoretically rigorous and testable argument for such distinctiveness. It was in the early to mid-1990s that the terms entrepreneurs' cognitions and entrepreneurial cognition (Busenitz & Lau, 1996) began to gain currency, and entrepreneurial cognition research emerged. Entrepreneurial cognition-based constructs were first used to distinguish entrepreneurs from non-entrepreneurs (Mitchell, 1994). Then Palich and Bagby (1995) used cognitive theory to explain entrepreneurial risk-taking, and Mitchell and Chesteen (1995) demonstrated how a cognition-based entrepreneurial instruction pedagogy was superior to the traditional "business plan only" approach to teaching entrepreneurial expertise.

The next wave of entrepreneurial cognition research was led by Baron (1998), who argued that consideration of several cognitive mechanisms such as counterfactual thinking, attribution style, the planning fallacy and self-justification, might have significant usefulness in explaining why entrepreneurs do the things that they do. Then McGrath (1999), and Simon, Houghton, and Aquino (2000) provided analyses of how cognitive errors, such as overconfidence, illusion of control, and misguided belief in the law of small numbers, and so forth shape such phenomena as the creation of real options for entrepreneurs. Busenitz and colleagues (Alvarez & Busenitz, 2001) have now utilized cognitive models to explain how the heuristic-based logic that appears to be stronger in entrepreneurs, helps to explain how entrepreneurs think and make strategic decisions; and Mitchell *et al.* (2000) have utilized entrepreneurial cognition constructs to explain the venture creation decision in the cross cultural setting. Most recently, the use of cognitive constructs has been further extended to explain cognitive complexity in aboriginal economic development and in family business (Mitchell & Morse, 2002s).

Distinctive Qualities that Make the Entrepreneur's Cognitive Behaviour Successful

Entrepreneurs are not carbon copies of each other. Nor do they all exhibit precisely exact characteristics. Yet, there is surprising similarity in a lot of what they do, and in how they go about doing it. The most highly successful entrepreneurs:

1. Actively Bank Experiences;
2. Systematically Think and Act;
3. Continually Test Limits;
4. Embrace Competence;
5. Commit to a "Cause";
6. Are Situationists;
7. Take Fast Action; and
8. Seek Significant and Enduring Change.

These "backdrop patterns" are what make the entrepreneur's cognitive behaviour successful. These are the behavioural forces that make entrepreneurs entrepreneurial (Mitton, 1997). The other common traits of the right entrepreneurs (Laurie, 2001) are:

1. They make what seems impossible, possible
2. They flirt with danger to achieve their vision
3. They create the demand for their products and/or services

4. They do it themselves
5. They are fiercely independent
6. They find order in chaos
7. They are highly focused
8. They have enormous energy
9. They move quickly and adapt quickly
10. They have a high tolerance for failure and are comfortable with uncertainty.

These personality traits of the entrepreneurs make them unique from non-entrepreneurs and successful in their ventures.

Outcome of Entrepreneurial Cognitions

The cognitive viewpoint may be seen to serve well as an effective tool in probing and explaining the previously unexplained phenomena within the entrepreneurship research domain. Examining both problematic and positive aspects of entrepreneurial cognitions is vital. For example, some of the problematic consequences of entrepreneurial cognitions occur in entrepreneurial environments characterized by information overload, high uncertainty or novelty, strong emotions, time pressure, and fatigue. These include counterfactual thinking affecting infusion, self-serving bias, planning fallacy, and self-justification (Baron, 1998); overconfidence or representativeness errors (Busenitz & Barney, 1997); and illusion of control, and misguided belief in the law of small numbers (Simon, Houghton, & Aquino, 2000). Some of the positive consequences include making the venture creation decision using cognitive mechanisms, such as expert scripts (Mitchell *et al.*, 2000). Some of these important consequences of entrepreneurial cognitions are explained below.

Opportunity Recognition and Venture Creation

Over the last decade, research and theory development in the field of entrepreneurship has moved from the study of individual differences/personal characteristics (Kalleberg & Leicht, 1991), toward integrated models of entrepreneurship as a process (Lumpkin & Dess, 1996). Bygrave (1989) calls the founding of an organization to pursue an entrepreneurial opportunity the "Entrepreneurial Event." Similarly, Stevenson and Jarillo-Mossi (1986) view entrepreneurship as the process of creating value by combining resources to exploit an opportunity. The recognition of the opportunity may be the critical first step of the entrepreneurship process (Hills, 1995).

Entrepreneurial activity involves new venture creation (Vesper, 1996) and new entry into promising markets (Lumpkin & Dess, 1996). These efforts revolve around a core process: recognizing opportunity (Kirzner, 1973). Opportunity recognition does have distinctive characteristics that can be identified and tested. In particular, the opportunity search and identification characteristics of individual entrepreneurs tend to fall into two broad categories: a solo activity that involves creativity by opportunistic entrepreneurs who have a good feel for the market and a network activity, that is, entrepreneurs who learn of opportunities through contacts with others and assess their viability through open discussion and trial and error; a sequence of activities carried on by the entrepreneurs who learn of opportunities on their efforts and assess them using their cognitive skills. These two opportunity recognition modes, in turn, are uniquely related to other personal preferences and features of business creation.

Many definitions of entrepreneurship have increasingly focused on opportunity as central to understanding the phenomenon. There is still little known about the sensitivity of entrepreneurs to opportunities or the cognitive processes they use to identify opportunities. The following is the cognitive process entrepreneurs generally use to identify the relevant opportunity and thereby create a new venture (Hills, 1997).

1. *Entrepreneurs' Opportunity Recognition Capabilities*

Developing the capabilities for the identification of new business opportunities is a must for entrepreneurs. It would be easy for those entrepreneurs who have considerable experience base with opportunities. "Identifying opportunities is really several learning steps over time, rather than a one time occurrence". Generally, Network Entrepreneurs (NEs) identify more potential opportunities as they use their networks for accessing more information pertaining to the existing business environment. It is noted that entrepreneurs with adequate capabilities could recognize opportunity than others.

2. *Self-Perceived Entrepreneurial Alertness*

Many entrepreneurs strongly see themselves as "entrepreneurially alert." Overwhelmingly, entrepreneurs have a 'special alertness' toward opportunities; see new business opportunities 'naturally'; and even enjoy casually thinking about new opportunities.

3. *Importance of Venture Ideas and Creativity*

A "venture idea" is not necessarily an "opportunity". However, it is striking that most of the successful entrepreneurs agree that, "New venture ideas are a dime a dozen. Evaluation is the key". Generally, entrepreneurs do not have problems coming up with ideas for businesses. They do accept that creativity is important and like to be creative. Entrepreneurs who are networked to opportunity sources may not need to be creative as those who are not, because they have access to a wider range of information and 'creativity' through network ties.

4. *Evaluation of Opportunities*

The entrepreneurs consider intuitive judgment or "gut feels" to be an important part of judging market potential. Their intuitive judgment process is supported by the Business Skills Cognition of the entrepreneurs for assessing the identified opportunities and thereby choosing the best one which is, then, transformed as a venture. Hence, this stage is very significant for the entrepreneurs in the process of recognition of opportunities.

5. *Venture Creation*

New ventures are the source of considerable economic growth and a primary source of wealth creation. Venture creation greatly depends on venture support capabilities, space for innovation, compensation that encourages risk taking and an entrepreneurial culture and heritage. Every venture strategy requires capital and an enlightened and forward-looking entrepreneur.

The Venture-Building Process (Laurie, 2001) consists of the following five phases:

1. Mining opportunities,
2. Refining and strengthening the business model,
3. Developing the product, platform and business,
4. Executing the business-building process and
5. Growth,

At the core of most successful business-building processes is the capability to be first to market. The core competence, the ability to move quickly from idea to market, is a key enabler of success.

Entrepreneurial independence demands space for action and trust and the entrepreneurial speed demands agility, experimentation, adaption, and rapid response in order to be first to market. The entrepreneur launching a venture is eager to experiment, adapt, go for gold, and – in the event of failure – pick up and start again. For a venture, the funding mechanism is the angel or the venture capitalist (Laurie, 2001).

Corning (2001) has identified the following steps to turning a business idea into a successful business venture:

1. Building Knowledge,
2. Determining Feasibility,
3. Testing Practicality,
4. Proving Profitability, and
5. Creating Venture.

Creative entrepreneurs find themselves sitting in the middle of data that would be confusing if they are not also deeply involved with every aspect of the consumer, the technology, the product development, the hiring decisions, the capital-raising process and the milestone achievement. He or she defines the value-added activities, the competencies, the people with the competencies, and the metrics (Laurie, 2001).

In general, the performance implications of the opportunity recognition process is another area that remains largely unexplored in the opportunity recognition literature to investigate how opportunity recognition and performance are linked. Network Entrepreneurs pursue more opportunities than Solo Entrepreneurs (SE's). They have access to more opportunities through their contacts while SEs take a more cautious approach, requiring that they fully understand and have personal experience with the entrepreneurial opportunity. Apparently two things are involved simultaneously: propensity to start an entrepreneurial venture and skills to run the venture successfully (Petrin, 1994).

Counterfactual Thinking

One aspect of cognition which appears to be potentially relevant to entrepreneurship, but which has not yet been investigated, a mechanism known as counterfactual thinking (Mandel & Lehman, 1996). This involves the tendency to imagine "what might have been" in a specific situation if the person in question had acted differently in it, and it appears to be relevant to entrepreneurship for several reasons. First, counterfactual thinking is closely linked to the experience of regret over missed opportunities. In fact, it appears that thinking over about what might have happened if these opportunities had not been missed is one important cause of the intense feelings of regret many persons experience in such situations. It seemed possible that because of their concern with identifying and acting on opportunities, entrepreneurs might be more likely to experience such reactions than other persons and that this, coupled with a strong desire to avoid such feelings of regret, would contribute to their initial decision to become an entrepreneur.

Second, recent findings (Roese, 1997) suggest that counterfactual thinking is especially likely in situations where individuals experience disappointing outcomes. Entrepreneurs, of course, often meet with such setbacks in the early days of their new ventures (Hatten, 1997). Moreover, their commitment to their ideas, businesses, and products, is frequently intense, thus magnifying the negative emotions generated by these disappointments. For these reasons, too, therefore, it seemed possible that entrepreneurs would be more likely than other persons to engage in counterfactual thinking. Consistent with this reasoning attempts could be made to understand whether entrepreneurs are more likely than other persons to engage in counterfactual thinking with respect to situations involving missed opportunities and if so, they experience more or stronger feelings of regret over missed opportunities than other persons.

Entrepreneurs and other persons differ with respect to several cognitive processes – that is, in the ways in which they think about certain events and situations. Entrepreneurs and non-entrepreneurs differ in terms of counterfactual thinking, the tendency to imagine what might have occurred in situations involving missed opportunities if different actions had been taken. The precise role of counterfactual thinking and the regrets over missed opportunities it often generates, remain to be explained.

Evolving Training Model on the Basis of Entrepreneurial Cognitions

Even though there are plenty of entrepreneurial training models available, the need for developing a model using cognitive approach is imperative. It is because of the quintessence of the cognitive approach in entrepreneurship. The process of identifying such a model is explained below:

1. *Identifying Aspirants for Training*

The entrepreneurial training process starts with the identification of potential participants who really want to become entrepreneurs. This is very significant because, by doing so, only the aspiring entrepreneurs can be identified and trained well. For identifying the aspirants, questionnaire can be used for assessing their entrepreneurial motivation and cognitions.

2. *Identifying Entrepreneurial Training Needs*

The second important stage in the process of developing an entrepreneurial training model is the identification of training needs/ requirements of the aspiring entrepreneurs. The training needs of the aspiring entrepreneurs, based on entrepreneurial cognitions, may be:

- *(a)* imparting the knowledge structure required for assessments and judgments.
- *(b)* developing the opportunity recognition capabilities.
- *(c)* improving their ability to evaluate the available opportunities.
- *(d)* giving the required inputs for venture creation.
- *(e)* managing counterfactual thinking.
- *(f)* acquiring/retaining the essential behavioural forces that make entrepreneurs entrepreneurial, etc.

3. *Evolving Entrepreneurial Training Model*

On the basis of the entrepreneurial training needs, suitable training models, which must satisfy those needs of the aspiring entrepreneurs, have to be evolved. Based on cognitive approach, a model has been developed by the authors for the purpose of giving training to the aspiring entrepreneurs, is shown in Table 2.1

The model consists of the following contents:

(a) Activity

An activity means the action that is to be carried on in the process of giving training to the aspiring entrepreneurs. This model contains five significant activities, namely Engage, Explore, Elaborate, Execute and Experience, which form The Learning Cycle—5Es. 'Engage'

Figure 2.1 : Entrepreneurial Training Model Based on Cognitive Approach

Aim : Managing Counterfactual Thinking (For Example)

Trainer : Mr. Ram

Duration : Three Hours

Activity (The Learning Cycle – 5E's)	*Trainer Cues (Behaviours)*	*Participants' Responses to Cues*	*Environment (Milieu)*
Engage			
Explore			
Elaborate			
Execute			
Experience (Feedback)			

indicates the trainer to fit the trainees into the place well and comfortable. 'Explore' indicates the trainer to make the trainees looking at the concepts taught and understanding them thoroughly. 'Elaborate' indicates the trainer to make the trainees going into detail of the concepts and investigating why/how the concept is. 'Execute' indicates the trainer to enable the trainees to carry out the concepts on their own. And 'Experience' indicates the trainer to make the trainees familiar with the concepts taught and learning the 'know-how' of the concepts comprehensively.

(b) Trainer's cues

For carrying out each of the above activities effectively, the trainer has to give necessary cues and directions to the trainees to perform their assigned tasks. These directions and cues have to be identified well in advance by the trainer to make the trainees carry out each activity easily and effectively.

(c) Participant's Responses to the cues

The trainer has to encourage the trainees to respond his/her cues and directions. The trainees must be allowed to clarify their doubts while carrying out their assigned tasks. If the responses are more for each activity, it means that the training is effective.

(d) Environment

It indicates that the setting, atmosphere (surrounding) and the materials required for the trainees for carrying out each activity effectively. Different environments may be required for carrying out different activities. Hence the trainer is required to define the precise environment for each activity well in advance.

Conclusion

Cognitive mechanisms into the study of entrepreneurship may provide researchers with important conceptual tools invaluable in understanding not only "the mind of the entrepreneur" (Timmons, 1994), but also factors that influence entrepreneurs' success as well. Entrepreneurial cognition theory reveals that cognition is associated with entrepreneurship, entrepreneurial performance, and the creation of economic independence by individuals, and within firms, industries, and economies. The utility of the entrepreneurial cognition perspective to be sufficient to suggest that within entrepreneurial cognition research, sufficient technical machinery is available to give researchers the means to better define and measure the contribution of "entrepreneurial people" to the tasks of entrepreneurship: opportunity recognition, opportunity evaluation, venture creation, and wealth building in general. The entrepreneurial training model developed by the authors based on the cognitive approach, would be of immense help for transforming the entrepreneurial aspirants into successful entrepreneurs in the society which will, in turn, make the nation wealthy and competitively advantageous.

REFERENCES

Alvarez, S. & Busenitz, L. (2001). The entrepreneurship of resource-based theory. *Journal of Management*, 27, 755–775.

Baron, R.A. (1998). Cognitive mechanisms in entrepreneurship: Why and when entrepreneurs think differently than other people. *Journal of Business Venturing*, 13, 275–294.

Barsalou, L.W. (1992). *Cognitive Psychology: An Overview for Cognitive Scientists.* Hillsdale, NJ: Erlbaum.

Bosire, Joseph & Martin Etyang (2003), The Effect of Education on Business Skills Cognitition: The Case of Indigenous Microscale Enterprise Owners in Kenya. *Journal of Vocational Education and Training*, Vol. 55, No.1, pp. 5-11.

Busenitz, L. & Lau, C. (1996). A cross-cultural cognitive model of new venture creation. *Entrepreneurship Theory and Practice*, 20(4), 25–39.

Estes, W.K. (1975). *Handbook of Learning and Cognitive Processes*, Vol. 1. Hillsdale, NJ: Lawrence Erlbaum.

Herron, L. (1990). *The Effects of Characteristics of the Entrepreneur on New Venture Performance*. Columbia, SC: University of South Carolina Press.

Hills, G. E. (1995). *Opportunity Recognition by Successful Entrepreneurs: A Pilot Study*. Frontiers of Entrepreneurship Research. Wellesley, MA: Babson College.

Johnsrud (1991) Entrepreneurship in the development of a rural area Keynote paper presented at the Fourth FAO/REU International Rural Development Summer School, Mikkeli, Finland, 16-20 September 1991.

Kahneman, D., & Lovallo, D. (1994). Timid choices and bold forecasts: A cognitive perspective on risk taking. In R.P. Rumelt, D.E. Schendel, & D.J. Teece (eds.), *Fundamental Issues in Strategy: A Research Agenda*, pp. 71–96.

Kalleberg, A. L. & Leicht, K. T. (1991). Gender and Organizational Performance: Determinants of Small Business Survival and Success. *Academy of Management Journal*, 34(1), 136-161.

MacMillan, I.C. & Day, D. (1987). Corporate ventures into industrial markets: Dynamics of aggressive entry, Journal of Business Venturing, 2(1), 29–39.

McGrath, R.G. (1999). Falling forward: Real options reasoning and entrepreneurial failure. *Academy of Management Review*, 24 (1), 13–30.

Mitchell, R.K. (1994). The composition, classification, and creation of new venture formation expertise. Ph.D. Dissertation, Management Department, University of Utah, Salt Lake City, UT.

Mitton, Daryl G. (1997), *Entrepreneurship: One More Time – Non–cognitive Characteristics that Make the Cognitive Click*, Frontiers of Entrepreneurship Research.

Palich, L.E., & Bagby, D.R. (1995). Using cognitive theory to explain entrepreneurial risk-taking: Challenging conventional wisdom. *Journal of Business Venturing*, 10, 425–438.

Robert A. Baron (1997), *Cognitive mechanisms in the decision to become an entrepreneur: the role of counterfactual thinking and the experience of regret*, Frontiers of Entrepreneurship Research.

Shaver, K.G. (1995). The entrepreneurial personality myth. *B&E Review*, April–June, 20–23.

Simon, M., Houghton, S.M., & Aquino, K. (2000). Cognitive biases, risk perception, and venture formation: How individuals decide to start companies. *Journal of Business Venturing*, 14(5), 113–134.

Wright, Russell W. (1997). *From Knowledge to Competence to Entrepreneurship,* Frontiers of Entrepreneurship Research.

Yukl, G. (1994). *Leadership in Organizations.* (3rd ed.) Englewood Cliffs, NJ: Prentice-Hall.

4

Innovative Training to Create Rural Women Entrepreneurs—A Case Study

Dr. S. David Amirtha Rajan and Dr. Mrs. P. Gnana Soundari

Introduction

The word 'entrepreneur' is derived originally from French Word "entrepredre" which means an organizer of musical or other entertainment. Oxford English Dictionary also defined the same as director or a manager of a public musical institution, one who 'gets up' entertainment, especially musical performance. But it was meant to those who were engaged in military expeditions, in 16th century. Later in 17th century, the term entrepreneur covered civil engineers. From 18th century onwards this term was used to refer to economic aspects. According to J.B "An entrepreneur is the economic agent who unites all means of production, land of one, the labour of another and the capital of yet another and thus produces a product. By selling the product in the market he pays rent of land, wages to labour, interest on capital and what remains is his profit". Therefore an entrepreneur is a director who combines various factors of production to produce a socially viable product.

A women entrepreneur is defined as "an enterprise owned and controlled by a women having a minimum financial interest of 51 per cent of the capital and giving at least 51 per cent of the employment generation in the enterprise to women". On the other side, rural entrepreneurship is defined with the term rural industrialization. Accordingly any industry located in rural area, village, or town with a population of 20,000 and below and an investment of Rs. 3 crores in plant and machinery is classified as a village industry". Therefore a rural women entrepreneur is means a woman in village or town with a population of 20,000 and below, having a minimum financial interest of 51 per cent of capital employed and providing employment at least to not less than 51per cent to women. Further women folk form about half of the India's population. In this juncture it is a need to analyse the training programme of rural women entrepreneurs. In this context a case study was developed on the following objectives:

(a) To study the rural women entrepreneur in general.

(b) To analyse the innovative training.

Rural Women Entrepreneur

Women need to be empowered to exercise their judgment. Only those who empowered can be able to create an enterprise. The women at present are gradually capturing the jobs and services, traditionally believed to be in a man's domain. As it is a known factor that the women constitute half of the population in India. However their participation in employment is negligible. In the case of rural, the employments as well as entrepreneurship are not up to the remarks. Because, rural women lack motivation to undertake any non-traditional economic activities. She will be reared for a traditional role of wife and a mother. Further she not only lacks motivation to take up non-traditional economic activity but also totally lacks any skill of her own. She is totally unfit and not prepared mentally.

Further, Rural women entrepreneurs face several risks. Mostly, they are social risks and technological risks. They face social risk in going out of home and developing relationships related to the new activity. The risk also lies in the village communities and castes perception of the new activity. There is also risk inherent in dropping old relationships of economic and social significance. In fact, the women who are working as labourers will face new risks at the time choosing self-employment. Women in rural areas also face technical risks such as lack of skill, knowledge and information to carryout any independent economic activity. Hence, entrepreneurship development among rural women should first prepare them through motivation training for entrepreneurship training.

Innovative Training

Training may be defined as any procedure, initiated by an enterprise, which intends to foster and enhance learning among the employee working in the enterprises. Such training may be given either by owner of enterprises himself or herself or with help of others who specialized in a needed field. However, training to rural woman is quiet different. Because they one unskilled as it is stated earlier. In this case, it is needed to provide training in innovative manners. This is evolved on the basis of the experience gained by organizers of such programme in Lady Doak College and The American College, Madurai. Based on the information collected, the innovative training programme is inculcated. These findings along with new ideas for a successful training programme are presented as follow:

(a) Initial Survey

Before starting any training programme to rural women, it is considered that initial survey would be conducted. This survey should be based on certain basic objectives as such as: *(i)* To know the socio-economic condition of the village households *(ii)* To find out their attitude towards entrepreneurship *(iii)* To identify the various training programmes already they attended *(iv)* To know the effect of training programmes *(v)* To initiate new approach on training women.

(b) Analyse the Survey Conducted

Based on the objective, data would be collected through interview schedule. The data are usually collected with help of students. The collected information are analysed properly.

(c) Identification of Need

The need of the society and thereby, reduce poverty, is found through the analysis of the collected data. The need is arranged on priority and necessity-wise.

(d) Conducting Camp

The rural camp is organized with help of college and respective panchayat, by the students and staffs. The main motto of this camp is to organize a programme without affecting the routine work of the people who are trainees to this programme. The programme is scheduled as such it is suited in all situations and circumstances to a trainee. This is otherwise called as outreach programme. In conducting training, a well qualified person on a specific field is invited to teach and demonstrate to trainee on those need identified through schedule. In the case of demonstration, in each case, trainee is instructed well and allowed them to demonstrate the same to other participants. Some competition is also conducted and prizes are distributed.

(e) Sale Talk

Apart from training, trainee may be taught, with new techniques in management, marketing and finance. They are encouraged to establish any type of industry producing at least one product. The motivational talk or speech is also arranged to instigate the trainee to undertake a venture. In motivating people, Cultural programme is also conducted to create emotion for the growth of rural economy. Further bank is also requested to arrange loan for the trainee to set up a new organization.

(f) Feedback and Follow-up

At the end of training programme, feedback is collected. Based on these, some relevant addition and modification may be done for the betterment of training programme. Further follow-up work is also undertaken to check how they proceed. Once it is started, the new entrepreneurs are allowed to do independently.

Experience on Rural Camp

The rural entrepreneurship training programmes were organized at Matharai, Chekkanoorani and Mattapparai. The expertises are provided by centre for Entrepreneurship Development and Madurai District Tiny and Small Scale Industrialists Association.

Matharai

Matharai locates 36 kms away from Madurai City. Women are having school education up to 10th standard and below. Only 5 per cent of women are educated up to UG. Most of them go for agricultural jobs. Which is seasonal and during off-season they find no job. Hence they are very much interested in entrepreneur-ship training. Twenty-four women attended and enthusiastically participated. The training programmes given to them are *(i)* Motivational training, *(ii)* Preparation of agarpathi, computer sambirani, detergent soap powder, shampoo, *(iii)* making papads, pickles, jam, juice, *(iv)* candle making, glass painting and fabric painting.

They are motivated that though they are not able to produce at a large scale but they can sell at least they can make use of themselves. They are also given lectures on how to market their products and guidance is given to them on how to approach DIC and Banks for financial help.

Chekkanoorani

Chekkanoorani locates 20 kms away from Madurai. Women here are going for both agricultural and constructional job. Those who involved in constructional work did not turn up for this training. They feel that they get adequate wage in the constructional work. Hence only 18 women are participated in the training on vermiculture. The women who get training felt that they can use it for their own land and they can organize a vermiculture unit in their village and start selling it to nearly villages.

Mattaparai

Mattaparai locates 30 kms away from Madurai. The beneficiaries are 20 women who are all housewives with school education. They are given training on plate mat and market making out of palm leaves and paper bags as they are eco-friendly products. They are also given environmental awareness. Moreover lectures are conducted on motivation, self-employment and sustenance. They are also given information on where to get raw-materials, financial help and how to sell their products. Really the rural women are benefited out of this training.

Conclusion

Women catering business is not anything new. It is phenomenon all over the world. Women all exercise their entrepreneurial spirit with more experience and training. In the light of such development of women and despite numerous constraints, women owned business are becoming increasingly popular in the economies of all countries. Hence it is essential to impact knowledge and awareness to rural women on entrepreneurial training.

REFERENCES

Nayan Barua and Aparajeeta Borkakoty, (2005). *Women Entrepreneur-ship*, APH Publishing Corporation, New Delhi.

Verma. S.B. (2005). *Status of Women in Modern India*, Deep and Deep Publications, New Delhi.

Rathore B.S. and Chhabra, Rama, "Promotion of women entrepreneur-ship – Training Strategies", *SEDME*, Vol. 18 No. 1 March 1991.

5

Diversity Training—A Need for Innovative Entrepreneur Training

Prof. M.D. Manoharan and Mr. K.R.Srinivasan

Introduction

Success in any venture depends upon foresight, knowledge, optimism, hard work, persistence and efficient management. Some of these are possessed by individuals due to inheritance *i.e.*, by birth in a particular family; whilst others can be acquired from the environment through education, training and self-experience.

In recent past the training approach to entrepreneurial development addresses itself to two broad categories of people *viz.*, *(a)* entrepreneurs in status whether by choice or circumstances, and *(b)* those who are potential entrepreneurs may engaged in non-entrepreneurial activities. Training to first group is directed at improving business performance and raising aspiration levels higher, as indicated by grater readiness in expanding business and taking risks of introducing change. Training for second group entails the convincing of individuals of the social and economic advantages of industrial activity.

In this paper, we would like to present a brief study about the need of diversity training to the entrepreneurs. Diversity training is a practical guide to the entrepreneurs to understand the changing attitudes of people and institutions. Diversity training has become a pervasive element in many organizational training programmes.

What Diversity Means?

Diversity is 'otherness' or those human qualities that are different from our own and outside the groups to which we belong, yet are present in other individuals and groups. (University of Maryland, *www.inform.umd.edu*)

Diversity takes many forms. It is usually thought of in terms of obvious attributes-age differences, race, gender, physical ability, sexual orientation, religion and language. Diversity in terms of background professional experience, skill and specialization, values and culture, as well as social class, is a prevailing pattern (United Nations, 2000).

Diversity training should thus be viewed as an inclusive concept, encompaning a broader focus than employment equality would suggest. It requires one to look at the mindset and the culture of an organization and the different perspectives people bring to an organization on account of their ethnicity, social background, professional values, styles, disabilities or other differences (United Nations, 2000).

Whatever the drivers for diversity, the UN identified five qualities, which contribute to the successful management of diversity?

Leadership

Demonstrable commitment and support including the establishment of steering and advisory groups and effective communication plans.

Valid and Reliable Performance Measurements

Pan organizational assessments, benchmarking and comparative analysis.

Education

Awareness training, development of in-house expertice.

Cultural and Management Exchange

Devising and implementing effective HRM strategies.

Follow up

Longtitudinal education, performance management systems, and knowledge management.

A Model for Diversity Training

Figure 5.1 : Model for Diversity Training in EDPs

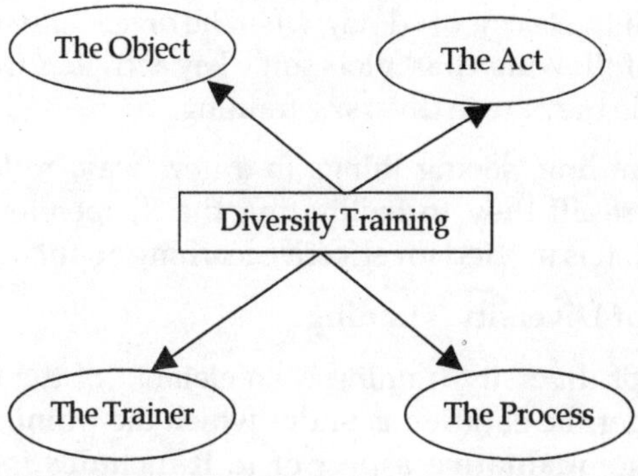

Source: Philclements and John Jones, *The Diversity Training Handbook*, p. 40.

The Object of Diversity Training

The major objects of good diversity training are 'raising awareness'. When people's awareness is raised truly, it may increase their knowledge of themselves as well as knowledge of things outside of themselves, and sometimes outside of their own experience of life. The crucial aspects of this self-knowledge are their way of seeing the world. To gain an understanding of one's world-view, which itself bound into attitudes, values and beliefs, will be the key to recognizing and valuing the fact that others' world-view may be different. This may represent value diversity.

Figure 5.g : Values of Diversity

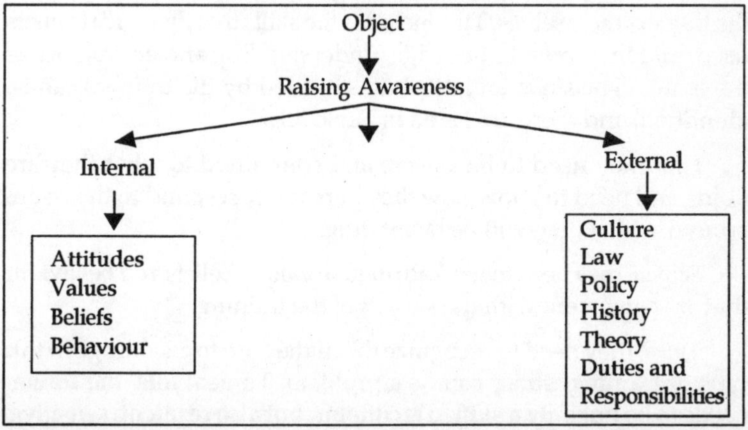

The Act of Diversity Training

The act of diversity training is an element of the model that has its focus on what the learner is doing when he or she engages in such training. The following chart plots some key activities that learners engaged while they are in diversity training.

Understanding, seeing things in a new way, reflection and realization are all they to facilitating the deeper level of self-exploration that is needed for effective learning about diversity.

The Process of Diversity Training

The process of diversity training is an element of the model that relates to either the conditions under which the training is taking place or some qualitative aspect of it. It includes issues about authority to engage and discomfort/pain for the learner. Several trainers describe the process in terms of being on a journey.

Figure 5.3 : Process of Diversity Training

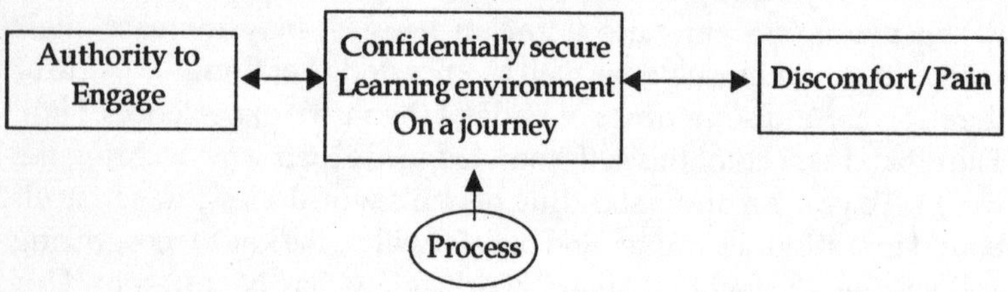

The Trainers in Diversity Training

The final element of diversity training model includes themes about the trainers themselves. This includes the skills that diversity trainers need, and their own knowledge, understanding and acceptance of the issues. The skills and attributes needed by the trainers can be identified; and these are listed in Table 5.1.

First they need to be sincere and committed to what they are doing and need to know how they personally respond to the issues around which they will be facilitating.

Second, they need to have attributed, values, beliefs and behaviour that are congruent with the subject of the training.

Third, they need to recognize that if they are to encourage in this type of training, stress can be a problem. To deal this, the trainer needs to be not only a skilled facilitator, but also resilient, sensitive, flexible, able to read body language, skilled in recognizing and responding to group dynamics and difficulties.

Table–5.1
Skills and Attributes Needed by Trainers

Skills	*Attributes*
Intervention	Resilience (take it on the chin)
Facilitation	Belief in what you are doing
Conflict management	Mental ability
Asking though questions	Deep understanding of issues
Flexibility	Positive outlook
Managing group dynamics	Recognizing own limits
Knowledge of law, policy issues, own attitudes	Been through the process, sensitive to to people's need, walk the talk, own the ethos
Values and beliefs	Motivation in the subject, well trained in diversity

Figure 5.4 : Support System for Trainers

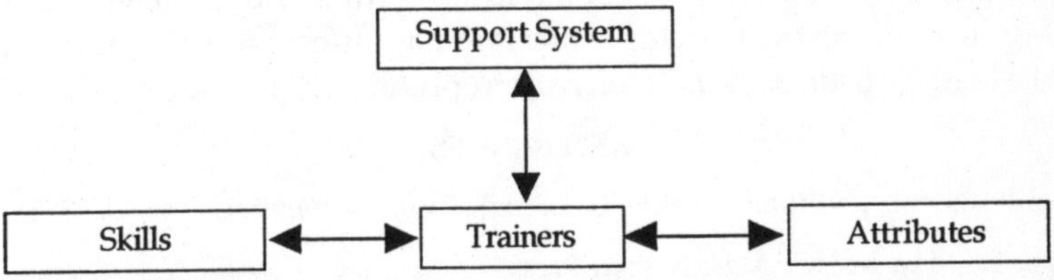

The trainer should supported by any supporting system managed by his own or organizational supporting system which based on the information previously available.

Significance of Diversity Training in Entrepreneur Development

- Planning and research on changing business psychology (bench marking and research)
- Designing programme for recruitment and selection
- Quality assurance/monitoring
- Reduction of stress
- Skill improvement
- Motivation and mental strength

Conclusion

The major aim of entrepreneur development training is to make the entrepreneur skilled and enhance rate of success in their attempt.

The rate of success is depend upon the effort they done and behaviour of them with others. The behavioural part of the entrepreneur is multi-dynamic in nature. It will not fulfil by merely training for skill improvement. It needs a training with empower the entrepreneur by skill, knowledge and character. This can be possible by diversity training.

The major aim of diversity training is to empower the learners towards variation including:

- Variation in people's life experience
- Variation in culture
- Variation in value system
- Variation in beliefs
- Variations in what can be assumed

Finally diversity training is needful for studying relationship between attitudes and behaviour and response to dominance, which determine the success of an entrepreneur. The major difficulty of this training is the stress involved in studying various subjects and having a support system for analysis. It may affect the easy adoption of diversity training for effective entrepreneurship.

REFERENCES

Phil clements and John Jones, *The Diversity Training Handbook*, pp. 40, 45, 51.

The HRM issues, ICFAI University Press.

University of Maryland, *www.inform.umd.edu*

6

Designing Innovative EDPs for Potential Rural Entrepreneurs

Dr. Ayub Khan Dawood

Introduction

It is the lack of investment in the development of human resources that has led us to our failure to exploit our largest resource, *i.e.*, people living in rural areas where most of our population dwells. What is required at the moment is an approach to decentralized planning in India with special reference to agro-climatic regional planning approach and making it operational through rural entrepreneurships development. The various services like financial support, guidance, counselling, marketing, testing and quality control, etc., may be polled together for common use by budding rural entrepreneurs. Industrial organizations and technical institutions in the country should be stimulated to identify, train and retain young entrepreneurs in village and give them full assistance in the form of initial capital and other infrastructure facilities for their projects. With proper encouragement, right kind of training and assistance the talent available in our villages can be utilized for value addition enterprises like handlooms, handicrafts and agro based units, etc. There can be 100 per cent export oriented units as there exists a vast potential of foreign markets for the goods/ articles produced by some of these units.

Process of Entrepreneurship Development

According to most of the behavioural scientists like David C. Mc-Clelland C. Ram Prasad, entrepreneurs can be groomed and all of us are not born entrepreneurs. It is the bunch of traits and a few characteristics of a person which need to be recognized and these can be further polished through scientific and systematically well designed EDPs their effective implementation and strong follow up. The process of entrepreneurship development for rural areas is shown through Figure 6.1.

Objectives of EDP

Some of the suggestive objectives for an EDP for rural areas can be:

(a) To make trainees of changing and existing business scenario;
(b) To awaken the sleeping entrepreneurial characteristics of the passive participants;
(c) To motivate and develop risk taking capabilities of potential entrepreneurs;
(d) To impart managerial skills and develop decision-making powers among the participants;
(e) To make the participants ready for self-employment is instead of wage employment in the fields of their own aptitude;
(f) To assist the rural entrepreneurs in project selection and working out its feasibility details ;and

Figure 6.1 : Process of Entrepreneurship Development

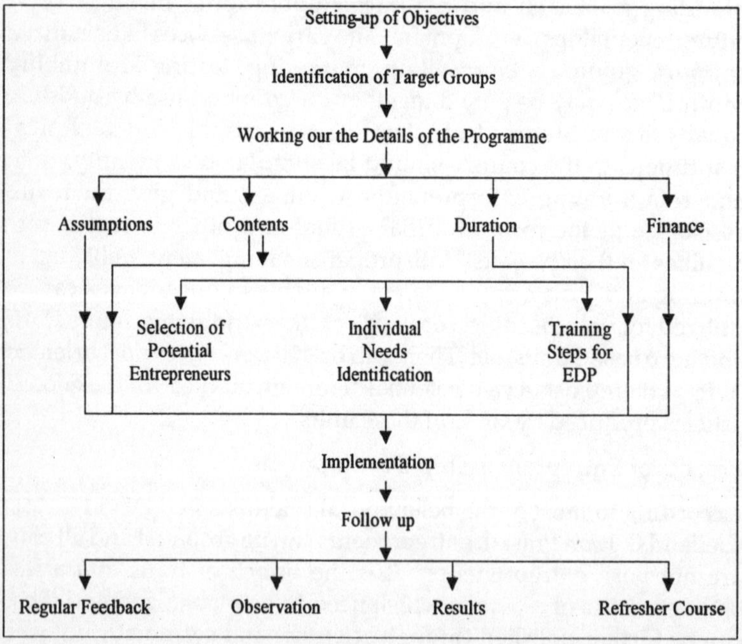

(g) To update the knowledge of the participants about process, rules, regulations, various programmes/schemes and help them in launching their own projects and setting-up of units.

Identification of Target Group

The rural population comprises of many groups of individuals ranging from illiterates, young, old, males and females having different backgrounds and aptitudes. The intensification and selection of a group which has been trained during EDP is of prime importance. Usually an individual falling in the age group of 20-35 years is most receptive and assimilating. However, all these factors may vary from one particular programme to another. Hence, flexibility should be kept in mind during the selection process of the target group for a particular EDP.

Working Out Details of the Programme

For any EDP to be successful, especially in the rural setting, a lot of home work needs to be done by the organizers. They have to work out the minutest detail of the programme in consultation with the local population, especially the opinion makers in the villages, panches/sarpanches, members of panchayat samitis, zila parishads, and municipal committees along with various agencies of district administration working for rural development. No programme can succeed till wholehearted involvement and full support from various agencies is not ensured.

Assumptions

Before actual designing of an EDP module some assumptions are necessary to be made by the trainers. The success of programmes depends upon the basic intelligence of the trainer as to what is the nature of assumptions his module is based on. What needs to be stressed is that assumptions should be very close to the reality and overall objectives of the programme.

Contents

The Programme contents have to be chalked out as per the expected outcomes.

Selection of Potential Entrepreneurs

For the selection of Potential entrepreneurs the local population has to be contacted and applications have to be sought. Contracts can be made through personal meetings or using multimedia approach. However, in rural areas, personal contacts with the help of village panches, sarpanches and opinion makers can be made more effectively. Selection can be done in an integrated manner involving following steps:

(a) Receiving applications;
(b) Analyzing, screening and short–listing applicants;
(c) Psychological tests;
(d) Group discussion; and
(e) Personal interviews.

Individual Needs Identification

As per the behavioural scientists an individual falls into one of the guardians shown in Figure 6.2. So we have to study each and every applicant and place him/her in the correct guardian. The ultimate target of the trainer is to develop the following features in a potential entrepreneur:

Figure 6.2 : Individual Needs Identification

Q – 1 Irrational/Dominant/Hostile (Always think that they are correct. Proper homework needed to bring them to point) DOMINANT	Q – 4 Warm/Dominant/Rational (Best Entrepreneurs) WARM
Q – 2 Irrational/Hostile/Submissive (Always suspicious. Most difficult to bring them to point) HOSTILE	Q – 3 Warm/Submissive/Irrational (Always need to be pushed) SUBMISSIVE

(a) Sense of risk taking,
(b) Sense of self-responsibility,
(c) Sense of self-achievement,
(d) Sense of self-esteem,
(e) Sense of self-control,
(f) Sense of confidence, and
(g) Sense of high efficacy.

This can be done by developing in a potential entrepreneur the leadership qualities, risk–taking capabilities and flexibility. Most of the people failing in the category of Q-4 have all these qualities. However, people failing in other quadrants need to be garnished through EDP.

Training Steps for EDP

Following steps are suggested for the conduct of a rural EDP

(a) *Opening of the session:* It should be, as far as possible, an informal set up–informal talks to observe in what way programme needs to be designed/modified and to know what the general moods and needs of the participants are. The talks can range from participants needs to their future fears/expectations about the programme.

(b) *Introduction and Induction course:* Explain opportunities; existing national, regional and local scenario arousing their need of achieving, sense of risk-taking, self-responsibility, achievement satisfaction, esteem, control, confidence and high efficacy. This shall develop traits of leader ship, risk-taking and flexibility among the participants.

(c) *Market research:* Equip the participants about techniques of analyzing local needs of the market, government schemes, and agencies ready to sponsor finances. Certain projects can tie up with large/medium scale industries which need to be developed as ancillary units. Discussions among the particulars and response of banks, DICs, Khadi Boards, State Industrial Development Corporation, State Small Scale Industries and Export Corporation, Rural Development agencies/departments, State Financial Corporations etc., have to be arranged.

(d) *Intensive training:* Once the participants come to know the opportunities and assistance available to them, the potential entrepreneurs are now developed and prepared through more intensive training/brain storming sessions. At the centre their survey reports are analyzed one by one and they are helped in finalizing their product. They are then briefed on the role of the financial and other organizations in making their ventures successful and given managerial inputs relating to finances, accounts, personnel, resource optimization and market management. They are also briefed on the legal aspects of the business.

(e) *Closing:* The Programme can be designed to last for a particular period. In this final exercise, a sort of 'loan mela' is organized with the help of representatives from local banks, DICs, and other agencies that can finance the units identified by the participants.

Duration

An EDP can be conducted as per following schedule:

1. Opening – 1 day
2. Introduction and induction – 5 day
3. Market research – 1 week
4. Intensive training – 3 weeks
5. Project reports preparation and finalization – 1 week
6. Closing – 1 day

However, duration of the course should be flexible depending upon nature and understanding of participants.

Finance

Conducting such programmes needs finance. It is the duty of the designer of the programme to work out the costs involved in organizing such a programme and suggest promoters for conducting these courses.

Implementation

After working out the details of the EDP for rural areas it should be implemented in the spirit of fulfilling overall objectives with which it is designed. Wherever needed experts may be invited to deliver lectures and interact with participants. The help from local government and non–government officials is necessary for the success of the programme.

Follow-up

Follow–up is the process to enable the client to understand and realize where he/she stands *vis–a–vis* his/her enterprise launching process. Apart from other significant reasons, failure can occur mainly due to lack of proper follow–up on the part of the training organizations. Follow–up activities start as soon as the EDP is over. The organization conducting the EDP must maintain regular contact with the trainees after the implementation of EDP and may have to conduct refresher course depending upon the feedback and results. This will also help the trainers to re-design and modify future programmes.

Conclusion

A well conceived integrated programme is necessary to tackle the problem of development of entrepreneurship in rural areas as only through rural entrepreneurs the general economic standard of living of the villages can be improved. It is necessary to mobilize the capital and skill resources of rural areas for promotion of industrialization, adopting decentralized approach, giving special incentives and emphasis to rural entrepreneurs. What is essential is to train and develop a corps of entrepreneurs who can usefully integrate the aspirations of the community with the overall economic and social development of the region.

REFERENCES

David C. McClelland and Winter D.G. *Motivating Economic Achievement*, The Free Press, New York, 1969.

Howard Stevenson and David Gumpert. The Heart of Entrepreneurship, *Harvard Business Review.*

Cochran, T.C., *Entrepreneurial Behaviour and Motivation, Exploration and Entrepreneurial History*, 1950, Volume 2.

"Liberating the Entrepreneurial Spirit", Accenture Report of a Study from Jan. 2000 to July 2001.

Singh, N.P., *Emerging Trends in Entrepreneurship Development – Theories and Practices*, IFDM, New Delhi, 1985.

Gaikwad, V.R. and Tripathy, R.N., *Socio-Physiological Factors Influencing Industrial Entrepreneurship*, Hyderabad, 1990.

Kao, J., *Entrepreneurship*, Harward Business School, 1990.

Davis H. Holt., *Entrepreneur – New Venture Creation*, Printice Hall of India (P) Ltd, New Delhi.

Dr. Arun Kaulgud., *Entrepreneurship Management*, Vikas Publishing House, 2003.

Akkauri, M.M.P. and Vinod Gupta, *Sustaining Entrepreneurs*, NIESBUD, New Delhi, 1990.

Tandon, B., *Environment and Entrepreneurship*, Chaugh Publications, Allahabad.

Brouwer, Maria., *Entrepreneurship and Un-certainty: Innovation and Competition Among the Many*. Small Business Economics, Volume 15.

Prasad, R., *Entrepreneurship Concepts and Cases*, ICFAI, 2002.

7

Action Oriented Training for Entrepreneurial Development

Mr. Mu. Subrahmanian and Dr. M. Jeyarathnam

Introduction

Entrepreneurship is a purposeful activity indulged in initiating promoting and maintaining economic activities for the production and distribution of wealth. Therefore Entrepreneurship has been recognized as an essential ingredient of economic development and an integral part of socio–economic transformation. The basic concept of entrepreneurship connotes effectiveness, an urge to take risk in the face of uncertainties and an intuition *i.e.,* a capacity for showing things in such a way which afterwards prove to be true.

Entrepreneurship is the creative and innovative response to the environment, which can take place in variety of fields of social work and the like and it is the potent limiting factor in economic development.

Training is an integral input of Entrepreneurial Development. The lack of adequate and skilled personnel is one of the bottlenecks in a developing economy. Training is essential for entrepreneurs and workers employed in small enterprise.

Need for Entrepreneurial Training

Entrepreneurship development training programme are primarily designed to enable the trainees to acquire and demonstrate a set of relevant competencies in areas such as problem-solving, analysis, creativity, motivation, communication and leadership. Use of conventional training methods by teachers such as lecture, talks and general discussion do not facilitate development of these competencies.

In the present scenario where development and promotion happen more rarely everyone still needs training, or rather needs it even more; if a job at any level became drudgery, then it connote be effectively performed. The role of training is to develop the critical awareness of trainees and prevent in growth.

Inputs for Entrepreneurship Development Training

The objective of the training programme in entrepreneurship development is to develop motivation of potential entrepreneurs, help them in taking up suitable enterprises and activities, enable them to prepare economically viable and technically feasible project reports and enhance their enterprise-building skills. The motivational inputs include psychological games, tests, goal setting exercise and role play. The objective of these inputs is to enable the participants to understand their own entrepreneurial personality and behaviour and bring about through self study changes in self concept, values and skills leading to positive entrepreneurial behaviour.

The training programme further enables entrepreneurs to develop skills in identifying suitable items for manufacturing or other self-employment ventures. The technique of conducting studies, market surveys and research should further be covered in the programme of training based on which project reports have to be prepared.

Any programme of training should not only develop proper entrepreneurial motivation and skill for project preparation but should also ensure that entrepreneurs are able to develop their enterprises well by application of scientific managerial techniques in various fields of management. The managerial contents of programme of training should be considered as vital for developing enterprise building skills and such various aspects of management such as financial management, marketing management, production management, inventory management, labour laws and taxation should be covered in the programme.

Designing an Entrepreneurship Development Training Programme

Designing the Entrepreneurship development training programme involves setting training objectives, developing the course curriculum and choosing appropriate methods. The programme designed is prescribed by the training needs of the target clientele. The training objective should be stated clearly, be trainee centered, employ observable action words can be concerned with ends rather than means. When objectives are set, the course curriculum can be developed. The elements of curriculum are knowledge, habits, skills, control of emotion. The material to be included should be accorded priority according to its relative depth of importance to achieving training objectives. Certain sequential can be followed in arranging the curriculum. Developing the course curriculum involves several stages, starting from analyzing training needs and stating outcome. In choosing the appropriate training methods, the factors to be considered are the subject area, the nature of learning, the trainee population, the trainers themselves and time and material factors. There are three process involved in designing the training programme, setting training objective, developing the course curriculum and choosing appropriate training methods.

Figure 7.1 : Building up an Action Oriented Training Programme

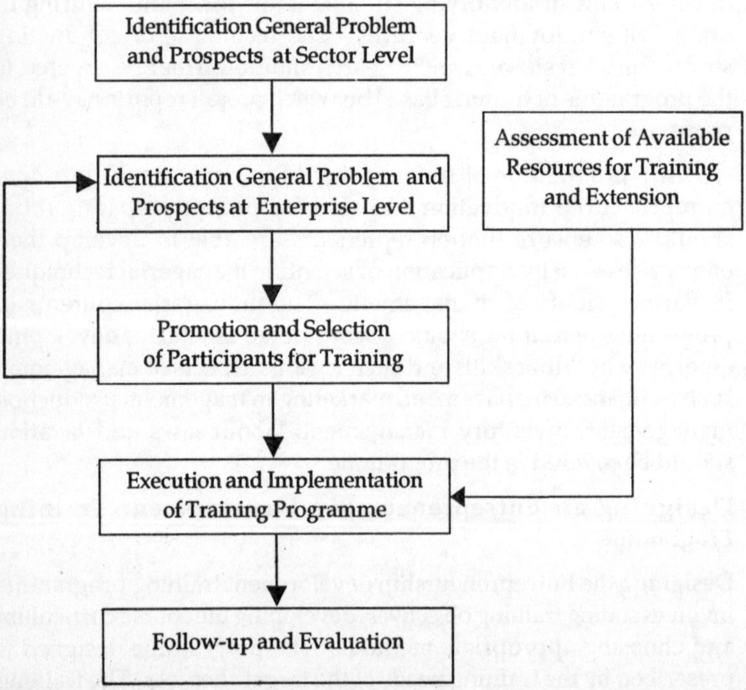

Dimensions of Training Methods

Active involvement of the trainees in the teaching-learning experience to the real situations encountered by entrepreneurs, and opportunities to acquire learn skills are same of the important dimensions of teaching methods.

Range of Training Methods

Apart from conventional training methods, there is a need for use of range of trainee centered and resource based learning methods for enabling trainees to effectively acquire and use the competencies.

Some of these methods are Role Model, Peer Groups, Power Buttons, Case Studies, Simulations, SWOT Analysis, Experimental Learning and Business Game. As a trainee, one should be fully conversant with these methods for their effective use in the training programme.

Areas of Training for Entrepreneur

Figure 7.2 : Skills of an Entrepreneur

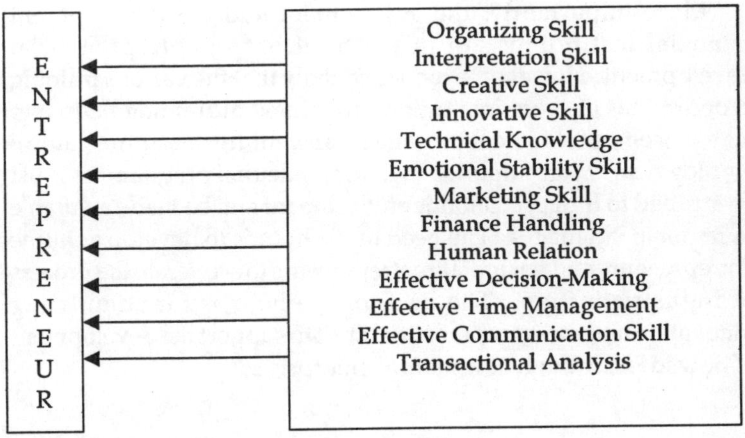

Training Curriculum for Entrepreneurs

1. Determining the potential of Entrepreneurs
2. Development of business plans
3. Understanding the nature of business
4. Planning the marketing strategies
5. Dealing with business
6. Protection of business

7. Managing Human Resource
8. Managing Finance
9. Handling of Customer

While formulating the curriculum, the planner must be guided by the results of the training need assessment and analysis and of course, by the training objectives.

While the training objectives serve as the skeletal frame work of the training, the curriculum represents its flesh and blood. If embodies the subject matter or learning promotes that will be put across to enable the trainees to attain the training objectives.

Conclusion

Training refers to the process of increasing knowledge and skill of an employee for doing a particular job. Soon after a worker is selected and inducted into a job, the entrepreneurs may not expect full contribution from him in attaining the objectives of the factory, as he is just a "raw" human resource. For ensuring satisfactory job performance, training is essential at all levels of management.

More importantly, the government and the development financial institutions are in the forefront in entrepreneurial development. However, experience show that the various training programmes of these institutions are aimed at training people to take up self-employment or some small venture or acquire gainful employment. More importantly, entrepreneurial programmes must be attuned to Indian economic environment and be made available in regional languages. The need of the hour is to develop genuine entrepreneurs and not imitate entrepreneurs to accelerate the process of industrialization. The need of the hour is for stimulating innovation and the entrepreneurial sprit to support the development of new ideas through new mature enterprise.

8

An Entrepreneurship Training Model for Prospective Entrepreneurs

Dr. T. Ramasamy

Self-employment and development of entrepreneurship among youth requires the inculcation of confidence building among them apart from training. The prospective entrepreneurs have to over come several obstacles to be an entrepreneur.

Entrepreneurship lies at the centre of economic development. It is an integral part of the strategy of industrialization, particularly in small-scale sector. The resources of production remain resources and can never become products or services in the absence of entrepreneurship.

An entrepreneur is a person who is responsible for setting-up a business or an enterprise.

Entrepreneurship is an activity that aims at starting, establishing and increasing the size of an enterprise that produces and sells goods or services in a market.

Importance of Entrepreneurship

The importance of entrepreneurship can be understood in the light of the declining rate of growth of employment in India. Moreover, the entrepreneurship development has enabled the society to generate productive human resources as well as to mobilize and solution them for the subsequent process of development.

Entrepreneurship is a complex and multifaceted phenomenon. Since economic reforms, there has been lots of restructuring in the Indian labour markets in terms of employee's qualifications, nature of work contents and work contracts. These changes have raised the profile and importance of entrepreneurship in the Indian economy.

The Planning Commission of India has set-up a Task Force on employment opportunities to examine the employment and unemployment situation in the country and suggest strategies of employment generation. Besides, efforts are also being made to accelerate the process of entrepreneurship development, particularly, at the small-scale and micro level.

Entrepreneurial Opportunities

Various researches have been conducted to find out the entrepreneurial opportunities in India. The areas such as tourism and hospitality, auto ancillaries, two wheelers, garments, software, light and medium engineering industries, trading/supplies, education and training, poultry, food processing, manufacture of business attires, fruits and vegetable processing, corporate gifting, herbal medicine and skin care products, mineral water, paints, enamels and varnishes, organic farming, music and entertainment, writing instruments, plastics, toys, floriculture, health care sector bio technology, IT–enabled services, educational portals, organized retailing, processing, refrigeration and transportation of food, vegetables and fruits, cruising business, courier services, summer solution related business, insurance, restaurant and bio–fertilizers which can be explored for gainful projects in India.

Entrepreneurship Training

Entrepreneurs are not born but made through training. Entrepreneurship cannot grow in vacuum. It requires an environment in which an entrepreneur can learn and discharge his functions. The required environment can be created in the Entrepreneurship Training Institute (ETI).

The establishment of ETI is an easy job. But, the running of ETI is a difficult task. The validity of ETI depends upon the number of industrial units established after getting training. The task of ETI begins with the feeding of the concept of entrepreneur in the minds of the prospective entrepreneurs and ends with the establishment of an industrial unit at the small-scale and micro level. This chapter highlights a training model for prospective entrepreneurs.

Gate Way to Entrepreneurship

The ETI imparts the concept of entrepreneur and entrepreneurship in the minds of prospective entrepreneurs *i.e.* trainees. This is just like the foundation of multistoried building. The ETI can spend four days for this purpose. An involvement of trainee is created by the institute. It means psychologically the trainee to become an entrepreneur.

Field Visit

The trainees are requested to make a field visit. They can meet the entrepreneurs for discussion and understand the ground reality of the functioning of the industrial unit. The trainees themselves identify the lacuna prevailing in the need of a particular product/ unit. The area of the field visit should be the area in which the trainees are going to establish their proposed units. The trainees can spend eight days for this purpose. A report may be received from the trainees at the end of the field visit. The report contains only the observation and findings of the concerned trainee.

Review of Report

The submitted reports of the trainees should be reviewed by group discussion. The group discussion can be facilitated by the trainer. Single report is reviewed by the trainees at a time. The discussion focus the areas like marketability, technology available, need of skilled labour force, quantum of finance required, sources of finance, gestation period of the project etc. Ten days may be allotted for the review of the report. The project may be finalized in this stage. If not so, the concerned trainee is requested to select some other project.

Finding of Location

Only the trainees who have finalized their projects alone enter this stage. The exact location of the proposed unit is to be finalized by the trainee. The trainee has the full freedom to select the site but he/she should consider the merits and demerits connected with the particular site. The location may be either in urban area or in rural area. Hence, initially theoretical knowledge is given to trainees relating to the merits and demerits of the urban and rural area. Both the Central and State Governments incentives are also listed out before the trainees. Then, only the trainees can select a suitable place. Six days may be allotted for this purpose.

Selection of Form of Business Organization

Each form of business organization has its own merits and demerits. The trainees can adopt anyone of the form of business organisation. Hence, it is need of the hour to discuss about the form of business organization with the help of exciting leading entrepreneurs. The practical experience of the existing entrepreneurs will give more insight into the weighing and adoption of suitable form of business organization. Four days may be allotted for this purpose.

Incentives and Subsidies

Different incentives and subsidies are given by Central and State Governments to each industrial sector. For time being, the quantum of incentives and subsidies are changing according to the changing industrial policy of the governments. Hence, the latest rate of incentives and subsidies of both the governments are given to the trainees in white and black form according to the projects selected by them. Three days may be spending for this purpose. The procedure of getting incentives and subsidies are also explained. The copy of forms used for getting the incentives and subsidies are also supplied to the trainees.

Finance

Finance is the lifeblood to any business. Now, the trainee has to calculate the amount of finance required to establish and start the proposed unit. The amount of margin money is the main criteria to get financial assistance from the Banks and Financial Institutions. If the trainee has enough margin money, he/she can get adequate financial assistance from the Banks and Financial Institutions easily. The quantum of financial assistance is differing from project to project. Eight days is enough to supply the information relating to finance to the trainees. Seed capital assistance is also available to the specified projects. The trainee has to decide and finalize the sources of finance to the projects in this stage.

Preparation of Project Report

Most of the trainees (prospective entrepreneurs) does not have entire amount to establish and start the unit. Hence it is the duty of the trainees to know the preparation of the project report. The Banks and Financial Institutions extend their financial assistance only on the basis of the project report. The contents of the project report are explained in a detailed manner. The trainees should understand general contents of the project report according to their proposed unit. Five days may be spending to supply the information regarding the preparation of project report.

Submission of a Project Report

The trainees are requested to prepare their project report independently. Eight days are given to the trainees for project preparation. The trainees can get the assistance from the member of Chamber of Commerce, Chartered Accountant, Successful Entrepreneurs, Non-Government Organisation and officer of Lead Bank at this stage.

Finalize the Project Report

The ETI takes the responsibility to finalize the project reports of all the trainees. An officer of District Industries Centre (DIC) may be called for to finalize the project report. Four days may be allotted for this purpose. The trainees may be requested to re-submit their project reports if major corrections have taken place. The final project report should be routed through DIC for getting financial assistance. The trainees can submit an application with DIC to register their proposed units.

Establishment of a Unit

Now, two months are over. The trainees are ready to establish their units. If the trainees have site and factory building already, the ETI can take one more month to establish the proposed unit. It means that one more entrepreneur should be developed at the expiry of three months by the ETI. If the trainees have no site and factory building and basic any technical qualification, six months may be granted to finalize the site and construct a building for a factory. More over, the same trainees are requested to familiar with technical qualification. Then the ETI can take one more month to establish the proposed units for these types of trainees. It means that all the trainees are converted into an entrepreneur at the expiry of nine months.

Pattern of Training Institute

The pattern of the training institute has the following persons.

1. One Academician

He imparts the concept of entrepreneur and entrepreneurship and guides the trainees in the project report in a systematic way.

2. A member of Chamber of Commerce

He must be an office beanery of Chamber of Commerce at district level. He explains the past and present business environments and gives a guideline regarding the changing scenario of business environment.

3. A member of NGO

Trainees are expecting a lot of assistance at every stage. The NGO member can regulate the trainees in the right bath to become an entrepreneur and develops self-confidence in the minds of the trainees.

4. An officer of Central Government

He gives the informalities like incentives and subsidies of Central Government in sector-wise and issues the forms to get such incentives and subsidies to the trainees. He should take the follow-up action of getting incentives and subsidies as early as possible. If there are any changes, he communicates the same immediately.

5. An officer of State Government

He gives the information like incentives and subsidies of State Government in sector-wise and issues the forms to get such incentives and subsidies to the trainees. He should take the follow up action of getting incentives and subsides as early as possible. If there are any changes, he communicates the same immediately.

6. An officer of Lead Bank

Financial assistance is necessary to establish and start an industrial unit. Hence, the officer of Lead Bank takes all steps relating to getting loans and financial assistance from the banks and financial institutions. He explains the procedure to be followed for getting the loans and financial assistance from the banks and financial institutions.

7. Chartered Accountant

The trainees are not well versed with regard to accounts maintenance. The names of books of accounts and register are not known to the trainees. Moreover, the maintenance of books of accounts and registers is differing from one type of industrial unit to another. Hence, the auditor helps the trainees in the way of keeping the books of accounts and registers independently.

8. Cost Accountant

The profitability of a unit is increased by reducing the expenses. Hence, the trainees should understand the cost control techniques. Besides, selling price of a product is a main factor for the marketability of the product. The trainees cannot able to fix the reasonable price without knowing the cost of the product. Here, the Cost Accountant plays in a vital role. He guides the trainees in this area.

9. District Collector

He can solve the problems faced by the trainees in the establishment and functioning of an industrial unit. He may visit the ETI once in a month. If so, the trainees are self motivated and became an entrepreneur as early as possible.

Number of Trainees

The number of trainees may be restricted to 25. The reason is that more concentration is necessary to import the training and establishment of an industrial unit. Moreover, the involvement of trainees in training may be reduced if the number of trainees increased which is beyond control.

Feedback

The task of ETI is not completed with the more establishment of an industrial unit. The functioning of every industrial unit should be watched over by the ETI periodically at least two years. If the new entrepreneurs are steady and develop the self-confidence, the task of ETI comes to an end.

REFERENCES

Reddy, C.R. and Satya Pal Sharma, N.K., "Self-Employment Programmers: An Analysis", *Southern Economist*, July 15, 2005, pp. 26-28.

Ashes Bhattacharyya., "Entrepreneurship Education", *Kurukshetra*, September, 2005, pp. 28-29.

Anuradha Mathu and Nilam Shukla., "Women Entrepreneurship in India—Some Concerns", *Social Welfare*, September 2005, pp. 8-11.

Pulak Mishra and Ramakanta Prusty., "Developing Entrepreneurship in India", *Yojana*, December 2003, pp. 15-18.

Arundhati Chattopadhyay, "Women and Entrepreneurship", *Yojana*, January 2005, pp. 27-33.

Gupta, C.B. and Srinivasan, N.P. (1998). *Entrepreneurship Development in India*, Sultan Chand & Sons, New Delhi.

9

Women Entrepreneurs and Training

Ms. K. Leelavathy and Ms. S. Subadra

"Freedom depends up on economic conditions even more than political. If women are not economically free and self-earning, she will have to depend on her husband or some one else, and the dependents are never free." – *Pandit Jawaharlal Nehru*

So, in order to improve the status and position of women at home and in the larger society, it is necessary that she achieves economic independence. Today, we find that the government is more concerned about the overall economic development of women and for this, development of entrepreneurship among women has become an important aspect of plan priorities. A broad based organisational arrangement for disseminating information, women oriented programmes by the banks and financial institutions, better linkages between the institute of entrepreneurship development and the entrepreneurs associations at state level could pave the way for speedy development in this directions. The Eight and subsequent plan focuses in a big way on generation of self employment among women.

Women Entrepreneurship Promotional Measures

In India, three types of roles are played by Government and Non-governmental agencies in promoting entrepreneurship. They are:

- Promotional
- Supportive
- Regulatory

Promotional

- Mass entrepreneurial awareness programmes

- Entrepreneurial education and motivation
- Guidance and counselling about equality and economic independence of women
- Identifying the targeted population
- Setting up local promotional agencies
- Programmes for personality development and achievement motivation
- Establishing favourable socio and political environment
- Lowering the entrepreneurial constraints
- Availability of suitable business and markets
- Encouragement from family, society and Government.

Supportive

- Skill training programmes
- Assistance for project selection and preparation
- Simplified registration and licensing
- Policy support, incentives and subsidies
- Availability of initial finance
- Development of infra structure
- Tax relief and concessions
- Initial marketing assistance
- Encouraging entrepreneurs association

Regulatory

- Modernization, diversification and expansion services
- Availability of additional working capital
- Industrial advisory services
- Reservation of products and factory sheds
- Quality testing and improving services
- Protection against globalization.
- Internal and overseas marketing assistance
- Group entrepreneurship

The Government and promotional organisations should evolve a suitable promotional policy and programmes including all these activities and implement with efficiently and effectively to have better women entrepreneurship development in the country.

With view to empowering and emancipating women folk, the Government has been implementing a host of gender focused schemes. These schemes aim at capacity building, skill formation and ultimately provision of sustainable livelihood for the unemployed and underemployed. In IRDP Scheme was launched with the above objectives. This scheme had five components *viz.,*

- Training of Rural Youth for Self-Employment (TRYSEM)
- Development of Women and Children in Rural Areas (DWCRA)
- Ganga Kalyan Yojana (GKY)
- Million Well Schemes (MWS)
- Supply of Improved Tool-Kits to Rural Artisans (SITRA)

For shedding the disfunctionalities in the existing individual schemes and streamlining the fool-proof delivery of service to the poor, in April, 1999, the IRDP was restructured as the Swarnajayanthi Gram Swarozgar Yojana (SGSY).

The SWSY, the only self-employment programme is currently being implemented. It aim at promoting micro enterprises and to bringing the assisted poor families (Swarozgaris) above the poverty line by organising them in to Self-Help Group through the process of social mobilization, training and capacity-building and provision of income-generation assets through a mix of Bank credit and Government subsidy .

Self-Help Groups

At all-India level, the number of Self -Help Groups formed have totaled 12.78 lakhs; out of these 1.08 lakhs have already taken up productive economic activities. The concept of Self-Help Group has been propagated by the NABARD. The NABARD has been taken keen interest in developing SHGs in order to empower the womenfolk economically since 1992-93. During the nine-year period ending 2000-01, 28590 SHGs were formed in the state. Bank loan disbursed was Rs. 7992.90 lakhs and NABARD refinance were at Rs. 7935.52 lakhs. The NABARD has conceptualized the Vikas Volunteers Vahini (VVV). It is an experiment in social engineering in the field of rural banking, by adopting a multi-pronged strategy on the part of the lending institutions.

The crucial factor that is indispensable for the success of the SHGs in mutual understanding and reciprocal co-operation. It is incumbent upon the SHGs to find the gap in market and fill the gap with its product to be successful. To help the SHGs realize this objective institutional support and facilitation is required. Even the corporate sector is playing its part in this aspect.

Mahalir Membattu Thittam

The Tamil Nadu Government support for the development of SHGs is through the Tamil Nadu Corporation for Development of Women set up in 1983 . "Mahalir Membattu Thittam " implemented by the Corporation is defined as a device for ameliorating the socio-economic conditions of the rural poor women folk , through formation of SHGs and empowering them to be self-supportive. The scheme is being implemented on a cost-sharing ratio of 75:25 between the Centre and States. The Directorate of Rural Development is implementing this scheme.

The objectives of the SHGs are:

- Promote saving habits;
- Meet small and urgent credit requirements by themselves;
- Utilise the amount borrowed frugally and develop the habit of repaying the loans;
- Augment family income;
- Uplift economic conditions by earning independently;
- Avail bank loan; and
- Governments financial assistance continuously;
- Shun the local money lenders who charge usurious rate of interest;
- Develop expertise to market the products with put the interference of middlemen; and
- Purchase immovable property in the name of women or jointly with her husband.

As on June 19, 2002 it covered 18.59 lakhs women who got enrolled in 1.08 lakhs SHGs in both rural and urban areas. Women below poverty line are the focused group. It also pays attention on welfare of widows, destitutes, divorcees, physically handicapped women, women belonging to weaker sections and adolescent girls. About 47 per cent of the members belonged to SC/STs. The training programmes are being conducted to upgrade the skill of the trainees. The training courses covered the following wide spectrum of activities – Nursing, Computer training, export garments making, mat weaving, silk reeling and twisting, handloom spinning and weaving, cement hollow block making, micro concrete roofing, seed production, leather goods making, etc. The women corporation works in close partnership with 320 NGOs.

Thus the SHGs have made significant progress in ameliorating the socio-economic conditions of the poor mostly along expected lines. But nevertheless, it is imperative for the implementing agencies to sustain this momentum.

Following the empowerment policies adopted by the Government, women are now increasingly coming forward to occupy their place in the sun.

Educational Empowerment

- The government should run continuing education centres of Arivoli Iyakkum, corporation of Chennai, through SHGs. This could serve as information and dissemination centres for implementation of various Welfare activities.
- The government should conduct Technical and service oriented Vocational Training Courses for adolescent girls.
- To ensure 100 per cent literacy among women, the government should take serious efforts in implementation.
- The government should run one year transit schools for school drop-outs and child labourers (A model developed by Tamil Nadu Slum Clearance Board) and admit them in to regular schools after one year of training.
- The government and NGOs should encourage SHGs to run tuition centres and night schools for girl children.

Economic Empowerment

- The government should construct cottage industry or work shed for starting economic activation by the SHGs. Since space is a constraint in most of the slum areas for expanding their business.
- The government should establish SHG bazaars, as followed by the Government of Andhra Pradesh and SEWA for marketing products manufactured by SHGs.
- SHGs should be encouraged to take up new innovative for creating jobs in the areas of catering, fast food, courier service, hardware maintenance, computer, photography etc.

Environment Empowerment

- The government should provide protected drinking water

supply and household and public convenience units, garbage disposal, roads, streetlights and storm water drains to all slum areas. Otherwise the SHGs should be made to demand the facilities they lack.

- Training on testing water quality levels could be imported the SHGs members.
- Tree planting and kitchen garden can be promoted through SHGs to protect environment.

Suggestions are offered for better implementation of EDP and for further promotion of women entrepreneurship in the country.

- Counselling and career guidance programme
- Periodical meeting and conferences
- Women entrepreneur grievance cell
- Reservation of factory sheds and products
- Special industrial park
- Setting-up raw material banks
- Establishing separate financial institution
- Sale promotion campaign
- Rehabilitation programme

Micro level study may be conducted on each common factor on women entrepreneur to suggest appropriate promotional measures in different stages for promotion of women entrepreneurship in the country.

Designing an Entrepreneurial Training Programme

- Setting-up objectives
- Developing course content
- Selection of training methods
- Training process
    - Setting up training objectives
    - Developing course content
    - Choosing a training methods

Apart from the character and quality an entrepreneur must possess, an individual may also acquire through the experience *i.e.*, trail and error, which can be expensive and discouraging. Training, therefore is the preferred method through which an individual can learn to become an entrepreneur. There are various institutions at the Union and State Government level that provide training to build knowledge and skill. Training increase the potential ability to improve performance, minimize the chance of failure, increase efficiency assumes better quality results, helps improve employer-employee and consumer and customer relationships and prepare the entrepreneur to accept challenges, systematize the work place and motivate work force towards improved performance. Entrepreneur training programmes are designed with special attention to achieve their objective.

Selections of Methods

- The lecture method to cover theoretical aspect through oral communication
  - Practice to be followed.
- The demonstration method
  - Physical performance is given
  - Practical aspects are exhibited.
- The written instruction method
  - Medium of training covers written courses and reading reference.
- The conference method
- Expert shares their ideas and experience and discuss new ideas/new techniques.

Meetings

- Involving group of people.
- Discuss problem faced by them.
- Exchange ideas/views.
- Consider proposal/alternatives.

Conclusion

The steps taken by the Government for emancipating women had made significant headway. The multi-pronged strategy encompassing education, capacity-building and self-employment, employment in organised and unorganised sector and participation in decision-making, etc., have made a tangible dent in the socio-economic conditions of the women folk . They have indeed become a force to be reckoned with. The fact that women have always been at the forefront of Green Movement, Protection of Human Rights, Campaign for Prevention of Cruelty to Animals etc. Is an acid test for increased participation and sensitisation of issues surrounding them? For all the positive impact made by women movement, equality at work place need to be emphasized through continuation of awareness campaign policy measures and legal efforts is to be curbed through guaranteeing safe and non-discriminatory working environment. Failure to tackle the widening socio-economic inequalities would adversely affect both social and economic cohesion and framework.

PART II

Challenges and Opportunities in Entrepreneurial Training

10

Changing Trends in Entrepreneurial Training

Mr. V. Ramesh Kumar and Mr. M. Vinod

Introduction

Entrepreneurship literature reveals general agreement that entrepreneurship flourishes where environmental conditions are most favourable. The environmental factors important for the decision to start a business include: examples of entrepreneurial action, knowledge about entrepreneurship, societal attitudes towards entrepreneurship, salary and taxation levels, availability of venture capital, availability of personnel and supporting services, accessibility of customers, accessibility to universities, opportunities to take advantage of interim consulting and general economic conditions. These environmental factors can be grouped into socio-cultural factors, economic factors, governmental factors and individual differences.

Entrepreneurship

"Entrepreneurship is the process of creating something new with value by devoting the necessary time and effort, assuming the accompanying financial, psychic, social risks and receiving the resulting rewards of monetary and personal satisfaction and independence."

British economists such as Adam Smith, David Ricardo, and John Stuart Mill briefly touched upon the concept of entrepreneurship, though they referred to it under the broad English term "business management". Whereas the writings of Smith and Ricardo suggest that they undervalued the importance of entrepreneurship, Mill goes out of his way to stress the significance of entrepreneurship for economic growth. In his writings, Mill claims that entrepreneurship requires "no ordinary skills", and he laments the fact that there is no good English equivalent word to encompass the specific meaning of the French term 'entrepreneur'.

Apparently, it can be said that the starting point of entrepreneurship would define its type. The two types of entrepreneurship may be classified as:

1. *Opportunity-based entrepreneurship:* an entrepreneur perceives a business opportunity and chooses to pursue this as an active career choice.
2. *Necessity-based entrepreneurship*: an entrepreneur is left with no other viable option to earn a living. It is not the choice but compulsion, which makes him/her, choose entrepreneurship as a career.

Entrepreneurial Training

Opportunity identification and evaluation is quite a difficult task. Most good business opportunities do not suddenly appear, but rather result from an entrepreneur's alertness to possibilities or, in some cases, the establishment of mechanisms that identify potential opportunities.

Although most entrepreneurs do not have formal mechanisms for identifying business opportunities, some sources are often fruitful: consumers and business associates, members of the distribution systems, and technical people.

Training Programmes for Entrepreneurs of Small and Medium-sized Enterprises improves productivity, quality, performance management, competitiveness and sustainability. Training Programmes are effective solutions to improve major performance indicators, productivity, quality, competitiveness, sustainability and knowledge management of multiple enterprises in particular industrial sectors.

Relevance in Today's World

The study of entrepreneurship has relevance today, not only because it helps entrepreneurs to better fulfil their personal needs but because of the economic contribution of the new ventures. More than increasing national income by creating new jobs, entrepreneurship acts as a positive force in economic growth by serving as the bridge between innovation and market place. Although government gives great support to basic and applied research, it has great success in translating the technological innovations to products or services. Although intrapreneurship offers a promise of marriage of those research capabilities and business skills that one expects from a large corporation, the results have not been spectacular. This leaves the entrepreneur, who frequently lacks both technical and business skills, to serve as the major link in the process of innovation, development, and economic growth and revitalization. The study of entrepreneurship and education of potential entrepreneurs are essential parts of any attempt to strengthen this link so essential to a country's economic well-being.

In spite of all these difficulties, entrepreneurship is presently the most effective method for bridging the gap between science and the marketplace, creating new enterprises, and bringing new products and services to the market. These entrepreneurial activities significantly affect the economy of an area by building the economic base and providing jobs. Given its impact on both the overall economy and the employment of an area, it is surprising that entrepreneurship has not become even more of a focal point in economic development.

Need for Entrepreneurial Training

There is a need for entrepreneurial training as it faces the challenges of globalization and the knowledge-based economy. Only with entrepreneurship at various levels in society including the government, can continue to thrive. There is now a renewed effort in place to encourage entrepreneurship. The government has realized that changes are necessary in order to encourage entrepreneurship. The preference on the part of a majority of its citizens, particularly its graduates, for careers as employees rather than as entrepreneurs is somewhat disturbing. Over the past few years, there has been some consensus that failure, particularly business failure, should not be stigmatized. One step to address this has been to reduce the arcane punishment element in bankruptcy law, where the bankrupt person must publicly account for his/her errors and is discharged from bankruptcy only upon payment of much of the debt. This law was amended in 1995 in order to encourage entrepreneurship. The most recent amendments were made in 1999 to encourage technopreneurial activity (technology-based entrepreneurial start-ups) and to enhance entrepreneurial climate.

Challenges to Entrepreneurial Training

Unfortunately, the opportunities for entrepreneurs are often limited by economic environment, which surrounds them. Additionally, although entrepreneurs share some common abilities, all entrepreneurs are different, and their success depend on the economic situations in which they attempt their endeavours.

Though the idea that entrepreneurs are innovators is largely acceptable, it can be difficult to apply this theory of entrepreneurship to less developed countries. Often in less developed countries, entrepreneurs are not truly innovators in the traditional sense of the word. Entrepreneurs in less developed countries rarely produce brand new products: rather they imitate the products and production processes that have been invented elsewhere in the world (typically in developed countries). This process, which occurs in developed countries as well, is called "creative imitation". Creative imitation takes place when the imitators better understand how an innovation can be applied, used, or sold in their particular market niche (namely, their own countries) than do the people who actually created or discovered the original innovation. Thus, the innovation process in less developed countries is often that of imitating and adapting, instead of traditional notion of new product or process discovery and development.

The decision to start an entrepreneurial venture consists of several sequential steps:

1. The decision to leave a present career or lifestyle,
2. The decision that an entrepreneurial venture is desirable, and
3. The decision that both external and internal factors make new venture creation possible.

Although the decision-making process is applicable to each of the three types of start-up companies, the emphasis in each one is certainly different. Because of their differing natures, foundation companies and high potential ventures requires a more conscious efforts to reach a defensible decision on these points than do lifestyle firms.

Latest Trends in Entrepreneurial Training

Entrepreneurial Training must be in such a way, so as to provide the individuals with proper skills in order to enrich themselves. The basic skills that have been identified can be classified into three main areas: Technical skills, Business Management skills and Personal Entrepreneurial skills.

Technical Skills

- Writing
- Oral communication
- Listening
- Monitoring Environment
- Technology
- Technological Business Management
- Ability to Organize
- Interpersonal
- Network building
- Management style
- Being a team player

Business Management Skills

- Planning and Goal setting
- Decision-making
- Human Relation
- Marketing
- Accounting
- Management
- Control
- Negotiation
- Venture launch
- Managing Growth

Personal Entrepreneurial Skills

- Inner control/disciplined
- Risk taker
- Innovative
- Change oriented
- Persistent
- Ability to manage change

Too-fast growth or uncontrolled growth can lead to a situation known as "hitting the wall". This is when a venture grows too fast and loses control of cash, inventory, and customers and eventually profits. Although the situation does not always result in bankruptcy or disaster, it is something that the entrepreneur can be prepared for by establishing good control and managing growth rather than letting it just run rampant.

One of the important role of an entrepreneur during ventures' growth stage is to establish an effective organization culture. This can be accomplished through good communication, being a good listener, delegating responsibility, providing employees with consistent and regular feedback, establishing employee incentives, maintaining a focus on the mission and goals set in the plan and establishing a "we" spirit rather than a "me" spirit.

Procedure for Effective Entrepreneurial Training

Today's knowledge based economy is fertile ground for entrepreneurs, in India. It is rightly believed that India has an extraordinary talent pool with virtually limitless potential to become entrepreneurs. Therefore, it is important to get committed to creating the right environment to develop successful entrepreneurs. To achieve this, India must focus on four areas.

1. *Create the Right Environment for Success*

Entrepreneurs should find it easy to start a business. To do so, most Indians would start slow with capital borrowed from family and friends, the CEO playing the role of salesman and strategist, a professional team assembled months or perhaps years after the business was created, and few, if any, external partners. A major challenge for India is to create a handful of areas of excellence—the breeding ground where ideas grow into businesses. For example, Gurgaon and Hyderabad for remote services, or Bangalore for IT. One-way of strengthening these areas are to consider the role of universities and educational institutions-places where excellence typically thrives.

2. *Ensure that Entrepreneurs have Access to the Right Skill*

A survey conducted by McKinsey and Company last year revealed that most Indian start-up businesses face two skill gaps: entrepreneurial (how to manage business risks, build a team, identify and get funding) and functional (product development know-how, marketing skills, etc.) India can move toward ensuring that the curriculum at universities is modified to address today's changing business landscape, particularly in emerging markets, and to build 'centres of entrepreneurial excellence' in institutes that will actively assist entrepreneurs.

3. *Ensure that Entrepreneurs have Access to 'Smart Capital'*

For a long time, Indian entrepreneurs have had little access to capital. It is true that in the last few years, several Venture Funds have entered in the Indian Market. And, while the sector is still in infancy in India (with estimated total disbursement of less than US$ 0.5 billion in the year 2003), VCs are providing capital as well as critical knowledge and access to potential partners, suppliers, and clients across the globe.

4. Enable Networking and Exchange

Entrepreneurs learn from experience – theirs and that of others. The rapid pace of globalization and fast growth of Asian economies present tremendous opportunities and challenges for India. Through planning and focus, India can aspire to create a pool of entrepreneurs who will be the region's – and the world's leaders of tomorrow.

Conclusion

The definition of entrepreneurship has evolved over time as the world's economic structure has changed and become more complex. Risk taking, innovation, and creation of wealth are the criteria that have been developed as the study of new business creations has evolved. Entrepreneurial role involves doing things in a new and better way, A businessman, who simply behaves in traditional ways, cannot be an entrepreneur, An entrepreneur has to make decisions under uncertainty and he has to take actions with unknown and unpredictable results.

REFERENCES

C.B. Gupta, and N.P. Srinivasan, *Entrepreneurship Development, Sultan* Chand & Sons, 6th Edition, pp. 1-75.

Robert, D., Hisrich, Michael. P. Peters, *Entrepreneurship,* Tata McGraw-Hill, 7th Ed.

Dr. Aruna Kaulgud, *Entrepreneurship Management,* Vikas Publishing House, pp. 21-32.

Prof. Satish. C. Ailawadi, *Entrepreneurship Challenges in 21st Century,* ICFAI Business School, Mumbai.

http://www.choice.humanitarian.org/

11
Why People Deviate from Entrepreneurship?

Mr. P. S. Nagarajan and Dr. S. Kaliyamoorthy

Globalization has sprawled its stretch even from manufacturing pins to the hi-tech concealed technology. Though it has entrenched its span all over the areas still people feel unemployed. The main objective of the initiation of globalization is to increase employment. Employment doesn't means direct radiation, also concerns the indirect employment. While defining the psychology of individuals some people wish to take adventurous venture, which should only be initiated by them, some people don't like to take any risk, but some people take risk not to be borne by them. These are the types of people, which can be psychologically segregated. Of all the sets people impart something to the growth of our economy, no man in this country is born for the degradation of the economy, because each one is born with a style to earn something, to save something. Earning something can be considered as an order of day, but saving cannot be considered as an order of day. The practice of savings should not be cherished because it makes the young generation not to think not to go on further proceedings to the venturesome. If any need arises, then only man starts to averse the fulfillment of need. To the satisfaction of need there should be deprivation, because if all the things are provided with man, he doesn't think anything, the order of the day is to make man all in this world to think something useful, to do something useful.

Aspiration

Man may think beyond his limit or he may contain within a limit. In economics we have known that the wants and needs are unlimited but the resources are scarce. Of course, at that time there might be any shortage of resources. But today, with all the blessings, man is provided with all the natural and artificial resources. Natural resources include the human and other non-human resources. The artificial resources comprise the machinery, material and money.

Natural resources include the human and other non-human resources. The artificial resources comprise the machinery, material and money.

Aspiration not need to be bounded, the only boundless and the immaterial source man has is the thoughts, dreams and aspirations. All the things can be made fertile if he plans and does all the things as per some periodical calculations, forecasting etc.

Aspiration is formed by some demographic events and some other time bound attributes. It starts with the family of the aspirant *i.e.* his father, mother, brothers, sisters, relatives etc. It may be regard to size of the family, monetary aspects of the family, mentality of the family member's etc. Personality of the family members, the initiation, motivation, perception, locus of control, believes, fatalism and other behaviour related attributes. Similarly the personality of the aspirant also influences in deciding or aspiring something. It is a continuum of highly risky venture to the layman venturesome. Personality in sense comprises all the backups, which surmounts to the personality of a man, then the economic condition of the aspirant. Here, there arise two conceptual assumptions. The sound economic backup aspirant may not venture into some business or to be an entrepreneur, but at the other extent some may wish to have some adventurous things. At the other extreme the aspirant may not have good economic backup they may start business by getting amount from the renewable sources or they may keep aside from Entrepreneurship. Then the important thing, which builds the strength of the aspirant, is the brought up *i.e.* how their family members explore an aspirant to the society, even by their relatives. Some may be orthodox, culture bound, ethical norms, believes and atheism and theism etc. For example TVS has some ethical norm, culture in which all should be truthful to the organisation that all the organization wishes to have but TVS stress more on that. Environment makes man, who is the general accepted fact that all oblique to it, likewise in case of venturesome it needs a good environment and good surroundings. Today's order of the day is indeed true, because if we go on analyzing entrepreneurs the education of the aspirant doesn't only influence to aspire but also the educational aspect of the family, *i.e.* father, mother, spouse etc. Inspiration effects and affects a lot in all the aspects particularly in venturing into business, because motivation can do a lot in inspiring. Inspiration itself is an output of internal motivation.

The above-discussed points influence a person to aspire something, which can be seen in the following.

Forms of Aspiration

It is indeed important for our economy to be developed only by means of Entrepreneurship. So the government promotes Entrepreneurship programmes, which may probably effects a subtle amount of people to be tailored into the Entrepreneurship venture. Other person may which to become higher government officials, which is highly impossible in the present government status. Some percentage of people which is very less take over their family business which cannot be run successfully unless the aspirant has some good innovative ideas to be implemented there. Similarly, to the private companies' job also, a few number of aspirants' aspiration may be fulfilled even if they have potential to perform. A very mere amount of aspirant's wish may be fulfilled with the ample college's providing higher education. Some aspirant fly abroad for work in which they are highly deserved for a feeble work. This is the nature of the present employment scenario. Some aspirants wish to be politicians in which they too even occupy some floor level posts in the political parties. Some renders social service by accompanying with some service groups. The groups are very less comparing other aspirant groups. In the other category people who have no aim comes here. We cannot say that there are people without aim. Anyway, they are the unscheduled groups that don't come under any category mentioned above.

The attributes that here discussed come under the pre-collegiate, *i.e.* before entering into the college. In the collegiate education they may be educated in a college for a maximum period of five years. Again they have to search something to accompany and fulfill their aspiration. Some go along with their aspiration, which they have previously determined. Some deviate from their aspiration.

The problem here discussed is the deviation from Entrepreneurship, which obviously confines to a particular area of Entrepreneurship. So, after the college education the aspirant further scans the environment by analyzing the strength, weakness, opportunity and threat entrenches to the individuals and environment.

Criteria Under Which People Deviate from Entrepreneurship

Of all the deviations in the Entrepreneurship venture the foremost all would say is the behavioural aspects, because the behavioural aspect influences all the activities which are encountered with the individuals. The following clearly demonstrates the conceptual aspects, which ceases the aspirant not to choose the pre-determined aspiration.

Personality

Sometimes both the personalities affect venturesome because introvert and extrovert aspect both has some implications over the behavioural consequences of a man. To some the introvert character may alter similarly with the extrovert, so the person may degrade their spirit of initiation and aspiration towards not to enter into the aspired events.

Locus of Control

Two concepts *i.e.* internal and external locus of control have some subtle influence over the aspirant. Irrespective of all these things the aspirant may aspire before enter into any venture, but at the time of analyzing the contributions needed to start a business the locus of control, particularly external locus of control—whatever happened is only because of some external forces, affect a lot.

Believes

Here theism and atheism influences to an extent. Some religious people while analyzing may not start business, which their religious propaganda will not accede. For example, Muslims would not start finance business.

Thoughts

Optimism and pessimism on all the foundation aspect of any event influences a lot, even in case of small venturesome if person thinks that the future may not be feasible the wishes to go away from the business proceeds.

Motivation

Lack of motivation impacts all the eventual proceedings, because if a person is not motivated self or by external agency he thinks all the negative corners of the events that may not make him to start any business.

Inspiration

At the time of having the aspiration he would have inspired by some model but at the time of analyzing because of the lack in inspiration he deviates against the venturing into business.

Family and Dependents

Man alone cannot live in a society, he needs family and he should have obligations it is indeed an important factor which contributes and makes man to deviate while entering into any business. The large members of dependents may make him to venture or may not. The family surroundings may initiate him to do any adventurous events.

Age and Experience

Aspirant himself may thing the age and experience he has with him may not sufficient to start any business, if he has the same initiation, spirit surely that individual will start only business after getting experience in the social environment.

Monetary Background

If the aspirant is not financially sound it may also make the aspirant net to involve in any business also contrary and *vice versa.*

Environment/Surroundings

The aspirant may be in an environment where there exist a large number of entrepreneurs, there the aspirant boldly enters into any venture, otherwise, and the aspirants will not enter into any business, adventurously.

Political Hindrance

The one, all would say, while not starting a business is the political environment, i.e. the political instability doesn't facilitate any individual to enter into any venture adventurously.

Legal Formalities

Generally people won't bound to the legal formalities we have in our constitution even though there are loopholes that may also be a hindrance which deviates the aspirant not to enter into any business.

Figure 11.1 : Chart Showing the Aspiration and Deviation

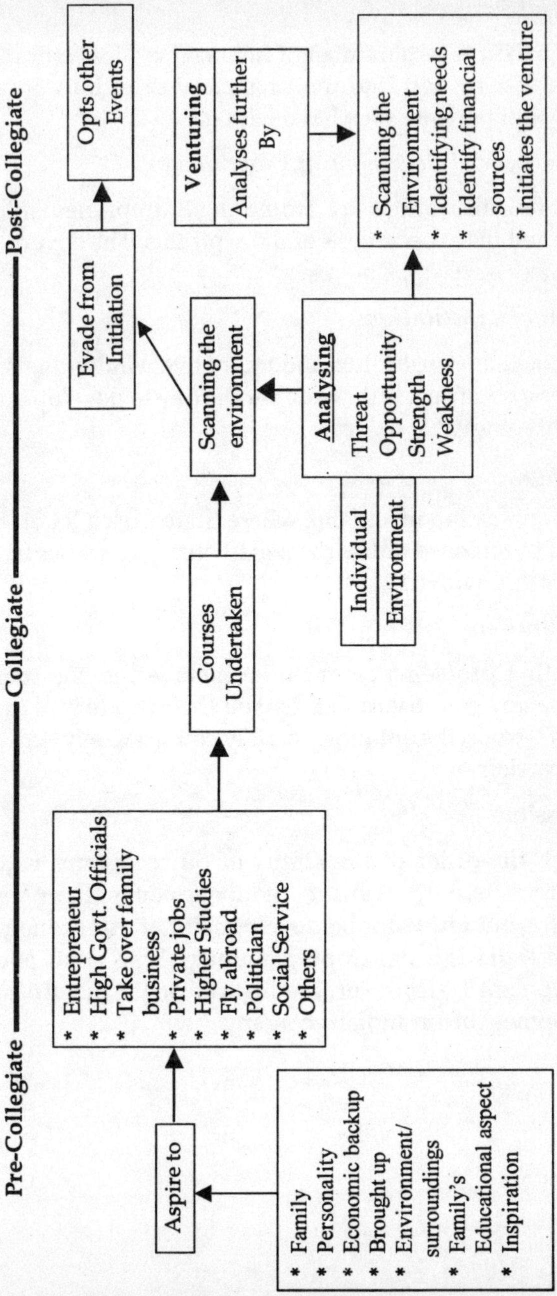

Financial Services

Though there exist a number of financial service institutions people have a fear to step into the financial institutions because of the previous experience they have with it.

Entrepreneurial Development Programmes

Only a few institutions are promoting Entrepreneurship that to do not exceed the expectations of the aspirants. The government has to make necessary steps in this.

Educational Institutions

The educational institution should motivate individuals to start any business, because it is the order of the day to develop our economy with this renovable source.

Economy

Our economy is a mixed one where there exist a lot of hurdles that can not be removed unless the neighbouring countries have a cordial relationship with us.

Trade Barriers

Marketing problems can also be included in the trade barriers because any country can easily sell their product in India but we couldn't export the optimum to other countries only because of some trade barriers.

Conclusion

Though the order of the status of our economy is to promote entrepreneurs, only because of the above points entrepreneurs could not come out fertile to the development of our economy. Still we believe India is a developing country there is no boundary for development. So let the proceedings are in the move of success and development of our Indian economy.

12

Entrepreneurial Training in a New Perspective

Mr. E. Josam Titus
Mr. S.R. John Jebaraj
Mr. M. Sivagnanasundarm

Introduction

The fundamental aspects of entrepreneurial education and training are with specific reference to creativity, innovation and opportunity identification as entrepreneurial skills. The importance of entrepreneurship and the accompanying training of entrepreneurs are not only supported by the current socio-economic situation in India, but are also catalyzed by it. The entrepreneurial trainer can be regarded as one of the favoured parties in this study. This party provides the scientific basis for the compilation of entrepreneurial curricula and the processing of this in the training situation. Discussed here is the way in which the potential compilation of an entrepreneurial curriculum in terms of entrepreneurial skills (creativity, innovation and opportunity identification) could be construed. The entrepreneur—the potential increase of entrepreneurial performance and the participation in a comparative entrepreneurial development programme as compiled by and developed from the $E/P = f[M(E/S \times B/S).]$ content model.

Training Within the Field of Entrepreneurship

Entrepreneurial training and education acts as a facilitator for entrepreneurial activities with the main focus being to stimulate entrepreneurial activity and performance. Training *per se* is defined as an intentional effort to teach specific abilities, which is knowledge bearing, to complete the project better. Training creates new opportunities and possibilities as well as a consciousness to attempt and complete certain tasks in a different way. Currently the problems of entrepreneurial training is seen in the lesser consensus that exists where the content of courses and curricula are involved. There is a big gap where substantial standardised components within the entrepreneurial training programme exist. More emphasis within the training situation should be placed on the complex and multi-disciplinary aspects of entrepreneurship. Those that are regarded as successful programmes vary between being exceptionally simplistic to being mostly abstract. Normally the problems with training programmes are:

- over-emphasis of theoretical and quantitative instruments;
- having too little relevant qualitative factors;
- placing too much emphasis on instruments, concepts and models;
- focusing on bureaucratic management only;
- placing too little emphasis on entrepreneurial activity; and
- Having facilitators that concentrate more on virtual than on real problems.

The New Perspective on Entrepreneurship Training

The new perspective consists of the following constructs: Entrepreneurial performance (E/P); performance motivation (M); entrepreneurial skills (E/S) and business skills (B/S). The composition of the constructs configures in a dynamic multiplication model:

$$E/P = f[M(E/S \times B/S)]$$

One can understand from this that the increase or decrease in entrepreneurial performance should be seen as the multiplication result of performance motivation (M); Entrepreneurial skills (E/S) and Business skills (B/S). The primary aim of this study is based on this content model with specific reference to the following concepts or entrepreneurial skills: Creativity, innovation and the identification of opportunity as primary elements in the training process. The backdrop of this new perspective is based on the following processes:

1. The entrepreneurial process.
2. Variables in the development of the entrepreneurial business.

Entrepreneurial Process

The entrepreneurial process, as indicated above, is based on four reciprocating contingencies. The entrepreneur forms the hub and core element in any entrepreneurial process. He or she (or entrepreneurial team) therefore needs certain characteristics and skills in order to explore feasible market opportunities. The significance of the entrepreneur in identifying and exploiting opportunities in the market in a differentiating manner elevates the importance of innovation as a differentiating entrepreneurial skill. An entrepreneurial organisation is therefore needed to produce the innovation and exploit the opportunity in the market place. Another differentiating skill (leadership) is needed to create an organisation which will grow and expand in an entrepreneurial performance context. The entrepreneur is also responsible for attracting the necessary resources or factors of production to fulfil the expected need on the side of the organisation and to achieve set objectives.

Figure 12.1 : Entrepreneurial Process

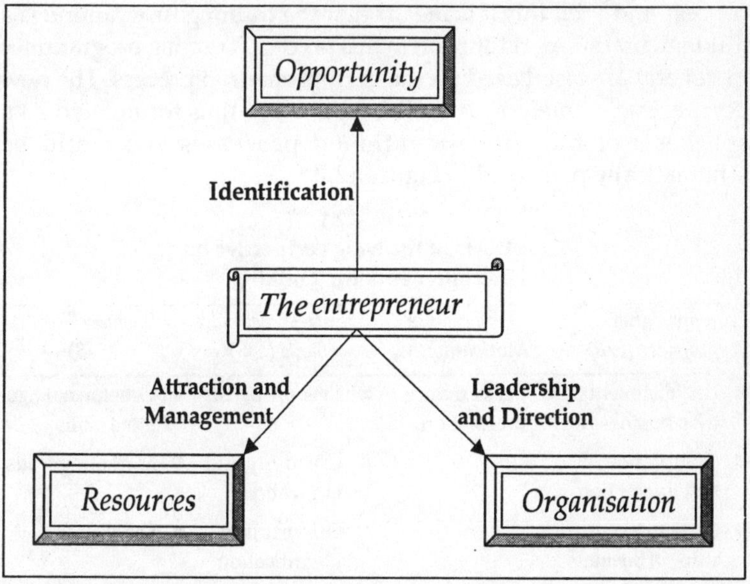

The process model sees the individual (entrepreneur) as an element with specific traits (need for achievements, locus of control, risk-taking, job satisfaction, work experience, role models, age and education); the organisation (type of firm; entrepreneurial environment; partners; strategic variable—cost, differentiation and focus as well as competitive entry mechanisms); the process involved, as compared to the previous process, the business opportunity, resources, marketing of the products or services, the production of the product, organisational development and response to the institutional and societal impact. The environment, as such, forms a pivotal component of the process-model including the following variables: The role of venture capital; inclusion of experienced entrepreneurs–mentors; technical skilled labour force; accessibility of suppliers; access to customers and new markets; government influences; proximity of educational institutions; availability of land; transport; attitude of immediate population; access to support organisations and basic living conditions.

The role of entrepreneurial training as intervention in the successful achievement of objectives or the desired increase in entrepreneurial performance is a vital part of the entrepreneurial process and with this it is meant that the training programme is a fundamental support function in this process. Training programmes in general are also based on the entrepreneurial process. The new perspective, namely $E/P = f\,[M\,(E/S \times B/S)]$, is formulated as a synthesis of the above-mentioned processes and could be schematically presented in Figure 12.2.

Table–12.1
Constructs of the New Perspective on Entrepreneurship Training

Entrepreneurial Performance (E/P)	*Performance Motivation(M)*	*Entrepreneurial Skills (E/S)*	*Business Skills (B/S)*
■ Establishment of own business	■ Performance motivation	■ Risk propensity	■ General management skills
■ Completion of first transaction		■ Creativity and innovation	■ Marketing skills
■ Growth in net value of business		■ Opportunity identification	■ Legal skills
■ Recruitment of employees		■ Role models	■ Operational skills
■ Increasing productivity levels			■ Human resource management skills
■ Increasing profitability			■ Communication skills
			■ Business plan

Figure 12.2 : Schematic Representation of the Entrepreneurial Process

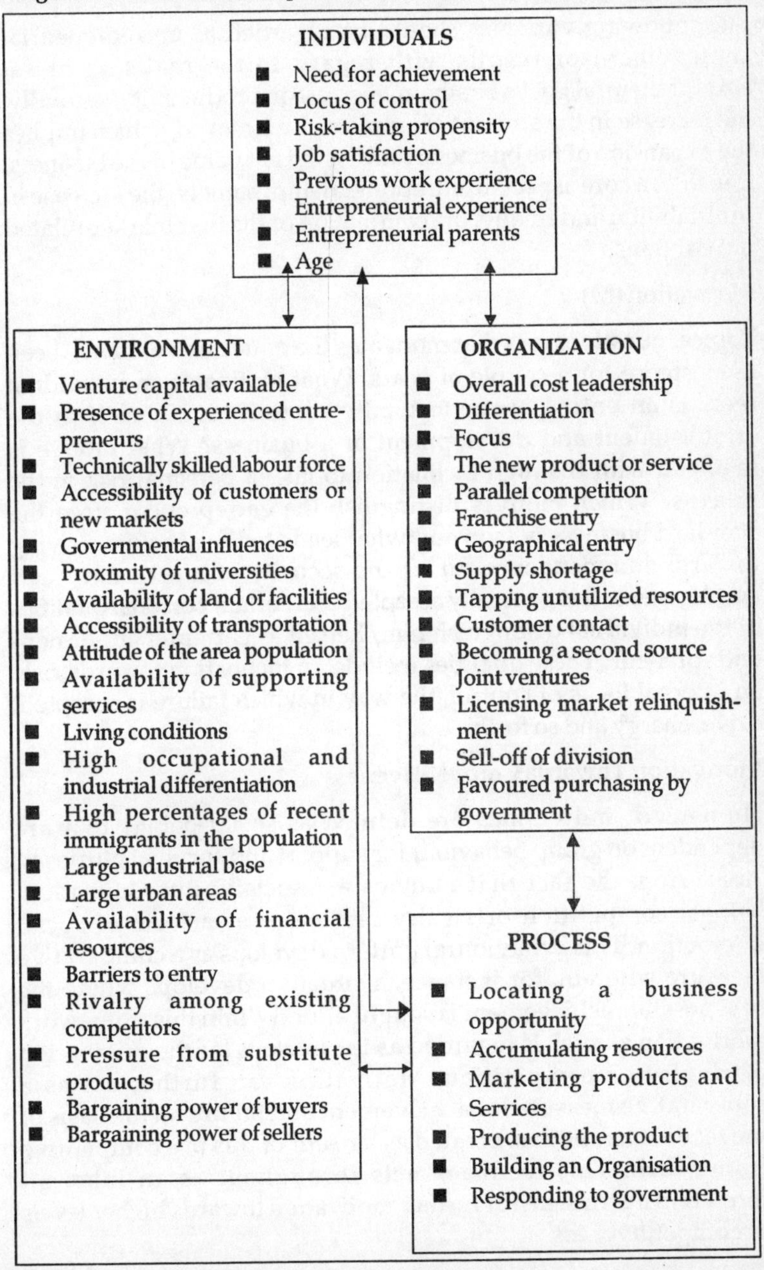

Entrepreneurial Performance

The following variables should be regarded as entrepreneurial achievement or results with regard to the realising of set entrepreneurial goals: Firstly, an increase in productivity; secondly, the increase in the amount of employees employed, which implies the expansion of the business; thirdly, the net value of the business; fourthly, a core aspect in entrepreneurship, namely, the increase in profitability; and finally, the completion of the first market-related transactions.

Motivation (M)

Topical questions on what motivates the entrepreneurs have been in existence for a couple of years. What motivates an individual seen as an entrepreneur to totally commit him/herself to the establishment and development of a business? What motive is involved with the high inclination to take a personal risk in the process? Which motives distinguish the entrepreneur from the standard business person and what leads to the absolute striving towards independence *versus* the security of a set salary and employment? It is generally accepted that certain personal qualities of the individual distinguish him/herself as entrepreneur or non-entrepreneur. These qualities include an inclination towards risk, an internal locus of control, the way in which failure is accepted, drive, energy and so forth.

Motivation Towards Competitiveness

Humans or individuals are defined as social beings that are dependent on group behaviour for support and survival purposes. Apart from the fact that humans are socially interdependent beings, competition or rivalry originates as a form of social interaction. This behavioural pattern develops as a comparative measure wherein, for instance, a situation develops where the best possible achievement is sought after. Within this framework motivation as such is regarded as the nucleus for the origination of rivalry or competition. Motivation can further act as a comparative measure for achievement and failure on the basis of the feedback function, created as a result of this in a competitive framework. This feedback acts throughout as an inherent formation instrument for further motivation towards higher levels of competitiveness.

Innate Incentive

The construct motivation is further described as a basic explorative incentive, which is derived from the inquisitive nature of man as such. Explorative behaviour is motivated by the search for new experience and the flexibility of man that enables him/her to adjust to these so-called new circumstances. This point to an individual who, due to his inquisitive nature, demands to go through a certain learning curve in order to gain the required knowledge to adjust to the "new". This process is driven by motivation.

Acquired Behaviour

It is generally accepted that motivation influences the learning process and learning *per se*. Accepting that learning does influence motivation can also turn around the argument. Motivation is thus placed on an equal footing with learning. Motivation is not only taught but represents a vital integration with the learning process. The individual doesn't learn effectively if the motivation does not exist. In addition, those individuals who do not learn effectively possibly are not motivated because they have never learnt how to be motivated. Motivation can therefore be a positive influence on learning as well as in the learning process: "The more you learned how to be motivated in the past, the more easily you transfer that motivation either to new learning, or more importantly, to new levels of incentives." Therefore, as soon as it is easier to move on to higher motivational levels the nature of motivation will change dramatically. Within this context it is of the utmost importance to investigate the entrepreneur and motivation as a characteristic of the entrepreneur. The motivation of the entrepreneur as an individual becomes absolute when placed within the entrepreneurial performance (E/P) perspective with the aim to integrate motivation as a driving force in the increase of entrepreneurial performance. Entrepreneurial performance as discussed as a result has the aim to increase for instance the profitability, productivity, the net value and growth of the venture. The so-called need to achieve (Nach) that is absolutely present within the entrepreneur is as a result discussed in detail.

The Entrepreneur's Need to Achieve

The typical quality of the entrepreneur as follows: They are well aware that big achievements do not come quickly or easily. Therefore they will mentally dig in for long, hard campaigns rather than hope for lucky breaks. Even their thinking is far more orientated towards the future, fuller of anticipation and attempts at logical predictions, than that of people without strong achievement needs. In view of the above quote it is obvious that in respect of the entrepreneur, motivation must be put in the context of achievement motivation.

Achievement training plays a large role in the development of achievement motivation and the generating of a need to achieve. Therefore, motivation on the one hand and achievement motivation on the other, plays a vital role throughout the training aimed at providing entrepreneurial as well as business skills.

Entrepreneurial Skills (E/S)

This study focuses primarily on the training to provide entrepreneurial skills (E/S), with specific emphasis on the concepts of creativity, innovation and opportunity finding. The other relevant concepts (E/S) will also be discussed in more detail. The scope of the study therefore excludes an intricate explanation of business skills (B/S), although the learner is intensely subjected to such skills training. Entrepreneurial skills (E/S) involve skills embraced by the following concepts: Risk propensity, Creativity and innovation, Opportunity identification and Role models.

Risk Propensity

Entrepreneurial risk as the result of insecurity that exists due to the fact that the success of market penetration can never really be determined beforehand. The correct prediction of the question by the entrepreneur would therefore be an indication of the success in the way of a decrease in risk. Hence, risk can be described as the possibility of innovation having an unwanted result. Regard risk as the conflict situation wherein the entrepreneur will find him/herself. Therefore all risk variables must be studied in depth with regards to the potential reward that could be a result of it. The authors refer to the successful entrepreneur as one who capitalizes on the constructive effect of the conflict situation that originates when a certain risk is taken. This includes the decrease of the negative reaction that can develop from the accompanying exhaustion and frustration, which results from continuous failure.

Time Risk

The time implication of taking a new idea right through the product development phase until it could be considered right for the market.

Investment Risk

This includes the cost of the establishment of a new venture, *i.e.* does the entrepreneur have access to enough capital to enable the venture to survive to the point of being an entrepreneurial institute? Other costs are those related to the total product development process, as well as those concerned with the physical manufacturing of the total product that will, for instance, satisfy the qualitative description.

Technical Risk

All the technical aspects associated with the product development process are considered with the final product having to satisfy the set technical quality standards.

Competitive Risk

The possibility exists that competitors could be offering the same or comparable products in the market, while the success rate of competitors in comparable markets is also an indication of risk. The financial strength and depth of the competitor should not be omitted as a "follower" strategy by the competitor could pose further risk. The existing market advantage of the competitor as well as it's existing distribution system, selling power and established relationships within the market place must be researched. The calculated risk-taking trait of the entrepreneur is regarded as important to distinguish between uncertainty and risk. The entrepreneur manages uncertainty by means of analysing and evaluating risk possibilities to be encountered in future. The calculated nature of managing uncertainty and risk is still, though only to a certain extent, dependent on the existence of "chance", "luck" and "timing". The projection of certain economic is not as predictable as in the past (*e.g.* inflation, exchange rates, interest rates and sales figures), and makes the risk evaluation process for especially the start-up entrepreneur, extremely strenuous. The whole opportunity identification process, which forms a core part of this study, integrates the assessment of risk factors.

Opportunity Identification

The identification of opportunities on a continuous basis is a differentiating characteristic of the true entrepreneur and therefore implying their relevance in a entrepreneurship training programme. These models vary from cognitive inclinations to economic variables. The discussion on opportunity finding forms an integral part of this training.

Role Models

The influence of role models in the choice of entrepreneurial action can, in the context of this study, not be omitted or underestimated. To observe another person as a successful businessperson will obviously lead to the entrepreneur colouring in the picture for him/herself. The entrepreneur could even regard him/herself as being more successful than what is in front of him/her. Role models have a huge impact in the majority of job or career choices. The same statement can be made in the entrepreneurial context. Role models can be parents, brothers, sisters, or family members but especially other entrepreneurs. For the potential entrepreneur the successful entrepreneur as outsider can act as a fundamental catalyst. Within the training context the usage of successful entrepreneurs as example could act as a massive motivational technique. This aspect can both indirectly and strongly support the need for achievement and the achievement variables. The entrepreneur can therefore realise that his/her chosen role model applies intensive innovation, took a calculated risk and strives towards unusual opportunities. Role insecurities could be removed as the entrepreneur can obviously see what is expected of the typical entrepreneur by making use of a role model to model him/herself on. The entrepreneur therefore places him/herself on an equal footing with the role model and in certain cases lets he/she be motivated to the extent that even better achievement than that of the role model could be the result.

Conclusion

This study endeavours to answer the "content" and "effectiveness of the entrepreneurship programme" issues, with regards to specific entrepreneurial skills. The fact that a need exists for further research in the field of entrepreneurship education and training supports the feasibility of this study. A primary focus is thus allocated to training in the following entrepreneurial skills: Creativity, innovation and opportunity finding.

13

Creative Process of Idea Management for Entrepreneurs

Mr. G. Muruganantham and Mr. K. Chandrasekar

Introduction

In the present era of hyper-competition, the need for new products and the entrepreneurial spirit have become so great. Entrepreneurial role involves doing things in a new and better way. Entrepreneurs are often struggling to generate new ideas to introduce new products or to expand their business. A good idea leads to sound business. Idea is the origin of any new venture. To generate new ideas, an entrepreneur can use the creative process of idea generating techniques.

Entrepreneur

According to Peter Drucker, an "entrepreneur is one who always searches for change, responds to it, and exploits it as an opportunity". Entrepreneurs innovate and innovations is a specific instrument of entrepreneurship. Successful entrepreneurs create new values or increase the values of what already exists. They convert a material into a resource or combine existing resources in a new or more productive configuration. Entrepreneurship is presently the most effective method for bridging the gap between science and the marketplace, creating new enterprises, and bringing new products and services to the market. A businessman, who simply behaves in traditional ways, cannot be an entrepreneur, an entrepreneur has to make decisions under uncertainty and he has to take actions with unknown and unpredictable results.

Creative Process

Creativity as it's commonly defined – the ability to come up with *brilliant novel ideas*. Creativity means have great, original ideas. No one knows exactly how the creative process works. It's often a painful process, fraught with uncertainty. Creative insight comes in unpredictable flashes, usually after extended periods of hard work, frustration, and incubation.

The lightening bolt of creative inspiration usually takes us by surprise, striking while we are in the shower, on the freeway, working in the garden sweating at the gym, hiking in the hills, swinging a golf club, reading a book, waking up, or in any of a thousand other settings. The really wild thing about creativity is that, one may not know how, when, or in what form, but it will come.

To keep a company innovative requires this leap of faith-faith that all people have the capacity to be creative, faith that there are lots of good ideas, faith in experimentation, and faith in giving people the freedom to act. Man is by nature an inventor, discoverer, and explorer. Ideation and innovation are not synonyms. The former deals with the generation of ideas; the latter, with their implementation. That is the way creative thinking will more likely be converted into innovation. To be an enduring, great company, it must have the ability to innovate continually to have a constant flow of new ideas. It's essential to keep in mind that many great ideas were at first thought to be stupid ideas.

The first element in making your company creative and innovative is to seek ideas from everywhere and, most important, to create a climate of receptivity to new ideas. There is no shortage of good ideas; there is only a lack of receptivity to ideas.

Entrepreneurial Personality must have a commitment to the systematic practice of innovation. Innovation is the specific function of entrepreneurship. What is often lacking is not creativity in the idea-creating sense but innovation in the action-producing sense, *i.e.,* putting ideas to work.

Innovation and Entrepreneurship

Entrepreneurship is based on purposeful and systematic innovation. "Systematic innovation consists in the purposeful and organized search for changes and in the systematic analysis of the opportunities such changes might offer for economic or social innovation". Essential characteristic of an entrepreneur was to take risks and create innovations.

Innovation may assume the following forms: *(i)* introduction of new goods, *(ii)* introduction of new methods of production, *(iii)* opening of a new market, *(iv)* conquest of new source of raw materials of half manufactured goods; and *(v)* carrying of new organization of any industry. What innovation requires is *hard, focused, purposeful work.*

The concept of innovation and newness is an integral part of entrepreneurship. Indeed, innovation, the act of introducing something new, is one of the most difficult tasks for the entrepreneur. It takes not only the ability to create and conceptualize but also the ability to understand all the forces at work in the environment. The newness can consist of anything from a new product to a new distribution system to a method for developing a new organizational structure.

Principles of Innovation

Purposeful, systematic innovation begins with the analysis of the source of new opportunities. Depending on the context, sources will have different importance at different times. Successful innovators use both the right and left sides of their brains. They work out analytically what the innovation has to be out and look at potential users to study their expectations, their values, and their needs.

To be effective, an innovation has to be simple, and it has to be focused. It should do only one thing; otherwise it confuses people. In fact, no one can foretell whether given information will end up a big business or a modest achievement. But even if the results are modest, the successful innovation aims from the beginning to become the standard setter, to determine the direction of a new technology or a new industry, to create the business that is—and remains—ahead of the pack. If an innovation does not aim at leadership from the beginning, it is unlikely to be innovative enough. Innovation requires knowledge. It often requires *ingenuity* and *focus.*

Establishing Entrepreneurial Systems

In order to establish an entrepreneurial system, an entrepreneur needs to take the following steps:

- Search for business ideas
- Process the ideas
- Select the best idea

- Assemble the necessary inputs resources
- Establish the enterprise

Figure 13.1 : The Process of Innovation

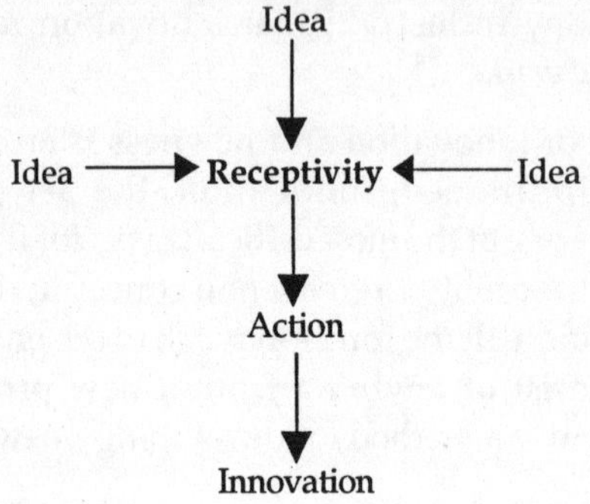

Search for Business Idea

The idea may originate from various sources *e.g.*, success story of a friend or relative, demand for certain products, chances of producing a substitute for an imported article, visits to trade fairs and exhibitions, study of project profiles and industrial potential surveys, meetings with Government agencies, etc.

Sources of Ideas: A business idea may be discovered from the following sources:

Observing Markets

Careful observation of markets can reveal a business idea. Market surveys can also reveal the demand and supply position for various products. It is necessary to estimate future demand and to take into account anticipated changes in fashions, income levels, technology, etc. In this connection, it will be useful to ascertain whether the demand is elastic or inelastic and whether the product is repeat purchase or not. Attempt should be made to determine the trend of demand and the composition and pattern of potential users of the product. A survey of the available channels of distribution should also be made so that the selling campaign can be properly planned well in advance of the production. Advice of professional experts like dealers, commercial consultants, bank managers, advertising agencies may also be obtained to supplement product analysis and market surveys.

Competitions and price trends can also be found through market surveys. From the date collected through market observation, one can identify the products, industries which are in demand and which require increase in supply.

Prospective Consumers

Consumer knows best what he wants and the habits/taste which are going to be popular in the near future. Contacts with prospective consumers can also reveal the features that should be built into a product/service. These days's good business firms generally conduct a survey among prospective consumers before choosing the product to be manufactured. These firms also conduct market test of the prototype product before launching it into the market. The customer is the foundation of a business and it is he who keeps it going. Therefore, data on consumer needs and preferences must be collected. Initially, a new enterprise should concentrate on one or a limited range of products. More products can be added to complete the line later on as the business becomes well established.

Being the Customer

One of the best ways to make and keep company innovation is to have people invent solutions to their own problems or needs. In other words, be your own customer and satisfy yourself.

In 1920, the **band-aid™** was invented by Earle Dickson, an employee of the fledgling Johnson and Johnson Company, whose wife was constantly cutting herself in the kitchen. The accidents occurred frequently enough that he finally decided to make a ready-to-use bandage that she could apply to herself. Laying out a long strip of surgical tape, he place small pieces of gauze on it at intervals, and to keep the adhesive from sticking, he covered it with a piece of cotton crinoline. Dickson mentioned his invention to colleagues at work, and thus sparked one of the most successful commercial products in history.

Hire customer. NIKE, for instance, has lots of athletes as employees. NIKE hires elite athletes as product testing consultants who are expected to test new products under the most severe circumstances and report back with ideas and problems. The nature of innovation is that it is fraught with the unknown. The best way to find out if something is a good idea is to experiment, to give it a try. This, of course, leads to mistakes-ideas that aren't good – but they are part of the process. Innovation requires experimentation and mistakes. You can't have one without the other two, period.

The idea of using microwave for cooking came about through a simple experiment. Les Vandt, an engineer working on microwave technology, bought some popcorn and held it in front of a microwave power tube.

Developments in Other Nations

People in underdeveloped countries generally follow the fashion trends of developed countries. For example, video, washing machines, micro ovens, etc. Which are now the 'in things' in India were being used in the United States and Europe before the eighties in touch with developments in advanced nations. Sometimes, entrepreneurs visit foreign countries in search of ideas for new products/processes. Trade delegations of various chambers of commerce, etc. visit foreign markets to explore foreign collaborations and other types of business ideas.

Existing Companies

Potential entrepreneurs and intrapreneurs should also establish a formal method for monitoring and evaluating competitive products and services on the market. Frequently, this analysis uncovers ways to improve on these offerings that may result in a new product that has more market appeals.

Distribution Channels

Members of the distribution channels are also excellent sources for new ideas because of their familiarity with the needs of the market. Not only do channel members frequently have suggestions for completely new products, but they can also help in marketing the entrepreneur's newly developed products.

Research and Development

The largest source of new ideas is the entrepreneur's own "research and development" efforts that may be a formal endeavour connected with one's current employment or an informal lab in the basement or garage. A more formal research and development department is often better equipped and enables the entrepreneur to conceptualize and develop successful new product ideas. R&D must respond to product ideas from salespeople and also to rotate R&D people into actual sales roles for a period of time or, at minimum, to send them out to the field to interact directly with customers.

Study of Project Profiles

Various Government and private agencies publish periodic profiles of various projects industries. These profiles describe in detail the technical, financial and market requirements and prevailing position. A careful scrutiny of such project profiles is very helpful in choosing the line of business; Technical and other types of experts may be employed to carry out a specialized study of project profiles and to suggest the most promising projects/industries for further evaluations.

Government Organizations

Several Government organizations now-a-days assist entrepreneurs in discovering and evaluating business ideas. Development banks, state industrial development/investment corporations, technical consultancy organizations, investment centers, export promotion councils, etc., provide advice and assistance in technical, financial, marketing and other areas of business. Government also identifies the priority sectors for investment through five years plans industrial policy resolutions and guidelines for industry. In this connection government publications on trade and industry can also be helpful in discovering business ideas. Items reserved for small sector will also indicate the potential areas.

Trade Fairs and Exhibitions

National and international trade fairs are a very good source of business ideas. At these fairs, producers and dealers in the concerned industry put up their products for display and/or sale. A visit to these fairs provides information about new products/machines.

Trade fairs and exhibitions provide opportunities for: *(i)* Assessing the market trends in terms of demand potential and types of products required, *(ii)* Meeting a large number of buyers from different states/countries, *(iii)* Assessing the attitude of the competitors in a particular product of marketing area, *(iv)* Comparing the price and quality of similar products, *(v)* Establishing personal contacts with dealers/importers customers, and *(vi)* Projecting new ideas on commercial publicity for promoting sales in the country and abroad.

Ideas from Inside

Of course, good ideas don't come only from outside; many of the best ideas and innovations bubble up from inside. An organization is a *natural incubator* of great ideas and innovations. For a company to get new ideas, encourage people (employees) to join technical, industry, trade or other groups where they will come in contact with interesting people and ideas. Allow people to travel to events otherwise spend time out in the world exposing themselves to new ideas. NIKE, for example, allocates a portion of its designers to get out of the office and see things, just to spark new ideas. Pay for subscriptions to journals and publications that might have interesting new insights, ideas, technologies and research results. Invite leading edge idea people to give a talk or seminar.

Pay for selected employees to attend education programmes, seminars and university-sponsored events, ask the people to present to others in the company (perhaps at a staff meeting) "the most intriguing ideas" they encountered at the event. Encourage people to read non-fiction materials unrelated to their work, and to share insights gleaned. In fact, research on creativity shows that significant creative contributors have wide interests, a breadth of perspective, and a need for novelty and diversity. Innovation often comes from seeing the relationship between unconnected ideas and melding them together.

Encourage and Help Shy People

Some good ideas never go anywhere because the people who have them are too shy to speak up. In fact, some of the best ideas come from quiet people. Quiet people tent to be excellent observers and thinkers; like cats, they're watchful and attentive, and often intensely curious.

Create Necessity

Human beings have an amazing ability to innovate there way out of seemingly impossible situations. "Necessity," as the cliché goes, "is the mother of invention." But cliché or not, it's true. In fact, many great ideas have emerged precisely because a company lacked the resource to do what it ideally would have liked.

Allow Time Away from the Fray

Certain highly creative individuals need solitary time to do their best thinking, time away, time to think in silence. Phil Knight, founder of NIKE, believes that people get their best ideas away from the office, at the beach, or running, which is one reason why NIKE has a wide ranging campus with running trails, tennis courts, basketball courts, weight rooms, and aerobics studios. Herman Miller lets its designers choose their venue for creativity and some choose to do much of their work at home or somewhere else off site.

In addition to the above business ideas can be discovered form other sources like a new invention awaiting commercial exploitation, an unexploited resource, an unsatisfied demand, an inferior product, etc. for example, housewives need a product that can tell them the quantity of gas left in the cylinder. But no such product is available in India at the moment.

Idea-Push or Market-Pull

On the one hand, classic business school dogma asserts that Entrepreneur should always define a market need first (via market research and other methods of analyzing customer benefit preferences, price sensitivities, etc.), and then develop innovations that meet that need (market-pull or, as it is sometimes called market focus). Yet, on the other hand, many market-successful innovations did not originate from market-pull, nor were they developed via classic market research techniques. Indeed, many breakthrough products wouldn't even if the companies that created them had relied solely on a market-pull approach to innovation.

The *fax machine* is an American invention; yet, as of 1990, not one fax machine sold on the market is American-made. Reason – market research convinced the Americans that there was no demand for such a gadget. The experiment that led to the unique adhesive behind the 3-M Post-it™ notepad was not driven by pre-defined market demand. Spencer Silver (the scientist) didn't start with the idea in mind that there was a market for his unique adhesive. On the contrary, the adhesive was a solution looking for a problem.

Furthermore, once the *Post-it™* product had been conceived it failed a four-city market research test! It was only after an intense period of giving the product away free-getting people addicted to the little note pads – that the product finally took hold. When Fed Smith conceived the idea for Federal Express (overnight nationwide deliver), UPS, Emery Air Freight, and the United States Postal Service, had all thought of the idea before. They had rejected it because they perceived no market need; no customers had ever asked for it.

The first *microwave oven* was built in 1946, based on radar technology imported to the United States from Britain. There was no market demand for a microwave oven.

In fact, according to Jack Kammerer, senior vice-president of marketing at Amana, who introduced the microwave: " If this project had been given to a very highly structured company that had spent a year and hundreds of thousands of dollars in market research, they'd have probably thrown it in the wastebasket and never done it. It was only a gut feeling of a couple of individuals that this is the right product for the right time." Furthermore, certain highly innovative companies are very clear that they consciously foster an idea-push approach to new product innovation.

Akio Morita of Sony wrote:

> "We seek to lead the public with new products rather that ask them what they want. Instead of doing a lot of market research, we refine our product and try to create a market for it by educating the public."

This notion of leading a market—of creating a market—is essential to breakthrough innovations. With dramatic, new innovations, customers will often not tell you what they want (because they do not know what is possible) until you show them what they can have—as was the case with the 3M Post-it™ notes, the radio, and the fax machine. This is very important to realize, or else companies might bypass tremendous opportunities. "Consumers, when confronted with something new and original, can be tempted by it, contradicting all the criteria previously applied to them". The total amount of innovation is higher by using both approaches, rather than relying exclusively on one.

Methods of Generating Ideas

Even with a wide variety of sources available, coming up with an idea to serve as the basis for a new venture can still be a difficult problem. The entrepreneur can use several methods to help generate and test new ideas, including focus groups, brain storming, and problem inventory analysis.

Focus Groups

Groups of individuals providing information in a structured format. *Focus groups* have been used for a variety of purposes since the 1950s. A moderator leads a group of people through an open, in-depth discussion rather than simply asking questions to solicit participant response. For a new product area, the moderator focuses the discussion of the group in either a directive or a non-directive manner. The group of 8 to 14 participants is stimulated by comments from other group members in creatively conceptualizing and developing a new product idea to fulfil a market need. In addition to generating new ideas, the focus group is an excellent method for initially screening ideas and concepts. Using one of several procedures available, the results can be analyzed more quantitatively, making the focus group a useful method for generating new product ideas.

Brainstorming

A Group method for obtaining new ideas and solution. *The brainstorming method* for generating new product ideas is based on the fact that people can be stimulated to greater creativity by meeting with others and participating in organized group experiences. Although most of the ideas generated from the group have no basis for further development, often a good idea emerges. This has a greater frequency of occurrence when the brainstorming effort focuses on a specific product or market area.

When using this method, the following four rules should be followed:

1. No criticism is allowed by anyone in the group – no negative comments.
2. Freewheeling is encouraged – the wilder the idea the better.
3. Quantity of ideas is desired – the greater the number of ideas, the greater the likelihood of the emergence of useful ideas.
4. Combinations and improvements of ideas are encouraged; ideas of others can be used to produce still another new idea.

The brainstorming session should be fun, with no one dominating or inhibiting the discussion.

Problem Inventory Analysis

A method for obtaining new ideas and solutions by focusing on problem. *Problem inventory analysis* uses individuals in a manner that is analogous to focus groups to generate new product ideas. However, instead of generating new ideas themselves, consumers are provided with a list of problems in a general product category. They are then asked to identify and discuss products in this category that have the particular problem. This method is often effective since it is easier to relate known products to suggested problems and arrive at a new product idea than to generate an entirely new product idea by itself. Problem inventory analysis can also be used to test a new product idea.

Results from product inventory analysis must be carefully evaluated, as they may not actually reflect a new business opportunity. For example, General Food's introduction of a compact cereal box in response to the problem that the available boxes did not fit well on the shelf was not successful. The perceived problem of package size had little effect on actual purchasing behaviour. To ensure the best results, problem inventory analysis should be used primarily to identify product ideas for further evaluation.

Free Association

Developing a new idea through a chain of word associations. One of the simplest yet most effective methods that entrepreneurs can use to generate new ideas is free association. This technique is helpful in developing an entirely new slant to a problem. First a word or phrase related to the problem is written down, then another and another, with each new word attempting to add something new to the on-going thought process, thereby creating a chain of ideas ending with a new product idea emerging.

Forced Relationships

Developing new idea by looking at product combination. *Forced relationship* as the name implies, is the process of forcing relationships among come product combinations. It is a technique that asks questions about objects or ideas in an effort to develop a new idea. The new combination and eventual concept is developed through a five-step process.

- Isolate the elements of the problem.
- Find the relationship between these elements.
- Record the relationships in an orderly form.
- Analyse the resulting relationship to find ideas or patterns.
- Develop new ideas from these patterns.

Heuristics

Developing a new idea through a thought process progression. *Heuristics* relies on the entrepreneur's ability to discover through a progression of thoughts, insights, and learning. The technique is probably used more than imagined, because entrepreneurs frequently must settle for an estimated outcome of a decision rather than a certainty. One specific Heuristic approach is called the heuristic ideation technique (HIT). The technique involves locating all relevant concepts that could be associated with a given product area and generating a set of all possible combinations of ideas.

Scientific Method

Developing new idea through inquiry and testing. The *scientific method,* widely used in various fields of inquiry, consists of principles and processes, conducting observations and experiments, and validating the hypothesis. The approach involves the entrepreneur defining the problem, analyzing the problem, gathering and analyzing data, developing and testing potential solutions and choosing the best solution.

Attribute Listing

Developing a new idea by looking at the positives and negatives. *Attribute listing* is an idea finding techniques that requires the entrepreneur to list the attributes of an item or problem and then look at each from a variety of viewpoints. Through this process, originally unrelated objects can be brought together to form a new combination and possible new uses that better satisfy a need.

Matrix Charting

Developing a new idea by listing important elements on two axes of a chart. *Matrix charting* is a systematic method of searching for new opportunities by listing important elements for the product area along two axes of a chart and then asking questions regarding each of these elements. The answers are recorded in the relevant boxes of the matrix. Example: Questions that can elicit creative new product ideas include: what can it be used for? Where can it be used? Who can use it? When can it be used? How can it be used?

Big-Dream Approach

Developing a new idea by thinking about constraints. The *big-dream approach* requires that the entrepreneur dream about the problem and its solution, in other words, thinking big. Every possibility should be recorded and investigated without regard to all the negatives involved or the resources required. Ideas should be conceptualized without any constraints until an idea is developed into a workable form.

Conclusion

Whatever the goals of a business may be, it must make money. To do that, it must get things done. But having ideas is seldom equivalent to getting things done in the business or organizational sense. Ideas do not implement themselves – neither in business nor in art, science, philosophy, politics, love, war. People implement ideas. Ideas are useless unless used. Conclusion keep in mind that there's no shortage of good, workable ideas, but that there's a tremendous shortage of receptivity to ideas. Indeed, ideas and innovation keep a company healthy and prosperous, it satisfies the basic human drive to create and, at the same time, moves humankind forward.

REFERENCES

Peter F. Drucker, "The Discipline of Innovation" *Harvard Business Review*, August 2002, pp. 95-102.

Theodore Levitt, "Creativity is not Enough" *Harvard Business Review*, August 2002, pp. 137-140.

James C. Collins & William C. Lazier (1992). *Beyond Entrepreneurship*, Prentice Hall, New Delhi.

Gupta C.B. and Srinivasan N.P. (2003). *Entrepreneurial Development*, Sultan Chand & Sons, New Delhi.

Aruna Kaulgud (2003). *Entrepreneurship Management*, Vikas Publishing, New Delhi.

Ideas, *Business Today*, January 18, 2004.

The New Entrepreneur, *Business Today*, Collector's Edition, 2002.

14

Role of Cooperative Sector—Entrepreneurship Development

Mr. M. Viswanathan and Mr. P.T. Vijaya Raja Kumar

Introduction

Industrialisation and agricultural development can be achieved both by collective means and individual efforts through innovative initiatives. These are all forms of entrepreneurship usually, the individuals and groups as entrepreneurs are the most important persons in economic life and natural resources gain value by their ingenuity if there is failure they forge success through knowledge to ensure social and economic stability in long-run. Entrepreneurship is neither science nor an art is actually in practice. An entrepreneur is essentially a creative person or an innovative person. He must be interested in acquainting himself with advancing technology and improving the quality of his services and products. He must also expand and re-invest in the organisation or enterprise of firm. The importance of entrepreneurship in socio-economic development through cooperative sector need not be overemphasized it is useful in the promotion of industrial growth and business ventures and also for the socio-economic prosperity of the community.

Objectives of STEP

STEP is being implemented to ensure well-being of women in traditional inform sectors. It aims at increasing self reliance and autonomy of women by enhancing their productivity and enabling them to take up income generation activities. Specific objective,

(i) To provide training for skill up-graduation.

(ii) To mobilize women in small viable groups and make facilities available through training and access to credit.

(iii) To enable groups of women to take up employment-*cum*-income generation programmes by providing backward and forward linkages.

(iv) To provide support services for further improving training and employment conditions of (women department of women and child development 1999) the target group covered under STEP programme includes marginalized, assetless rural women and urban poor. During 1987-2002, about 4.92 lakh women were covered under 96 project launched in various states.

Cooperative Entrepreneurship – A Profile

The Indian economic policy since 1991 had paradigmatically shifted and paved the way for new implications such as competitiveness, transparency, marketisation and operational efficiency. Productivity parameters have brought unimaginable shifts and switches in the economic environment. Cooperative sector is basically a democratic sector, but cooperative should naturally be guided and led by informed and entrepreneurial leaders. Leadership in cooperative is to ensure that, the organisation is developed and ventures become successful and also curry on the business in accordance with the cooperative principles.

The application of management principles and practices in cooperative entrepreneurship is highly desirable in this regard. The principle of voluntary and open membership and democratic member control remains vital in running enterprises. There is an urgent need to change the attitudes and business activities of the cooperative enterprises. Cooperatives perform two functions simultaneously, *viz.* services to members and achieve business goals. Survival of the cooperative enterprise is highly essential in the era of open market economy. Even though a number of successful stories, of cooperatives like 'Amul' remain the pillar stone in cooperative sector. It is surely the need of the hour, cooperative sector. Still we need and require cooperative entrepreneurship leadership in cooperatives. It is surely the need of the hour, cooperatives have the ability to transform the socio-economic condition of crores of underprivileged population in India, and therefore cooperative entrepreneurship leadership is required. Cooperative enterprises are formed to meet the needs of the members. The success of any cooperative primarily depends on the members' participation in its business and management, therefore the entrepreneurial culture among the members in essential.

The principle of self-help and voluntarism of cooperative is necessary and consistent with the entrepreneurial framework of the cooperative the new national policy on cooperatives organisation should recognise the need for inculcating the spirit of entrepreneurship culture in the cooperative sector. The guiding principle in formulating the national policy on cooperative must emanate from the elements and parameters of entrepreneurship growth and progress of cooperative sector in India one of the most notable factors in the cooperative sector is over when living quantitative growth of cooperative sector and parentage of share in the national economy it care be termed as extremely massive in quantitative terms but qualitatively low. The coverage is simply excellent it covers lagers part of the Indian economy, hence the need of the hour is to imbibe the culture of cooperative entrepreneurship.

Table–14.1
Growth and Progress of Cooperative Sector in India

Sl.No.	*Details*	*% share in the national economy*
1.	Rural network (Villages Covered)	100
2.	Agricultural Credit Disbursed (NABARD)	46.3
3.	Fertilizer disbursed (5.809 million tonnes)	31.0
4.	Sugar produced (7.062 million tonnes)	54.9
5.	Capacity utilization of sugar mills	90.1
6.	Wheat procurement	29.7
7.	Jute procurement (1995-96)	21.0
8.	Retail fair price shops (1,25,2000)	28.5
9.	Milk procurement to total production	6.7
10.	Milk procurement to marketable surplus	10.0
11.	Oil marketed (branded)	51.0
12.	Spindles in cooperative (3.27)	10.5
13.	Cotton marketed/procurement (1997)	72.9
14.	Cotton yarn/fabric production	19.3
15.	Cotton yarn export	8.0
16.	Handlooms in cooperatives	55.0
17.	Fisherman in cooperative (active)	21.5
18.	Storage facility (village level PACs)	62.0
19.	Soyabean Production	7.5
20.	Self-employment generated for persons (in millions)	12.5
21.	Salt manufactured	7.5

Developing Entrepreneurship in India

Although the existing government support systems in India includes a number of entrepreneurship promotional measures in terms of reservation of items for SSIs (though the number of items has been reduced drastically in the new industrial policy of 1991) reservation of items for government purchases price preference, priority for utility services, financial incentives, financial support systems, providing infrastructural facilities, marketing services, training, information dissemination monitoring of the system consultancy, very little attention has been paid in developing an enterprising conductive environment and entrepreneurial attitudes. Hence, the following measures, in addition to the above may be suggested to develop a comprehensive policy framework for entrepreneurship development in the country.

First of all it is necessary to create an enterprising environment in the economy as well as entrepreneurial attitudes among the unemployed youth. For this youngsters should be connected intimately with the business. The very trend of the middle class ideology has to be reshaped by complementing (even substituting, if necessary) the belief of traditional education to that of professional education, human moral code to a strong set of business ethics and the idea of a steady job to risk taking for better earnings. All these require extensive moral boosting and confidence building efforts on the part of the governments, academic (both traditional and professional) institutes, and the NGOs.

The organizers of various vocational training programmes, respective government agencies and local administration must work together with proper coordination among themselves to make these programmes effective and successful in terms of self-employment generation and entrepreneurship development. The youth should also come forward and join hands more professionally with these agencies to create wonders in the recent endeavours of governments (both at center and state level) in promoting entrepreneurship and thereby, helping in creating more employment opportunities in the country as well as accelerating the pace of economic growth and development of the nation.

Need for Promoting Entrepreneurship Develop Programme in Cooperative Sector

Entrepreneurship development deals with human resources,

motivation, skills, competencies and social and economic risks. It develops entrepreneurs through systematic entrepreneurship development programmes and developing the core business in a country like India with growing unemployment, the cooperative sector can promote industrial cooperatives, tiny and small industries, agricultural and non-agricultural activities and farm and non-farm activities for these, they need entrepreneurship culture and spirit the educated unemployed youth can be involved in the culture of cooperative entrepreneurship and the spirit will eventually grow. In areas such as IT and computerization young people can enter into entrepreneurship. Again the local indigenous entrepreneurship can be tapped and used by the new generation cooperatives (NGCs) all these can be possible through new perspective and approaches such as:

- *(i)* Effective and efficient training.
- *(ii)* Consultancy.
- *(iii)* Motivation and use of encouragement techniques.
- *(iv)* Development of management skill programmes.
- *(v)* Creation of awareness.
- *(vi)* Use of entrepreneurship development programmes (EDPs) through reputed institutions and centre for entrepreneur development (CED).
- *(vii)* Targeting the right groups such as, technical employees, young engineers, traders, artisans craftsman. They can be urged or motivated to create cooperative enterprises such as cooperative website creation etc.

The following Suggestions are Made to Improve the Effect of Entrepreneurship Programmes on Rural Development

1. Rural peoples should be made more aware to take up such programmes.
2. Activities of different programmes on rural development should be highly co-ordinated to avoid wastage of funds.
3. More emphasis should be given on rural industrialization rather than on agro-based economy as a policy matter.
4. Government should make sure that only needy section of rural areas gets the benefit of these programmes.
5. Government should also encourage private investment in such programmes.

Conclusion

Entrepreneurship development should be viewed a way of not only solving the problem of unemployment but also of overall economic and social advancement of the nation-wide scale development of entrepreneurship can help not only in generating self-employment opportunities and thereby, reducing unrest and social tension amongst the unemployed youths but also in introducing small business dynamism encouraging innovative actives and facilitating the process of balanced economic development.

15

Scenario of Entrepreneurship in the New Millennium: Some Recommendations

Dr. M. Abul Hasan Sathali and Dr. Ayub Khan Dawood

Indian economic structural reforms have been taking place (since July 1991) for making a transition form inward oriented and highly regulated policy regime to export oriented and internationally competitive Indian industry. The future entrepreneur of 21st century will have to face considerable challenges and severe competition not only from domestic industries but also from enterprises of global nature. With liberalization, the Indian entrepreneur is facing severe competition from the global players even in such areas like consumer products which till recently had some protection.

Presently the world is shrinking into a global village due to economic interdependence and revolution in communication technology. Globalization has become a password. Technology is perhaps the most important resource for any nation. Invention, innovation, adoption are the major processes in wealth creation and making the country technologically superior, which in turn lead to economic supremacy. Technology up gradation and modernization will continue to influence the entire sector. Quality assurance, total quality management and new managerial styles will also assume importance as years pass and need to be popularized in the small enterprise sector. Entrepreneurship is going to be one of the trends in the 21st Century as described in 1982 in the book *Megatrends* by John Naisbitt and Patricia Aburdene. There would be shifts from: Industrial society to information society, forced technology to high tech/high touch, national economy to world economy, representative democracy to participatory democracy, hierarchies to networking.

The megatrends which would be the gateway to the 21st Century and which would be influencing our lives are: The booming global economy of the nineties, the emergence of free market socialism, global lifestyles and cultural nationalism, the decade of women in leadership and entrepreneurship. However, in order to lead India towards real entrepreneurial society, the Government of India as well as the entrepreneurs has to take a number of steps to incubate the spirit of entrepreneurship among the educated youth of the country. The following are some of the recommendations to face the challenges.

Recommendations

1. Manufacturing of technology and management of technology will be two generic topics which will need utmost attention in the next century. It is in this context, that technical institutions in our country should rise to the occasion by launching a continuing education programme for the retraining of practicing engineers in industries after assessing the nature and extent of training necessary to be imparted to them.
2. The coming century will see a lot of entrepreneurial opportunities in the areas of electronics including repair and maintenance of electronic gadgets and equipments, electro-medical equipments, consumer electronics items, industrial electronics equipments and electrical home appliances, information technology, technology up gradation and modernization, tie-ups with joint ventures, telecommunications, consultancy services, agricultural sector including food processing and packaging, preservation of seasonal vegetables and fruits, seed processing and preservation, floriculture/cut flowers, fruit juices and pulp, mushroom processing, sweet meat exports, etc., equipments and technologies for abating environmental pollution including monitoring equipment, waste treatment plants, catalytic converters, filtration equipment for power station chimneys, solar cells, wind turbines, heat pumps and other energy recovery systems, venture capital industry, energy conservation measures, computer hardware and software, health care services in rural and semi urban areas including mobile hospitals, new simple and reliable

diagnostic equipment, mineral water industry, robotics, electronic power generation; photocopier, flexible packaging, toys. Inner wears, advertising, herbal cosmetics, express industry, education sector, cattle related items, etc. service sector will provide a tremendous scope for entrepreneurship.

3. Entrepreneurs will have to keep a balance between high tech and high touch in the 21st century because the human beings and their value systems will dominate the show.
4. For eradicating environmental hazards, the people at large will have to take a determined action and involve themselves fully. Mere dependence on various government agencies and Acts is not sufficient. It is also the foremost responsibility of the entrepreneurs to ensure proper steps against environmental degradation.
5. Evolution of an entrepreneurial society that can nurture and sustain steady and continuous entrepreneurial and innovative activities is the need of the hour. Thus, there is need for total reorientation in policies, attitudes and priorities in terms of review and reorientation of curricula, need for committed trainers, need for learning and self-learning with a view to inculcating creativity and innovation qualities in our youth and testing these qualities through entrepreneurial activity.
6. With a view to reaching large number of potential owner-managers of small enterprises, there is a need to try out alternate and cost effective approaches to enterprise education. One of these approaches could be a continuing education model which could be largely be delivered through the distance mode.
7. Total quality management is an effective system combining quality development, quality maintenance and quality improvement efforts of various departments in an organization so as to optimize marketing, engineering, production and after sales service for full customer satisfaction.
8. With the globalization of the Indian economy becoming a reality, small and medium enterprises should adopt ISO-9000 Standards with a view to gaining credibility in the market. Small scale industry sector being one of the major consumers of the energy deserves special attention and efforts in the direction of energy conservation.

9. In the 21st century only those entrepreneurs, who have professional approach, will survive and prosper. To help bring in professionalism, the existing and prospective entrepreneurs should be trained in the modern management skills and techniques.
10. Procedural formalities for availing of any entrepreneur scheme need to be simplified after a comprehensive review of the schemes. Vigorous efforts also need to be made with the help of an appropriate strategy to motivate new band of entrepreneurs in technical institutions.
11. Entrepreneurship awareness must be created in the minds of youth right from the level of primary and secondary education. Special courses need to be designed at college and university levels to impart education on entrepreneurial management.
12. National Employment Service Personnel need to be imparted professional training so that their skills can be upgraded in the context of bringing about entrepreneurial awareness, identifying and selecting the right candidates for entrepreneurship, motivating candidates for entrepreneurship and rendering assistance in launching and management of the enterprise.
13. Entrepreneurship in engineering education is very important with the modernization of industry and economy and in the light of rapid advances in technical education.
14. District Industries Centres should entrust the responsibility of conducting Entrepreneurship Development Programmes (EDPs) for Prime Minister's Rozgar Yojana beneficiaries only to those institutions that can organize EDPs in effective ways. The programme curriculum should be specifically designed.
15. Separate laws should be enacted for the tiny sector. This sector should also be granted exemption from the purview of central excise laws. Ten year tax holiday be given to SSIs for setting up industries in backward areas. SIDBI, CII and State Government agencies should coordinate in identifying the problems faced by SSIs and eradicate the sickness by properly monitoring the progress.
16. In view of plethora of problems being faced by SSIs, the government should come to the rescue of the small entrepreneurs by ensuring the fair distributors of raw

materials, raising of technological level, simplification of administrative procedures and enactment towards both socialistic aims of government and the desired industrial growth in the long-run. There is also a need to push the rural industrialization process.

17. Directories of women entrepreneurs and their enterprises and compilations of existing facilities granted by various agencies should be prepared on high priority. Media should play an important role in bringing about better awareness on issues related to women entrepreneurs. Special training-*cum*-orientation programmes for appraising officers of banks and state agencies should be planned to change their biased attitude while dealing with women entrepreneurs.
18. Entrepreneurial Awareness Camps need to be conducted in rural areas with a view to making rural women aware of their hidden entrepreneurial capabilities.
19. In the changing scenario with the advent of globalization, both small and medium enterprises are facing imminent change and competition, which also signals the need for innovation and thus arises the need for Entrepreneurship within the organization.
20. Women entrepreneurs face certain problems some of which are in addition to, or may be different from, those met by men in starting and managing businesses. The problems and constraints being faced by business women need to be addressed in the right perspective. Their training requirements need to be identified and training programmes should be conducted so that women entrepreneurs are successful in their enterprises and contribute substantially towards the socio-economic development of the country.

Conclusion

The emerging forces of globalization, deregulation and technology transfer as well as increasing and shifting demands of customers etc., are changing the contours of small scale industries. In the days to come, there will be a considerable shift in the way entrepreneurs can perceive business opportunities. Opportunities that are likely to emerge in the new environment can be categorized as follows:

Tie-ups for 'joint ventures' within and outside the sector, Growth in demand for 'differentiated products', Access to 'new technology and process of manufacture' base on a flexible manufacturing system to serve the demand for differentiated products, Access to 'markets which are non-homogenous, and rapidly changing, expanding 'service sector'.

However, in order to lead India towards real entrepreneurial society, the Government of India as well as the entrepreneurs have to take a number of steps to incubate the spirit of entrepreneurship among the educated youth of the country. These steps include integrating entrepreneurship in the education mainstream, cultivating an entrepreneurial culture by helping society to change its value system, increasing facilities and incentives, undertaking R&D and innovations, and assigning a bigger and broader role to entrepreneurs in economic development.

16
Fostering Entrepreneurial Culture

Prof. A.C. Anbudevi

Introduction

What is meant by entrepreneurial? Is it the ability to introduce vast selling new products? The conventional entrepreneur is identified by his/her willingness to take risks in order to seize a market opportunity. He/she may do so by introducing a novel product or service; or by copying what someone has succeeded in doing in another location.

What Makes an Entrepreneurial Culture? Culture has two meanings in the dictionary:

- The customs, arts, social institutions and achievements of a particular nation, people or social group.
- The cultivation of bacteria, tissues cells etc. in an artificial medium containing nutrients.

An Entrepreneur, in the same dictionary is a person who sets up a business or businesses, taking on greater than normal financial risks in order to do so.

The motivational model of entrepreneurship suggests that people are faced with the choice of becoming entrepreneurial at distinct phases in their lives – when changing jobs, moving location, during a period of discontent with their current working environment, when the work-life balance becomes lopsided, following redundancy, early retirement or a return to work after a career break. This model chimes well with the experience of entrepreneurs; makes entrepreneurship an opportunity that can be grasped in many and varied circumstances, and allows people to consider the risks of entrepreneurship in a proper balance with the other elements of their lives.

Entrepreneurial Characteristics

- *Innovation* – Constant striving to develop new products/services.
- *Risk taking* – Willingness to take risks – to face unestablished markets.
- *Leadership* – Striving to be the first to introduce the amazingly novel ideas/products/services.
- *Improvisation* – Willingness to act without plans worked out in advance, and to improvise as necessary.
- *Learning* – The willingness to tolerate mistakes and learn from them.

Entrepreneurial Culture

An entrepreneurial culture is one in which all employees think and act like entrepreneurs. An organization does not have an entrepreneurial culture if the founder who happens to be an Entrepreneur makes all the new products/ideas and decisions. The culture of such an organization could be very oppressive and bureaucratic if the founder/entrepreneur institutes strict procedures for the implementation of only his own ideas. Entrepreneurs in fact found many large and successful businesses; but their long-term success is at risk if they are sole source of initiatives. Therefore there is the need of entrepreneurial culture.

An organization's culture is the set of factors that lead employees to behave differently on a long-term basis from the employees in another organization. Organizations develop different cultures based on different set of values. Values are stronger than practices or habits. Values refer to patterns of behaviour that are either rewarded or punished. Deal and Kennedy (1982) see culture as "a system of informal rules that spells out how people are to behave most of the time."

Some of organizational values to illustrate are:

1. Relationship with employees respect, permanent jobs, promotion within selection and training, comment loyalty.
2. Method in which business is carried informally, team work, Hard work, Integrity, Decision-making, Functional focus.
3. Products/Service values, quality, service, price, cost, innovation, consistency or tradition.

4. Other non-business values: The environment, public service.

Culture influences behaviour. Employees will be motivated to behave as we wish to them to, if our firm's values are in some sense motivational for them. Common motivational factors are—Acceptance, Affiliation, Achievement, Recognition, Independence, Identification, Power, Responsibility, Self-development, Excitement, Nurturing, Creativity, Affection, Justice, Personal integrity, Security, and Money etc. Some of these corporate values relate primarily to retaining employees and only indirectly, to work performance.

Values for an Entrepreneurial Culture

The desire for independence may clash with other values. The innovative knowledge workers may be allowed to take risks with a minimum of central control. The clash between innovation (with its associated motivational desire for independence) and commitment or loyalty has profound implications for organizations. In these days of organizational decline and employees' increased mobility, the need is more than ever to cultivate a strong sense of loyalty among all employees in order to share the strain. In a crisis, a group is often more united than in other circumstances.

One can foster multiple visions of the future, all of which are developed bottom-up among different groups of product development leaders. Therefore instead of sharing the stress of uncertainty among all by encouraging every employee to accept a single vision, it may be more effective to spread the risk by facilitating the formation of multiple visions. But one should see that this diversity must result in the development of different products rather than different divisions offering virtually the same product on a competing basis.

Examples of Entrepreneurial Values

Innovation, Diversity, Risk taking, Respect, Decision-making, Learning, Informality, Networking, Partnership, Results, Intuition, and Disorganization etc.

New Motivational Factors to Cultivate

(a) *Independence:* Most of us has the desire for independence. We are also susceptible to the pressure to conform because of our stronger need for acceptance.

(b) *Creativity:* Independence without creativity yields stubborn rejection of existing practices; individuals with creativity have a natural and insatiable curiosity about how things work and why have to be the way they are. They are like explorers in their constant quest to discover a better way.

Despite the natural creativity of some individuals, everyone can be encouraged to think more creatively by a culture that explicitly and continuously challenges and reward employees to come up with something new.

(c) *Self-development:* It is a means for some people; for some others it is an end itself. To have a driving need to learn more, leads self-development. These people are always concerned to be better and better in their chosen profession, it is not a means to an end, but simply because they value knowledge and competence. As the work force generally becomes more knowledge oriented, many more employees will have this type of motivation.

All these three fundamental motivating factors will contribute to the entrepreneurial values of innovation, diversity, and risk taking.

(d) *Implementation:* An entrepreneurial employee should be motivated to implement new ideas.

(e) *Perseverance:* The entrepreneur must be motivated to persist with a strongly felt intuition in the face of discouragement by colleagues and even sometimes by initial rejection by the market.

(f) *Individualism:* The value of individual effort should not be forgotten.

Motivational Factors that Should be Discouraged in Fostering Entrepreneurial Culture

Just as certain personal motivational factors should be cultivated in order to foster and sustain an entrepreneurial culture; *some others that inhibit should be either discouraged or channeled harmlessly in some other direction.*

Security

The need for security should be channeled in the direction of individual competence and personal diversification. It works with the need for acceptance to increase the tendency to conform.

Acceptance

Often we need acceptance to an excessive degree precisely because we have not developed a very strong degree of self-reliance. An important objective of employee development should be to help them to learn to balance the need for acceptance with a healthy degree of independence.

Power

The need for power in small doses is necessary so that budding entrepreneurs can sell their ideas to those who have the resources they need to bring their ideas to fruition. Beyond this degree of power, the need to acquire authority for its own sake can very easily to produce a high degree of tension between an entrepreneurial culture and a hierarchical one. Those with strong power needs should be encouraged to focus on managing large but short-term projects or to specialize in the delivery task where the creativity of entrepreneurial culture is not very important.

Fostering to Achieve Efficient Entrepreneurial Culture

Creating an entrepreneurial culture is vital for on-going self-renewal. It is not enough to ensure profitability; it requires efficiency above all. The reliable delivery of existing products and services cannot be forgotten in the rush to create the future.

A large diversified enterprise should cultivate a continuum of cultures across the range of its various profit centers. Structure is important and it is designed to facilitate efficient coordination across departments. Empowerment in these units will not mean the freedom to take expensive risks or start entrepreneurial ventures. It will mean having the authority to solve local production or customer problems without consulting a superior. These units still need a minimum of creativity to introduce minor modifications to their products—may be packaging those changes.

For newest units, it is managerial efficiency rather than entrepreneurial culture, which is more needed in the volatile market conditions. Managerial efficiency ensures earning profits. There is no clash if we maintain continuum. The most dynamic markets are those where a firm's whole product line becomes obsolete suddenly, and where managers cannot easily forecast what new products they could launch successfully.

To help the organization to make the necessary transition to a more entrepreneurial cultured organization, managers need to find new roles for themselves, to discover new sources of identity and motivation. Few examples are – Opportunity Explorers, Coaches and Mentors, Purchasers of services, Project managers, Venture Capitalists, Strategists.

An Example of Change in Entrepreneurial Attitude from Ireland

As hard as it may be to believe, the ISA (Irish Software Association) – sponsored report said that money was not the prime motivator for the people behind many of Ireland's start-ups. Instead, the men and women behind many of Ireland's newest high-tech firms are driven to "be their own boss" and have "greater independence," the ISA said.

The survey, entitled "What Motivates Irish Entrepreneurs to Set-up their First Business," was conducted by Shane Davey of the Michael Smurfit Graduate School of Business under the supervision of Dr. Frank Roche. Around 180 entrepreneurs responded to the study, making it the largest published survey of Irish entrepreneurs and motivation to date, the ISA said.

According to the report, the top reason entrepreneurs gave for setting-up their business was "I wanted to be my own boss and have more independence." The number two reason, according to Davey's research, was "I want to do something that I enjoy." The third most popular answer was "I saw a niche in the market that was exploitable," suggesting that on some level, money motivated a few start-up founders.

The Irish Software Association Paul O'Dea said the report was evidence that the entrepreneurial culture in the Republic was beginning to change; a change that could boost indigenous industry. "This report is further evidence of the emergence of a new generation of Irish entrepreneurs," he said.

"If you go back a number of years to the dot-com bubble, there was much more of a get rich quick mentally among high-tech entrepreneurs," O'Dea told ElectricNews.Net. "But I think they are much more real today than they were in the past." He went on to say the change in mentality was driven in part from some business leaders that may have been "burned" in the dot-com hype, while other are emerging as first time business owners who had seen the carnage when the bubble burst.

Davey himself said that he was most surprised that "getting rich" was not the prime motivator for Irish entrepreneurs. "It seems that Irish entrepreneurs at least are more interested in having more control and independence and enjoying their work more than starting up a business to earn their fortune."

"That is not to say that some Irish entrepreneurs are not solely motivated by money just not as many as may be from other countries," Davey added.

Other statistics from the report said that women are more likely to start their companies later than men. According to the ISA-backed work, the average age of all entrepreneurs when starting their first business was 32 years old, although for women the average age was 35 and for men it was 31. Around 15 per cent of business founders in the survey were over 40 when starting their first company. Around 40 per cent were in their 30s and a further 40 per cent were in their 20s, Davey's work indicated. Just 5 per cent were under 20 years old.

Although 76 per cent of the respondents to Davey's questionnaire were men, he reported that women's primary motivations in starting a business are similar to those of men. However, "there is some evidence that instead of struggling to break through a glass ceiling, women feel they can better develop professionally and personally by starting a business," added Davey.

Conclusion

Organizational values are not quite so central to one's core sense of personal identity. The key is to recognize one's allegiance to managerial values and to loosen their grip to enable greater appreciation of entrepreneurial values. The manager should learn to value his/her strengths as being necessary for the present, while seeing entrepreneurial activity as essential for the future.

Based on success stories of other entrepreneurial ventures in an organization or within similar industries, one can develop one's own blend of managerial and entrepreneurial values.

Empowerment means multi-skilling people. When an organization or a small unit is described as a team, the idea is that everyone in the team shares the same values; but when a team is mainly to do with communication between individuals as members, they do not have a common culture. We should encourage teams in the first sense, to adhere to entrepreneurial culture.

REFERENCES

Mitch Mccrimmon (1995). *Unleash The Entrepreneur Within,* FT Pitman Publishing.

Peter Drucker (1985). *Innovations and Entrepreneurship,* Harper and Row.

Terrence Deal and Allen Kennedy (1982). *Corporate Cultures,* Addison- Wesley.

www.electricnews.net

17

Entrepreneurial Culture Among Proprietors of Small Business

Dr. S. David Amirtha Rajan and Dr. Mrs. P. Gnana Soundari

Introduction

The entrepreneur is the creator and manager of a business. Therefore the entrepreneur is not a single person. Further he/she is an economic agent who plays an important role in the economic development of a nation. However he is an individual with knowledge, skill, initiative, drive and sprit of innovation who aims at reaching goals. Richard Cantillon, an Irish man living in France, defined entrepreneur as an agent who buys factors of production at certain prices in order to combine them into a product with view to selling it at uncertain prices in future. Knight also expressed his view on entrepreneur as a specialized group of persons who bear uncertainty. Thus an entrepreneur is a person of having capability to bear risk due to uncertainty in order to attain goals. Such an entrepreneur keeps on changing his/her entrepreneurial character in order to suit with existing environment. Once it is reached, new formation may be established. This new formation is called as entrepreneurial culture. Therefore an attempt is made to study on "Entrepreneurial culture among proprietors of Small Business in Madurai". This chapter is evolved on the basis of the following objectives.

1. To study the personal factors of the entrepreneur.
2. To analyse the entrepreneurial culture.

These objectives are taken into consideration for constructing of a schedule to collect data. A sample of 50 respondents is chosen among various small business owners in Madurai. The convenient sampling technique is adhered. The scheduled is demonstrated among chosen respondents. Such collected information is properly edited, coded and classified. These results of analysis are presented in forth coming paragraph.

Personal Data

Personal data are mainly meant for knowing the ability of any respondents to think on any activity. Mostly it consists of many factors such age, sex, marital status, education and soon. These are presented as follows.

1. Age

The age of the respondents is a vital factor to assess the maturity of the entrepreneur. This provides certain guidance to develop a matured culture. Table 17.1 shows the age-wise classification of the respondents.

Table–17.1
Age of the Respondents

Age	*No. of Respondents*	*Percentage*
Up to 30	15	30
30–40	10	20
40 and above	25	50
Total	**50**	**100**

Source : Primary Data.

It is found from Table 17.1 that 50 per cent of the respondents are in 40 and above age group.

2. Sex

The sex is another factor shows what type culture and character exist among people due to sex. It is interesting to note that all respondents are male.

3. Marital Status

Marriage is another important weighing scale to measure how a new culture is being cultivated after getting themselves union to each other. It is noted that 80 per cent of respondents are married and the remaining 20 per cent are unmarried.

4. Education

Education imparts knowledge on entrepreneurial skill development. It also a mechanism for measuring the cultural factors existing among entrepreneur. Table 17.2 shows the education of the respondents.

Table–17.2
Education of the Respondents

Education	*No. of Respondents*	*Percentage*
SSLL and +2	15	30
Undergraduate	20	40
Postgraduate	15	30
Total	**50**	**100**

Source: Primary Data.

It is noted from Table 17.2 that all respondents are qualified with either school education or college education. However 40 per cent of the respondents have the qualification of undergraduate.

5. Family Size

Size of the family is also an important criterion for expressing one's views and ideas on others or oneself. If a family has a member up to 3, they lead peaceful and cheerful life. Therefore, and the entrepreneurial culture of the proprietor is high. Otherwise, it is in reverse condition. Table 17.3 discloses the family size of the respondents.

Table–17.3
Family Size

Size	*No. of Respondents*	*Percentage*
Up to 3	15	30
3–5	25	50
5 and above	10	20
Total	**50**	**100**

Source: Primary Data.

It is found from Table 17.3 that 50 per cent of respondents have family size of 3 – 5 members.

6. *Qualification of the Spouse*

There is a role of woman behind every successful man. This means, the effort and encouragement women are real strength for a person who is in any kind of work. In this connection, qualification of the spouse plays a vital role in their life for the development of family and society and nation. Table 17.4 shows the qualification of the spouse.

Table–17.4
Qualification of the Spouse

Qualification	*No. of Respondents*	*Percentage*
SSLC	8	20
Undergraduate	24	60
Postgraduate	8	20
Total	**40**	**100**

Source : Primary Data.

It is found from Table 17.4 that 60 per cent of the spouses of the married respondents are qualified with undergraduate. However it is clear that they are educated.

7. *Occupation of the Spouse*

The occupation is a supportive measure to economy of any house hold. Especially, the occupation of the spouse of the married respondents is a additional strength and power of economy of household. Further their earnings help a lot to the business also. On the other side, to some extend, it may be burden to husband or wife who is the proprietor of the business. The burden may be "no physical support", "not maintaining family" and so on. Table 17.5 shows the occupation of the spouse of the married respondents.

Table–17.5
Occupation of the Spouse

Occupation	*No. of Respondents*	*Percentage*
House Wife	16	40
Agency	8	20
Teacher	16	40
Total	**40**	**100**

Source : Primary Data.

Table 17.5 shows that 40 per cent of the spouses of the married respondents are house wife. This is very clear that the remaining that is 60 percent of them gave involved in either business or teaching.

General Awareness

1. *Nature of Business*

The nature of small business of the respondents is shown in Table 17.6.

Table–17.6
Nature of Business

Nature	*No. of Respondents*	*Percentage*
D.T.P. Work and Printing Technology	15	30
Agency	20	40
Automobile	5	10
Grocery Merchant	10	20
Total	**50**	**100**

Source : Primary Data.

It is inferred from Table 17.6 that 40 per cent of the respondents are agents and 30 per cent carry on D.T.P. Work and Printing and Technology.

2. *Experience in Business*

The experience in business is stated in Table 17.7.

Table–17.7
Experience in Business

Experience (in years)	*No. of Respondents*	*Percentage*
Up to 10	20	40
10–20	30	60
Total	**50**	**100**

Source: Primary Data.

It is found that 60 per cent of the respondents have experience in business for 10-20 year. In general they gained good experience in business.

3. *Owner of the Business*

It is observed that all are owners of the business.

4. *Forefathers Business*

60 per cent of the respondents stated that the present business is their own business.

5. *Initiator of Business*

It is very interesting to note that they have started business on their own self initiation.

6. *Motivation in Starting Business*

The persons who took pain in advising and motivating, are presented in Table 17.7.

Table–17.7
Motivation in Starting Business

Motivation	*No. of Respondents*	*Percentage*
Previous experience	5	10
Parents	10	20
Friends	5	10
Self	30	60
Total	**50**	**100**

Source : Primary Data.

It is observed that 60 per cent of the respondents stated that the business was started by the self-effort of the founders.

Attitude on Entrepreneurial–Culture

Table 17.8 shows the attitude of the respondents on entrepreneurial culture.

It is found from the Table 17.8 that most influenced entrepreneurial cultures are "Self confident and optimistic", "Take Initiative", "Responsive to Criticisms and Suggestions", "Creative need to achieve" and "Good memory".

Table-17.8
Entrepreneurial – Culture

Sl. No.	*Culture*	*No. of Respondents*					*Total Score*	*Rank*
		SA	A	NO	DA	SDA		
1.	Self Confident and Optimistic	40	10	-	-	-	240	1
2.	Able to take calculated risk	20	10	15	5	-	195	10
3.	Respond positively to changes	15	20	10	5	10	195	10
4.	Flexible and able to adopt	30	-	10	-	-	190	12.5
5.	Good knowledge of markets	15	20	10	5	-	195	10
6.	Good memory	20	20	-	5	5	190	12.5
7.	Independent minded	30	10	5	-	5	210	4.5
8.	Ability to learn from mistakes	20	15	10	5	-	200	7.5
9.	Energetic and diligent	15	15	10	10	-	185	14.5
10.	Dynamic leader	15	25	10	-	-	205	6
11.	Responsive to criticisms and suggestions	25	15	10	-	-	215	3
12.	Take initiative	20	30	-	-	-	220	2
13.	Resourceful and preserving	20	20	-	10	-	200	7.5
14.	Good planner	20	15	-	10	5	185	14.5
15.	Creative need to achieve	30	10	-	10	-	210	4.5

Source : Primary Data.

Conclusion

The well qualified – married – male dominates the small business. They are mostly above 30 years. They are also much experienced in their fields. The spouses are also qualified and good earners. It is a business, normally, started by self interest of oneself. Their properties are not a property of their forefathers. They feel that they gained a new culture from their business such as "Self confident and optimistic", "Take initiative", "Responsive to Criticisms and Suggestions", "Creative need to achieve" and "Good memory". Therefore, these cultures help them service in their field successfully for a long period.

REFERENCES

Khanka, S.S. (2003). *Entrepreneurial Development*, S. Chand and Company Ltd, New Delhi.

Anil Kumar, S. *et.al.* (2003). *Entrepreneurship Development*, New Age International (P) Limited, New Delhi.

Haynes, W. (2000). *Principles of Management and Entrepreneurship Development*, New Central Book Agency (P) Ltd., Calcutta.

18

Performance and Challenges of EDPs in Dharmapuri and Krishnagiri Districts

Dr. G. Jayabal and Mr. G. Prabakaran

Introduction

Entrepreneurial Development Programme (EDP) designed to help a person in strengthening and fulfilling his entrepreneurial motive and in acquiring skills and capabilities necessary for playing his entrepreneurial role effectively. A programme which seeks to do this can qualify to be called a programmer. This has to be stressed here, because there are a number of programmes which aim at providing informational or managerial inputs or focus on preparation of a project. Although all these inputs are required by a new entrepreneur, a programme not touching entrepreneurial motivation and behaviour cannot be called an EDP. EDP by itself therefore aims at achieving the specific objectives of the programmes and therefore cannot create any magical result. It is a continuous process of training and motivating then to set up profitable enterprises in large measure.

The EDPs are offered by both the Government Organizations as well as Non-Government Organizations (NGOs). Initially, the Small Industries Extension and Training Institute (SIET), Hyderabad selected 52 young persons in 1971 from business and industrial community and offered a three-months training programme and motivated the participants to be entrepreneurs. This was the humble beginning of a massive programme of entrepreneurial development. The central and state level financial institutions and public sector banks conducting EDPs. Even private companies have started offering entrepreneurial development programmes.

Objectives of EDPs

The important objectives of the Entrepreneurship Development Programmes (EDPs) are to:

1. develop and strengthen their entrepreneurial quality.
2. analysis environmental setup relating to small industry and small business.
3. select product.
4. formulate project for the product.
5. understand the process and procedure involved in setting up a small enterprise.
6. know the sources of help and support available for starting a small-scale industry.
7. acquire the necessary managerial skills required to run a small enterprise.
8. know the merits and limitations in becoming an entrepreneur.
9. appreciate the needed entrepreneurial discipline.

Course Contents and Curriculum of EDPs

On the basis of the above mentioned aims and objectives, the course content and curriculum of EDPs could consist of the following:

1. *General Introduction:* It includes factors affecting small-scale industries, the role of entrepreneurs in economic development, entrepreneurial behaviour and the facilities available for starting enterprises.
2. *Motivation Training:* It provides confidence and positive attitude and behaviour among the participants towards business. It ultimately tries to make the participants to start their own business enterprise after the completion of the training programme.
3. *Management Skills:* It provides basic and essential managerial skills in the functional areas. Knowledge of managerial skills enables an entrepreneur to run his/her enterprise smoothly and successfully.
4. *Support System and Procedure:* The participants also need to be exposed to the support available from different institutions and agencies for setting-up and running enterprises.
5. *Project Feasibility Study:* Under this, the participants are

provided guidelines on the effective analysis of feasibility of the particular project in view of marketing, organization, technical, financial and social aspects.

6. ***Plants Visits:*** In order to familiarize the participants with real life situations, plant visits are also arranged. Such trips help the participants know more about an entrepreneur's behaviour, personality, thoughts and aspirations.

Phases of EDPs

An EDP involves three phases. They are:

1. ***Pre-Training phase*** *(Initial Phase):* Through publicity and training programmes, awareness is created about the entrepreneurial opportunities.
2. ***Training phase*** *(Development Phase):* Through training programmes, motivation and managerial skills are developed.
3. ***Post-training phase*** *(Support Phase):* It involves assessment to judge how far the objectives of the programme have been achieved. It indicates drawbacks, if any and suggests guidelines for framing future policies to improve our performance.

Aims of the Study

The following are the specific objectives:

1. To study the performance of EDPs.
2. To study the relationship between the number of trained persons and number of trained persons who actually started enterprises.
3. To study the relationships between educational level and sex of the prospective entrepreneurs.
4. To study the sources of finance to establish enterprise.
5. To study the various challenges in EDPs.
6. To study the level of motivation, agencies support and follow-up action.
7. To provide suggestions to improve EDPs.

Research Methodology

In this research, both Primary and Secondary data was used. The secondary data was collected from previous research reports, EDP training institutes, District industries centre, Banks, Financial

Institutions, District project office etc. Primary data was collected by using structured interview and structured questionnaire. The sample for the survey was 100 respondents in Dharmapuri and Krishnagiri districts. The structured interview was analysed and interpreted with the help of statistical tools.

Analysis and Interpretation

In this study, the analysis and interpretation of performance and challenges of EDPs of Dharmapuri and Krishnagiri districts are presented here. We collected the necessary data for an understanding of the performance and challenges of EDPs by structured interview of 100 trained people through EDPs.

Table–18.1
Male and Female Respondents

Sex	*No. of Trained Respondents*	*No. of Trained Respondents who actually started enterprises*
Male	76	16
Female	24	5
Total	**100**	**21**

Table 18.1 reveals that the relationship between the trained male and female respondents and those who actually started enterprises out of total trained respondents.

It is hypothesized as follows:

H_0 – Male trained persons and who actually started enterprises are more than female.

H_1 – Female trained persons and who actually started enterprises out of total trained respondents will more than male.

$$X^2 = \sum_{i=1}^{n} \frac{(Oi-Ei)^2}{E\,i} \sim X^2(n-1)df$$

The calculated value of X^2 is less than the tabulated value, and hence H_0 is accepted.

According to X^2 goodness of fit, Table 18.1 says that out of 76 trained male, only 16 (21%) persons actually started enterprises. In the case of female, out of 24 trainees, only 5 (20.8%) female members started enterprises. Thus, the trained persons and those who become entrepreneurs more than trained female and those who became entrepreneurs.

Table–18.2
Performance of the EDPs

Respondents	*No. of Trained Respondents*	*Percentage*
Actually started enterprise	21	21
Blocked due to various reasons	7	7
No ideas for starting enterprise (engaged in other activities)	72	72
Total	**100**	**100**

Table 18.2 says that 72 per cent of trained persons who have no idea to start enterprises due to various reasons so that they are engaged in other activities. Out of 28 per cent respondents, 21 per cent of respondents actually started enterprise. Remaining 7 per cent of people attempted to start enterprise but it could not materialise due to various reasons.

Table–18.3
Sex and Educational Status

Educational Level	*Graduates*	*School Education*	*Total*
Sex			
Male	16	60	76
Female	6	18	24
Total	**22**	**78**	**100**

Table 18.3 reveals that there is a significant difference between the male and female with respect of educational status.

It is hypothesized as follows:

H_0 – Male who had more educational status than female.

H_1 – Female respondents will have more educational status than male.

$$X^2 = \sum_{i=1}^{n} \frac{(Oi-Ei)}{Ei} \sim X^2(r-1) \times (c-1)df = 0.36$$

X^2 tab = 3.841

If X^2 cal $<X^2$ tab => H_0 is accepted.

As seen in Table 18.3, chi-square test reveals that female respondents had less educational status than male respondents. Thus, the male had more educational status than female.

Table–18.4
Sex and Sources of Finance

Sex	*Male*	*Female*	*Total*
Sources			
Money Lenders	8	1	9
Banks and Financial Institutions	47	18	65
Own Capitals	15	4	19
Others	6	1	7
Total	**76**	**24**	**100**

Table 18.4 says that there is a significance difference between the various sources of finance with sex.

It is hypothesized as follows:

$$X^2 = \sum_{i=1}^{n} \frac{(Oi-Ei)}{Ei} \sim X^2(r\text{-}1) \times (c\text{-}1)df$$

X^2 cal = 1.4

X^2 tab = 7.82

If X^2 cal $<X^2$ tab => H_0 is accepted.

As seen in Table 18.4, chi-square test reveals that other sources and sources of money lender are less than sources of banks and financial institutions. Thus, the banks and financial institutions play vital role in EDPs.

Table 18.5 reveals that the main challenges are lack of follow-up action which is followed by poor selection of trainees and followed by poor training to existing entrepreneurs.

Findings and Recommendations

1. Number of female trained respondents is more less than male trained and educational status is also less than male.

Table-18.5
Challenges in EDPs

Challenges	*Good*	*Average*	*Poor*	*Total*
Commitment and Sincerity of ED Organisations	22	31	47	100
Support from Agencies	6	44	50	100
Environmental Conditions	20	53	27	100
Selection of Trainees	12	25	63	100
Follow-up	7	25	68	100
Operational Efficiency	12	40	48	100
Motivation	27	31	42	100
Training Methodology	26	44	30	100
Further Training to Existing Entrepreneurs	12	28	60	100
Total	**144 (16%)**	**321 (35%)**	**435 (49%)**	**900**

Female members are to be adequately encouraged to participate in the training programme and establish enterprises.

2. Financial support given by the banks and financial institutions is not adequate. In order to make the programme successful, the banks and financial institutions should provide adequate and timely credit and technical assistance to prospective entrepreneurs.
3. ED organizations have had lack of commitment and sincerity in conducting the EDPs. Necessary guidelines and sufficient financial support will be given to ED organizations so as it will lead to have enough commitment and sincerity.
4. Methods for selecting the candidates who undergo the EDP training programme are also poor. Selection of wrong trainees also leads to low success rate of EDPs. ED organizations should adopt scientific methods for selecting the prospective candidates.
5. Follow up action given by the ED organization is not adequate. Absolute surveillance is essential to identify the discrepancies, if any and rectify it.

6. Trainer–motivations are also poor. That is, trainer - motivations are not found up to the mark in motivating the trainees to start their own enterprises. Motivation is the central core of entrepreneurship. Without motivation, an individual cannot become a successful entrepreneur even though he may have access to finance.
7. There is ill-planned training methodology, inconsistency in programme design, its content, sequence and theme and focus of the programme. Management education and industrial training is needed to the development of entrepreneurship since entrepreneurial decisions have to be effectively supported by managerial decisions. Thus, an adequate number of training centres shall establish and strategic training modules should be evolved.
8. The study found out that the further training to existing entrepreneurs is lack. Over the years what already acquired through training programme become obsolete. Periodic training should be given to existing entrepreneurs according to the changing situations.
9. The study revealed that the environment is not conducive to make the programme success. Non-conducive environment makes the trainer–motivator's role ineffective. Conducive working environment should be ensured for the healthy development of such entrepreneurs in future.

Conclusion

It is now well recognised that entrepreneurs can be developed through appropriately designed EDPs. Commitment and sincerity of ED organizations, structuring of the programmes, motivation, training methodology, methodology for selection of the prospective entrepreneurs, support services after the training, surveillance after the training as well as further training to existing entrepreneurs have significant impact on the success of the EDPs. More importantly, the government and financial institutions are in forefront in entrepreneurial development. Lack of co-ordinated efforts between the various supporting agencies is another notable problem.

The performance of EDPs in these districts has not been well. The actual start-up rates are observed to 21 per cent as against the overall national start-up rate to about 26 per cent which cannot be considered as impressive performance. In this non-impressive performance lies the need for looking at the problems and constraints of EDPs so that the state and central governments have to take necessary measures to eradicate the problems and constraints of EDPs.

However, in the case of women, Tamil Nadu Government has taken necessary steps to cultivate entrepreneurial culture among the women through Tamil Nadu Corporation for Development of Women Ltd. Last four years, nearly 4 lakhs of women have been trained to be entrepreneurs but there are no immediate results. Recently our State Government has taken initiation to foster the entrepreneurial culture among the college students. Accordingly, Educational institutions have been directed to conduct the EDPs to students and submit their report to authorities concerned.

REFERENCES

Tandon. B.C., *Environment and Entrepreneurs*, Chugh Publications, Allahabad.

Khanka, S.S., *Entrepreneurial Development*, S. Chand & Company Ltd., New Delhi.

Vasant Desai, *Dynamics of Entrepreneurial Development and Management*, Himalaya publishing House.

Gupta C.B. and Srinivasan N.P., *Entrepreneurial Development*, Sultan Chand & Sons, New Delhi.

Srivastava, S.B., *A Practical Guide to Industrial Entrepreneurs*, Sultan Chand & Sons, New Delhi.

Jayashree Suresh, *Entrepreneurial Development*, Margham Publications, Chennai.

A Guide to Small Scale Entrepreneurs, Directorate of Industries and Commerce.

19

A SWOT on Successful Women Entrepreneurs—Their Yesterday, Today and Tomorrow

Dr. V. Saikumari and Mr. S.A.Vijayaraj

In the 60's there were white aprons, homemade cookies and hand-sewn clothing. In the 80's there were business suits, fast-food meals and a grab-and-go lifestyle. Now in the 90's, women are recreating their roles once again by starting home businesses at an unprecedented rate. For many women, working from home gives them the flexibility to spend more time with their children while continuing to contribute to the family's income. A large number of women around the world have set up and managed their own businesses. It was not easy for these women to succeed in business. They had to face a lot of difficulties and overcome a number of barriers to become successful in their ventures. They had to deal with discrimination and withstand the skepticism of society, and also put in more effort than men to prove their credibility to others. The entrepreneurial style adopted by women was different from that of men.

The modern Chennai woman is different from the homebound woman of the past to whom selling or running a business carried a stigma which she found difficult to shake off. The cultural contours and attitudes of the city have changed regarding gender. Now the woman entrepreneur can choose to be stationed at home and be in touch with the world outside, cater for the family's needs and yet pursue her dream of economic independence.

Entrepreneurship is not an easy road. One needs to be tough and strong and above all, tenacious. When you enter a big business, you have to learn to handle unpleasantness – coping with demands for bribes, warding off men who try to make passes, handling sexist remarks. Don't expect concessions because you are a woman. You have to fight it out, learn not to cry and complain constantly – that is entrepreneurship. Drive, dedication and the will to strive make a successful businessperson. Since the area is so vast, randomly selected interviewees give us an idea of what is happening in Chennai – why women have taken to a particular field and how well they are coping. But almost all those interviewed stress that it is still a woman's responsibility to look after the home and family and they have to juggle their jobs with cooking, cleaning and taking care of the needs of husband and children. But a double income certainly helps. Loans are a problem when you want to start a business.

This chapter is an empirical investigation among successful woman entrepreneurs in Chennai. A survey was conducted, the collected data was tabulated, all Respondents were SWOT analyzed individually, came out with useful findings. This chapter brings to light the problems existing in the present EDPs, the difficulties women face in setting up and running businesses, overcoming the bottlenecks, the future trends in woman entrepreneurship, the views of experts - women entrepreneurs operating in different fields, the way in which these women entrepreneurs overcame difficulties, their careers from the background in which they set-up their businesses to the success they have been able to achieve, the entrepreneurial traits of successful women entrepreneurs.

The entrepreneurial style of some of the successful women entrepreneurs of Chennai are featured in this chapter. All the women featured in this chapter came from different backgrounds and worked in different fields. These women were able to overcome various constraints to establish an extremely successful business model. By doing so, they set an example for other women.

Methodology Adopted

Sample	:	10
Segmentation	:	Gender Based – income based.
Area	:	Chennai
Limitation	:	Time consuming-interview method.

Opportunities, requirements and preferences of chennaities may vary with other cities.

Findings

1. Reasons for becoming an entrepreneur (own business maker)

Table-19.1
Reasons for Becoming an Entrepreneur (Own Business Maker)

Reasons	*Ranks*
Financial support	1
Financial independence	2
Need for achievement	3
Priority to children	4
Purpose to life	5
Others	6

2. *Background from which Respondents Entered this Field*

Table-19.2
Background Details

Reasons	*Ranks*
Business background	3
Educational/Technical background	2
None	1

3. *The Problems/Blocks Faced*

- Lack of Business education/business experience.
- Securing funding.
- Gender discrimination.
- Societal, cultural, and religious attitude.
- Lack of training and developmental facilities.
- Others.

4. *Ways to Overcome Problems*

- Change your attitude (problems get reduces in size–its all in how we look at it)
- Update yourself with latest news
- Be deterministic
- Self-motivation
- Hard work
- Read about famous successful woman entrepreneurs achievements

5. *Personality Traits to become a Successful Entrepreneur*

- Highly self-motivated

- Self-directed
- Risk taking propensity
- High energy level
- High internal locus of control
- High need for achievement
- Creativity
- Generate new ideas and ways of doing things
- Interpersonal skills
- General business management skills
- Social adroitness
- Ability to focus intensely (especially woman entrepreneurs)

6. The Future of Woman Entrepreneurs

- Wider opportunity
- Greater scope
- Government support and other supportive organizations
- Better training and development opportunities
- Ample loans, finance facilities
- Easier and faster loan approvals
- Skilled and qualified man power availability
- Better support from family
- Positive cultural changes
- Improvement in standard of living
- Increase in spending capacity
- Advancement in marketing activities
- Development on distribution channels

7. The Problems Existing in the Present for Woman Entrepreneurs in Setting-up and Running Businesses

- Lack of business education
- Lack of business experience
- Developing marketing and management skills
- Devising suitable business strategies to thrive in globalised social and economic environment
- Gender discrimination
- Other impediments for woman are societal, cultural and religious attitude.
- Financial institutions give less preference to micro enterprise credit (in which many women entrepreneurs are into)
- Technology, education and training issues are tightly

interwoven and can prevent woman entrepreneurs from reaching profitability potential

- Double shift and double burden – combination of two job one at work and one at home, is difficult for woman in a developing or transitional economy where poverty and lack of infrastructure can make the task harder and more time consuming.

8. Suggestions for Future Woman Entrepreneurs

- Discover your potential
- Develop your personality
- Develop the ability to take risks
- Develop the will to pursue one's passion
- One needs to be tough and strong and above all, tenacious
- Educational qualification is not that important but sound business sense in
- Develop the courage to take the right decision at the right time
- Gender plays no role in this field (according to many)
- Don't expect concessions because you are a woman
- Getting the right ideas at the right time can be crucial to success
- If the scheme is fairly new and it's better, if you go where no one has gone before, the odds are that you will win
- Should learn new skills
- Time management is important, though entrepreneurship offers you flexible time
- Take good care of employees (by providing school fee for their children and attending to their medical needs)
- Dedication and the will to strive

9. A SWOT Analysis on Successful Woman Entrepreneur (own business maker) (Table 19.3)

Conclusion

The success stories of successful woman entrepreneurs are surely a valuable guideline for future woman entrepreneurs. Individually woman entrepreneurship provides women with independence they crave and with the economic and social success they need. Nationally, woman entrepreneurship has great importance for future economic prosperity. Globally woman are enhancing, directing, and

Table–19.3
SWOT Analysis on Successful Woman Entrepreneur

Strength	*Weakness*
■ Self-confidence	■ Sensitivity
■ Determination	■ Worrying about rumors
■ Risk taking	■ Compete back to back with the men
■ Persistence	■ Handling sexist remarks
■ Need for achievement	■ Loans are a problem when you want to start a business
■ Independence	■ Prompt repayment of loans
■ Strong willed ■ Self-motivator ■ Good health ■ Foresight ■ Unique business idea ■ Sound business sense ■ Family support ■ Educational qualifications ■ Drive to run a huge business	■ Society's attitude and double standards can be irksome. If a man comes home late, people remark on how hard he works for the family. If a woman does so, they blame her for neglecting her family.

Opportunities	*Threats*
■ Improvement in technology	■ Ageing
■ Government support	■ Health
■ Development of entrepreneurial training and development centers	■ Competitors
■ Increase in the economic conditions of the people-purchasing power	■ Finance
■ Increase in standard of living	■ Coping up with change in cultural changes
■ Positive cultural changes	■ Coping up with change lifestyle
■ Wider markets-local, national, e-shopping	■ Change in new technology-e-international
■ Educational qualification	■ Compete back to back with the men
■ Diversification	■ Tough world out there
■ Availability of specialized manpower	■ Employee management
■ Change in customers expectations, behavioural patterns	

changing the face of how business is done today. Ultimately, woman entrepreneurs must be recognized for who they are, what they do, and how significantly they impact the world's global economy.

20

Role of Management Teachers in Developing an Entrepreneurship Culture in Business Schools

Prof. A.M. Suresh

Introduction

Entrepreneurship is said to be an attempt to create value through recognition of business opportunity, the management of risk taking appropriate to the opportunity and through the communicative and management skills to mobilize human, financial and material resources necessary to bring the project towards success. Innovation and risk bearing or regarded as the two basic elements involved in entrepreneurship. An Entrepreneur acts as an intermediary between capital and labour, originates and organizes new business ventures or brings in innovative changes in an existing business. Entrepreneurs are growth agents, who initiate and establish an economic activity.

Entrepreneurship promotes capital formation and provides large scale employment. It promotes balance regional development and helps to reduce the concentration of economic power. It encourages effective resource mobilization of capital and promotes country's export trade. Thus entrepreneurship serves as a catalyst of economic development. The role of entrepreneurship in economic development of a country can best be put as 'an economy is the effect for which entrepreneurship is the cause'.

Entrepreneurial development is essentially an educational process and an endeavour in human resource development. Development of an entrepreneur involves inculcating entrepreneurial traits in to a person by imparting the required knowledge, developing technical, financial, marketing and managerial skills to develop the entrepreneurial attitude. It involves equipping the entrepreneur with the information used for enterprise building and sharpening his entrepreneurial skills.

Entrepreneurial Efforts in India

The shining example of success set by the developed countries has proven to be role model for other countries. India in the early years of independence paid relatively more attention to planned economic development than to fostering individual entrepreneurial development. Subsequent years, however, saw many changes. In the 1960's Mcclelland (1961) based on his work in Kakinada District, Andhra Pradesh, demonstrated that entrepreneurial behaviour could be taught. By the 1970's the development strategy it self underwent gradual change moving away from the import substituting self reliance model to an outward looking open market economy. Recognizing the role of entrepreneurship in such an economy, India has been making a national effort to develop entrepreneurship. Entrepreneurship development programmes have been organized by various agencies like SISI, DIP, SIDCO, SIDO, DIC, SSIB and institutions like EDII, NIESBUD, RED, MDI, IIE, XISS, TCO, STEPs for overall economic development of the country by harnessing the vast untapped human resources, channelising them to accelerate industrialization process in Indian context. This has been strengthened by the changes in information and communication technology which has contributed for development of entre-preneurial spirit amongst the younger generation of India.

Management Education in India

The growth of management education has been phenomenal in last 15 years. Accordingly the visibility of management institutions, faculty and students has increased. It is expected that total number of institutions at post graduate level must have already crossed 1000 mark which means that India is second largest in the world, next to USA. The reasons for growth of management education in India are historical, economic, social, technological and policy related. This growth has led to issues like transition to mass education, miss match of supply and demand factors, changing composition of institutions, faculty members and students, heterogeneity, accessibility, quality and excellence of management education. Hence management education is not only huge but also has tremendous growth potential.

Entrepreneurial Training in Management Institutions

This growth in the Indian Management Education System can serve as a useful platform for nurturing an entrepreneurship culture among the diversified management students. Already IIMs have made modest efforts in entrepreneurship education. At IIM Lucknow the 'New Venture Planning' course gives perspectives from all functional areas like marketing, finance, operations, strategy and also preparation of business plans. IIM Bangalore offers electives covering the entire gamut - from the regulation 'Managing New Ventures' to the new subjects 'Entrepreneurship from the trenches – a real world perspective' and 'Social Entrepreneurship'. N.S. Raghavan Centre for entrepreneurial learning at IIM Bangalore has state of the art incubator to help entrepreneurs launch their business plans in to commercially viable products and services. Similarly IIM Ahmedabad has an elective course on 'Laboratory in entrepreneurial motivation'. In this direction, quite a few university departments have also taken up the responsibility of igniting the entrepreneurial fires through their 'Centers of entrepreneurial development', there by contributing towards entrepreneurial training.

Role of Management Teachers

Dr. S.L. Rao in his detailed road map for reinventing management education in the country has observed that management education appears more focused on the elimination of risk rather than on risk taking. He recommends for the efforts to teach students about risk assessment and risk taking. Management education can provide a significant exposure to entrepreneurship and risk taking. Since management teachers play a pivotal role in importing necessary business knowledge and managerial skills to the business management student to assume managerial responsibilities in the corporate world, they can even mould the MBA students to be successful entrepreneurs. A management teacher with a combination of his academic qualifications, research experience, industry background, creative teaching skills and mentor attitude can motivate and bring out meaningful thoughts and entrepreneurial efforts from his students. Thus he his not only transmitting the knowledge but also building the nation through the entrepreneurial spirits of next generations. Hence management teachers of an institution should initiate and involve in the following measures in the present context.

1. Must strongly recommend to the heads of the departments / management of the institution to open entrepreneurial cells in their institutions.
2. Conduct open sessions to promote entrepreneurship as a specialization and profession.
3. Provide in house guidance, encouragement and direction to the budding entrepreneurs to conceptualize, design, produce and market a product/service.
4. Promote interactive sessions with successful business personalities at the local, regional and national level.
5. Help students to develop business plans by integrating new business propositions with existing markets.
6. Establish network with venture capitalists, banks and financial institutions.
7. Make students think small and innovatively.
8. Extend support in understanding and completing legal formalities.
9. Counsel the family members to create supportive environment for entrepreneurial activities of the students.
10. Develop incubation cells to facilitate the students in fertilization of their dream ideas and provide help in identifying business opportunity.
11. Conduct seminars, fast track programmes and special sessions for developing entrepreneurship spirit amongst students.
12. Counsel the students to anticipate experience and manage failures.
13. Promote self study and experiential learning culture amongst students.
14. Ensure linkage of summer training and projects with entrepreneurial training of the students.
15. Involve in case study writing with the inputs of experiential learning of self and students.
16. Seek corporate and institutional financial support for augmenting the entrepreneurship development activities.
17. Conduct guest lecture of successful student entrepreneurs.
18. Develop a resource centre for training and guidance of local entrepreneurs.
19. Get networked with other institutes, agencies and organization for additional input supports.

20. An insight into Junior achievement scheme, Real entrepreneurship through action learning (REAL), Kauffman Foundation (K-14 Models), The National Foundation for Teaching Entrepreneurship (NFDE), The Iowa Entrepreneurial Consortium (IEC), The Dupree centre for entrepreneurship and new venture development, The Johnson centre for entrepreneurship and innovation, Dingman centre for entrepreneurship of USA, and Young Enterprise of UK and Europe provides useful professional inputs for fostering entrepreneurial culture at the institutional level.

Conclusion

In these changing times when per capita income is increasing, markets are expanding, access to information is enhancing and technology is fast changing, it is easy for entrepreneurs to venture forth and grow. What is needed today are a technology friendly environment, a right attitude, a good work plan, fund support and risk taking capacity. Once a few student entrepreneurs succeed, they will become agents of change. Management teachers must nurture these entrepreneurs and make them role models for the rest. The feeling of a successful student entrepreneur as expressed by Henry Brooks Adams "I am indebted to my father for a living, but to my teacher for living well" becomes true for management teachers.

REFERENCES

Jain P.C. (1983). *Handbook for New Entrepreneurs,* Oxford University Press, 1998, p. 3.

Nagarajan, K.V. and Elaine G. Porter (2000). *Women Entrepreneurship, The Current State of Business Disciplines,* Edited by Shri Bhagwan Dahiya, Spellbound Publications Pvt. Ltd., Rohtak, p. 845.

Sridhar, M.K., *Management Education in India – An Analysis,* Manage, House *Journal of Bangalore Management Association,* April 2005, pp. 15-16.

Business World, 6th September 2004, p. 48.

Rao, S.L. An agenda for proactive action, Indian Management, *Journal of All India Management Association,* September 2005, pp. 70-82.

Aryakumar and Umesh Dhyani, Nurturing an entrepreneurship culture - through Academia, *University News,* New Delhi, November 22–28, 2004, p. 12.

Lori, E. Williams, Entrepreneurial Education, Creating a usable economic community base, Rural research report, Illinious Institute for Rural Affairs Publication, Spring 2004, pp. 3-9.

21

Variations Personality and Innovative Personality Among the First Generation Entrepreneurs and the Second Generation Entrepreneurs

Ms. M.A. Vijaya and Dr. Mrs. K. Indumathi

Introduction

Studies on entrepreneurs with regard to their personality will lead to an understanding of the phenomenon of entrepreneurship and may provide a means to develop entrepreneurship. The psychological investigation of entrepreneurs gain significance from the angle and is required to fill gaps in the exciting research.

It is generally agreed that the role of entrepreneur is working with and through individuals and groups to accomplish organizational goals. The objectives of the present investigation may result to the enhancement of certain skills necessary for better personality development and development of entrepreneurial skills. Among the many interpersonal skills the ability to judge and understand the motivation of the employees is of prime concern. A study of entrepreneurial personal may contribute towards understanding of the psychological characteristics that influence human behaviour.

The available studies in the area of entrepreneurship, emphasises that typology of entrepreneurship has a unique contribution in making an entrepreneur. It is inevitable that First Generation Entrepreneurs (FGEs) and Second Generation Entrepreneurs (SGEs) coexist in the society. A comparison of entrepreneurs within themselves will contribute interesting findings in this area of research. A study on personality variations and innovative personality among FGEs and SGEs may reveal many unknown factors. A study of this kind is necessary to facilitate an understanding of entrepreneurs for the process of selection and training programmes.

Researches on typology of entrepreneurs are not new. Such distinction between different types of entrepreneurs has been studied by Collins (1964), Lessener (1973), Scanlan (1979) Venkatapathy (1984) and significant differences have been found among them. The available studies in the area of entrepreneurship, emphasises that typology of entrepreneurs has a unique contribution in making an entrepreneur. A recent focus on the typology resulted in unique patterns of behaviour. Unearthing this area will have greater benefit in uplifting the entrepreneurial population.

Abundant studies have been done with regard to the personality dimensions expanded by Eysenck in relation to varied phenomena such as conditioning, learning, perceptual motor processes and attitudes. The results of these investigations suggest that personality dimensions contribute to all the psychological processes investigated. The present study is encouraged by the trend of results of the studies first cited.

Psychological studies and profiles of entrepreneurs are interesting and revealing. But so far the psychological dimensions have not been able to predict successful entrepreneurship. Under such condition the personality characteristics of the entrepreneur is worth exploring. Hence the present study specifically aims to find out the possible similarity and difference among the FGEs and SGEs on a host of psychological variable, namely, personality trait and innovative personality trait.

Objectives of the Study

1. To find out the difference between the FGEs and SGEs on a host of personality variables, namely, extraversion, introversion and neuroticism, the overall personality and innovative personality.
2. To investigate how far the dependent variable "innovative personality trait" depends on the independent variable "personality trait" among the entrepreneurs.

Methodology

This chapter brings to light the methodology tools and techniques used in this investigation.

The present study is exploratory in nature.

Instrumentation

The following are the instruments used in the present study.

1. Eysenck personality inventory.
2. The Innovative personality inventory developed by Venkatachalam (1978) is an adopted version of the Kirton's innovation inventory.

Sample

A sample of 60 FGEs and 60 SGEs belonging to Coimbatore city has been randomly selected from the list obtained from District Industries Centre of Coimbatore (DIC), Coimbatore District Small Industries Association (CODISIA) have also been approached.

Method of Data Analysis

Statistical Analysis

The data collected using the inventory was scored using appropriate scoring procedures. The tabulated data was entered in the computer, and analysis was done with the SPSS package. The statistical tools used are:

Statistical Tools Used

1. *t*- test
2. Regression Analysis.

Results

Table-21.1
Showing the *t*-Test for FGEs and SGEs with Reference to Extraversion

Group	*Number of cases*	*Mean*	*Standard deviation*	*t-value*
FGEs	60	7.117	2.572	0.30^{NS}
SGEs	60	6.983	2.266	–

The details furnished in Table 21.1 show the mean, standard deviation standard, error and *t*-value between FGEs and SGEs on the dimension extraversion. The calculated *t*-value is found to be 0.30 which is not significant. It can be inferred that there is no significant difference between FGEs and SGEs with reference to extraversion.

Table-21.2

Showing the *t*-Test for FGEs and SGEs with Reference to Introversion

Group	*Number of cases*	*Mean*	*Standard deviation*	*t-value*
FGEs	60	4.517	1.127	0.46^{NS}
SGEs	60	4.417	1.253	

The details furnished in Table 21.2 show the mean, standard deviation, standard error and *t*-value between FGEs and SGEs on the dimension introversion. The calculated *t*-value is found to be 0.46 which is not significant. It can be inferred that there is no significant difference between FGEs and SGEs with reference to introversion.

Table-21.3

Showing the *t*-Test for FGEs and SGEs with Reference to Neuroticism

Group	*Number of cases*	*Mean*	*Standard deviation*	*t-value*
FGEs	60	11.033	3.268	0.62^{NS}
SGEs	60	11.383	2.871	

The details furnished Table 21.3 show the mean, standard deviation, standard error and *t*-value between FGEs and SGES on the dimension neuroticism. The calculated *t*-value is found to be 0.62 which is not significant. It can be inferred that there is no significant difference between FGEs and SGEs with reference to neuroticism.

Table-21.4

Showing the *t*-Test for FGEs and SGEs with Reference to Overall Personality Trait

Group	*Number of cases*	*Mean*	*Standard deviation*	*t-value*
FGEs	60	22.667	3.521	0.17^{NS}
SGEs	60	22.783	3.832	

The details furnished in Table 21.4 show the mean, standard deviation, standard error and *t*-value between FGEs and SGEs, on the overall personality trait. The calculated *t*-value is 0.17 which is not significant. It can be inferred that there is significant difference between FGEs and SGEs with reference to the overall personality trait.

Table–21.5
Showing the *t*-Test for FGEs and SGEs with Reference to Innovative Personality

Group	*Number of cases*	*Mean*	*Standard deviation*	*t-value*
FGEs	60	22.667	3.521	0.12^{NS}
SGEs	60	22.783	3.832	

The details furnished in Table 21.5 show the mean, standard deviation, standard error and *t*-value between FGEs and SGEs on the innovative personality trait. The calculated *t*-value is found to be 0.12 which is not significant. It can be inferred that there is no significant difference between FGEs and SGEs with reference to the innovative personality trait.

Table–21.6
Showing Regression Analysis for Relationship between Personality and Innovative Personality

Variable	*β*	*Standard Error*	*Correlation*	*t-value*
Personality score	-0.89	0.037	-0.219	-2.44*
Constant	9.112	0.849		

It has been hypothesized that the correlation co-efficient $r = 0.219$. The level of significance $\propto = 0.05$.

From Table 21.6, it has been concluded that the regression co-efficient is significant at 5 per cent level and personality trait is significantly related to innovative personality trait.

Findings

1. There is no significant difference between FGEs and SGEs with reference to extraversion.
2. There is no significant difference between FGEs and SGEs with reference to introversion.
3. There is no significant difference between FGEs and SGEs with reference to neuroticism.
4. There is no significant difference between FGEs and SGEs with reference to the overall personality.
5. There is no significant difference between FGEs and SGEs with reference to innovative personality.
6. The overall personality is significantly related to innovative personality.

Discussion

Findings of the study lead to the following discussions.

When the personality dimensions *viz.*, extraversion, introversion and neuroticism, overall personality and innovative personality are taken into account, there exists no significant difference between FGEs and SGEs. The present finding is in line with the views of Naffziger, Hornsby and Kurtado (1994), where a chronological scheme of entrepreneurial indicators has been devised, namely, early childhood exposure, trouble in school, problems with work, desire to risk and bliss in business independence. They are also considered as the personality traits, which are common to entrepreneurs in spite of the variations whether they are FGEs or SGEs.

The regression co-efficiency suggests that overall personality and innovative personality are related. Where innovation is considered as a dependent variable and personality as a independent variable. This finding is in line with the view of Kirton (1976) that innovation is a continuum of individuals' personality trait. Innovation and decision-making have been considered as important entrepreneurial characteristics according to McClelland (1961). Innovation may affect the performance and entrepreneurs who are innovative are dynamic in nature and also have been explored in number of investigation (Hazulhust, 1966; Sharma, 1973; Brevton, 1975; Subramaniam, 1975).

Recommendations

1. There found to be no significant difference between FGEs and SGEs on a host of personality variables and innovative personality. The world facing SGEs is more complicated than the one in which their parents had success. Technology, competition and workforce are ever changing in today's business environment and make up some of the most difficult challenges for "new" entrepreneurs. So entrepreneur in this competitive millennium could follow six important ways to achieve success.

   (i) Create your own fate
   (ii) Never stop learning
   (iii) Motivate yourself
   (iv) Trust yourself
   (v) Live your values

(vi) Give something back (Marci Syms, Syms corporation who have experienced as second Generation Entrepreneur).

2. Personality factor is significantly related to innovation. True entrepreneurs ventures for creative rather than economic reasons. Entrepreneurs 'intention should be, not the desire to glair economically was the primary motivator of entrepreneurial behaviour but should be the desire to create something as a societal concept. Entrepreneurialism should be meditated by an atmosphere that fosters innovation. So adaptation and innovation should be one of the entrepreneurial activities to face the dynamic world of today.
3. The entrepreneurial idea may be developed and cultivated over from childhood days onwards which may mould an individual to be creative and innovative where age should not be a criterion for entrepreneurship.
4. The entrepreneurs may think in terms of developing their nature of business bared on their personality for example father and son looking after the business planning and execution for introverts and trading for extroverts.
5. The findings of the present study reveals that there is no significant difference between FGEs and SGEs on a host of psychological variable personality dimension *viz.*, extraversion, introversion and neuroticism overall personality and innovative personality. From the foregoing conclusions it is pertinent to note that other more specific psychological factors such as self-concept, value orientation and subjective well-being may have variations between the two groups of entrepreneurs studied. Hence, it is recommended that further researchers are needed in these lines to find out whether generation plays a major role in shaping an entrepreneur.

REFERENCES

Abraham Zaleznik and MKD Vries (1975). *Myths and Realities of Entrepreneurship,* Power and the corporate Mind Houghton Miff in Co., New York.

Balakrishnan, R. (1985). A Study of Motivational and Personality Characteristics of Entrepreneurs, unpublished Doctoral thesis, submitted to Bharathiar University.

Christopher, K.J. (1969). *Socio–Psychological Factors Influencing the Adoption of the Innovation of Starting a Small Industry Unit,* SIET Institute.

Chandran, H.S. (1990 (d)). Study of Innovativeness in Relation to Target Achievement and Type A Behaviour, *Managerial Psychology.*

Ravichandran, K. (1991). *Entrepreneurial Success a Psychological Study,* sterling Publishers Private Limited, New Delhi.

Venkatapathy, R. (1983). Biographical Characteristics of First and Second Generation Entrepreneurs. *Journal of Small Enterprise Development Management and Extension,* 11(4), pp. 55-66.

Venkatapathy, R. (1989). Self-Concept (conative) in Relation to First and Second Generation Entrepreneurs, *Indian Journal of Industrial Relations,* 24, 3, 312-320.

Educated writing tutors, The Entrepreneur in Economics, Content provided by Term paper Edge's Hardvard www.Yahoo.com

Marci syms, *Second Generation Entrepreneurs in Family Business Face New Challenges,* George Rothman Institute of Entrepreneurial Students, www.Google.com

22

Entrepreneurship Development Programmes—A Solution for Unemployment

Mr. P.T. Vijaya Raja Kumar and Dr. S. Kaliyamoorthy

Introduction

"Employment generation is an issue of life and death for our democracy", says Amit Mithra, Secretary General of the Federation of Indian Chambers of Commerce and Industry.

Good Entrepreneur can create a healthy economy. Entrepreneurship is an important facet of industrial growth and development of a nation. It is the backbone of a nation that sets its eyes on maximizing its performance in every field. The spirit of entrepreneurship brings about enthusiasm, persistence and the ability to seek entrepreneurial opportunities that lead to success.

A nation's ability to generate a steady stream of business opportunities can only come about when its people take to entrepreneurial activities. Entrepreneurs are essentially the engines of growth for a nation. There are several factors that go into making a successful entrepreneur, and he or she need not necessarily possess a strong business and financial background. On the contrary, well-conceived and well-directed training can always produce an outstanding entrepreneur.

In addition, today's world with its burgeoning population offers limited avenues of employment. This makes entrepreneurship all the more necessary for self -employment and small-business.

The employment situation in our country is marred by a number of ugly marks. Large many are underemployed. Many are without work. Quite a number though educated find no or little work to use their talent or skill.

Basically unemployment in India is structural in nature. It is associated with the inadequacy of productive capacity to create enough jobs for all those able and will to work. In India not only is productivity capacity much below the needed quantity, it is also found increasing at a slow rate. As against this, additions to labour-force are being made at a fast rate on account of the rapidly growing population. Thus, while new productive jobs are on the increase, the rate of increase being low, the absolute number of unemployed persons is raising year to year.

This sort of unemployment is not a temporary phenomenon in the sense that it will pass off on its own after a lapse of time. It is chronic. It requires for its solution the application of long-term measures for remedying the defects in the economic structure. In other words, it is the development of the economy alone that can take care of unemployment.

While this is the basic nature of unemployment in the country, it has taken different forms, for example, disguised unemployment, underemployment and open employment. Besides, there are special problems of unemployment, *e.g.*, seasonal unemployment and educated unemployment.

Disguised Unemployment

This refers to unemployment that is not in the open for every one to see; it remains invisible. For example, in Indian villages, where most of the unemployment exists in this form, people are found to be apparently engaged in agricultural activities. But such employment is mostly a work-sharing device *i.e.*, the existing work is shared, howsoever large may be the number of workers. In such a situation, even if many workers are withdrawn, the same work will continue to be down by fewer people. It follows that all the workers are not needed to maintain the existing level of production. The contribution of such labourers to production is thus zero or near zero. There are some who feel that the very large number of workers on Indian farms actually hinder agricultural operations and thereby reduces production.

In the case of disguised unemployment, every one only seems to be fully employed. It is so because a larger number of workers than required are sharing a given amount of work. As such it appears that nobody is without work. But this, of course, conceals the fact that there is no full employment, as the workers are not working to their full capacity.

Underemployment

It is a situation under which employed people are contributing to production less than they are capable of. For example, a diploma holder in engineering, if for want of an appropriate job, starts shoe-shining may be said to be underemployed. Apparently, he may be deemed as working and earning in a productive activity and in this sense contributing something to production. But in reality he is not working to his capability, or to his full capacity. He is, therefore, not fully employed. Here, too, his underemployment is disguised.

Open Unemployment

Under this category fall those who have no work to do. They are able to work and are also willing to work. But there is no work for them. Such unemployment is in the nature of involuntary idleness. They are to be found partly in villages, but very largely in cities. Most of them come from villages in search of jobs; many originate in the cities themselves.

Seasonal Unemployment

It is so called because it occurs at certain seasons of the year. Associated mainly with agriculture, it is a widespread phenomenon in Indian villages. Agricultural operations, being dependent upon Nature, are such that in a certain period of the year there is heavy work, while in the rest, the work is lean. Around sowing and harvesting, for example, there is such an amount of work to be done that agriculturists may have to engage themselves day and night. As against this, the period between the post-harvest and before the next sowing is almost workless, rendering many without work.

Educated Unemployment

It is concerned with joblessness among the educated *i.e.,* matriculate and higher educated. Of these, there may be some suffering from open unemployment. There may again be others who are underemployed, belonging to the category of what we have earlier termed as underemployment. The latter type of unemployed persons may not be getting work suitable to their qualifications to enable them to make full use of their capacities. Mostly towns and cities are faced with this problem of educated unemployment. In developed economies there are two dominant types of unemployment. One is cyclical unemployment and the other frictional unemployment.

Cyclical Unemployment

Associated with the downswing and depression phases of business cycle, it is to be found in capitalist or market-oriented developed economies. Caused by the lack of coordination among the innumerable decision-makers in the fields of saving and investment, the trade cycle in its downward phase renders many unemployed. Falling income lowers demand for goods and services. As a result, the economy produces less than it is capable of, aggravating further the employment-income situation.

Frictional Unemployment

This type of unemployment characterizes developed economies as they push towards further development. At a higher level of development many changes take place in the industrial structure of these economies, with old industries contracting and dying out, and new industries coming up. This process seems to be endless. In fact without this no development is possible. The products, the resources and the technologies undergo changes, making the structure on an economy a picture of permanent change.

Causes of Unemployment

The major causes which have been responsible for the widespread unemployment can be spelt out as,

(i) Underdevelopment

In the context of vast and varied unutilized natural resources as also manpower, it is stressing the obvious that the Indian economy. The volume of economic activities at present, determined largely by agriculture, is low and the rate of rise in such activities is small. The non-agricultural sector, in particular the modern industrial sector, which was to provide increasing avenues of employment, is growing at a very slow pace.

(ii) Inadequate Employment Planning

Planning in India, has not contributed adequately to the solution of this problem. This is largely because of the lower priority to the employment objective and the under-rating of human resources.

To the overall inadequacy of planning may be added he weak manpower planning *i.e.,* balancing of manpower needs and supplies in the various branches of production, in the various regions of the country and in various skills. In some sectors of the economy there is more than we need, while in others there is less than required. So is the case with many regions and various skills. These imbalances have largely arisen in the sphere of educated and trained personnel such as engineers, cost accountants, administrators, etc. Even in these spheres, where large resources of the community were at stake and where manpower budgeting could take care of these problems, not much has been done.

(iii) Rapid Population Growth

The rapid growth of population has adversely affected the unemployment situation largely in two ways. In the first place, it has directly affected it by making large additions to labour force. Of course, how much of the evil of unemployment can be ascribed to this factor depends upon the rate of growth of job opportunities.

The second consequence of the rapid population growth has been to worsen indirectly the unemployment situation by reducing the resources for capital formation. In our country more resources get used up in private consumption, *i.e.,* food, clothing etc., and in public consumption *i.e.,* drinking water, electricity, medical and educational facilities etc. This has reduced the opportunities of diverting a larger proportion of incomes to saving and investment. Population growth has thus created hurdles in the way of fast growth of the economy and retarded the growth of job opportunities.

Entrepreneurship Awareness Camps

"Challenges make you discover things about yourself that you never really know."

In this era of Liberalization, Privatization, Globalization, the students flying out of the technical institutions and professional institutions are competing with each other in finding an entry into any public or private organizations. But most of them are left out with no chances, and to remain idle.

EACs are being organized with the objective of bringing to the limelight, the inner being of those qualified individuals to develop them into successful intrapreneurs. As such, EACs are targeted on the individuals from institutions like polytechnics, ITIs, Engineering colleges and professional colleges. That is very essential and important thing to create awareness about entrepreneurship among the students. Sometimes it may use to start a business with the help of their friends.

The EAC programme having different interesting module whereby the qualified individuals are provided opportunity to learn the aspects of becoming a successful entrepreneur and to interact with those officials, who will be providing supportive assistance in their endeavour. Real lifetime successful entrepreneurs are being invited for direct interaction, with visits to their units, for first-hand understanding of the benefits arising out of self-employment than underemployment. When they interact with the successful entrepreneurs, they can get an idea to start a new business or new concern. They can motivate with the help of hearing successful stories of successful entrepreneurs.

Entrepreneurship Development Programmes

Entrepreneurship development is a very important catalyst in context of the rapid growth of small and medium industries in a country. The efficient performance of this sub-sector is dependent on effective utilization of man, machine and materials and human factor plays more important role as compared to machine and tools.

Hence continuous effort for entrepreneurship development in the Small and Medium Enterprise (SME) sector is essential for effective utilization of the human resources. For creation of new SME and for operating these enterprises successfully, development of entrepreneurship is a recognized pre requisite and this target can be achieved only through systematic training programme. The objective of entrepreneurship development training programme is to develop entrepreneurial traits of entrepreneurs for motivating and enabling them to create new industries in the country and enhancing capabilities to manage their enterprise efficiently.

The Important Objectives of the EDP are as follows:

- To create entrepreneurial awareness to the young generation and motivate them to establish small and medium enterprises.
- To trained up the prospective new and young entrepreneurs to maintain and run their enterprises successfully.
- To enabling the entrepreneurs about the global production and market strategy in context of market economy.

- To encourage the entrepreneurs to establish pollution free SMEs.

Suggestions for Reduce Unemployment

In the light of the above mentioned causes of unemployment, we now discuss the measures that can help us in eradicating this evil.

(i) Expanding Volume of Work

The one and the foremost solution to the problem of unemployment lies in enlarging the opportunities for work. This needs to be done rapidly and at an increased scale so as to clear the backlog of unemployment which is substantial and to provide jobs to the large additions being made to the labour force. The work to be expanded has to be both in the sphere of wage-employment and the self-employment.

(ii) Raising Capital Formation

It is also necessary that the accumulation of capital is stepped up. It helps employment expansion in two principal ways. One, it becomes possible to maintain the existing activities, as also to expand the current activities and set up new ones. Secondly, capital formation directly generates employment in the capital goods sector. The production of mother machines' *i.e.* machines which provide machines give rise to employment. This also provides capital goods for the production of various other types of goods like consumer goods and services.

(iii) Appropriate Mix of Production Techniques

It is also necessary to choose such a combination of capital-intensive and labour-intensive technologies of production as it generates maximum employment.

(iv) Special Employment Programmes

The remedies suggested above amount to employment-generation through a faster growth of the economy, as well as an expansion of capital-intensive biased activities. This is in a sense an ultimate solution of the problem.

The need for the supplemental programmes is all the more important for the poor people residing mostly in the rural areas and small towns. These people do not have the necessary physical strength, adequate elementary education or skill. Nor do they have sufficient productive assets such as land, animals, equipment etc. There are then many large seasonally unemployed, mostly those associated with agriculture, who need supplementary seasonal employment. Quite many, though employed such as artisans, do not earn enough to meet their needs for even necessities.

(v) Manpower Planning

For achieving employment for all, it is necessary also to manage human resources in a scientific manner. This is essential to ensure that while employment it promoted, development of the economy is also realized. This requires measures of various types.

First one is, outside the narrow concept of manpower planning as related only to the demand and supply of skilled personnel, it is essential to adopt effective remedies to cut down the growth rate of population.

Secondly, the supply of skilled labours needs to be tailored to the requirements of the rate and pattern of employment-oriented development.

Thirdly, while high-level skill-formation through education and training will be confined to a small proportion of labour-force, it is essential to improve upon the capabilities for development of the vast masses of people.

Finally, in providing employment under special programmes, it is necessary to ensure that these accord with the characteristics of the targeted group area, as also with the overall development plans for the various sectors.

Conclusion

Thus, there are various opportunities to reduce the unemployment with the help of entrepreneurship in our country. Entrepreneurs can provide job opportunities for many people. There are vast enterpreneurial opportunities in our country. The important areas are poultry framing, food processing, fruits and vegetables processing, manufacturing writing instruments, floriculture, basket making, toy making, preparing garments, match sticks, covers, paper cups, brushes, bags and organic manure, bakery, dairying, sericulture, nursery farming, preparation of coconut husk cake and so on. The budding entrepreneurs can get ideas from District

Industries Centre, Tamil Nadu Industrial Investment Corporation and so on. The Government Agencies are also giving guidelines to the budding and blooming entrepreneurs as well as the existing entrepreneurs for establishing their business.

REFERENCES

C.B. Gupta, N.P. Srinivasan (1999). *Entrepreneurial Development*, Sultan Chand & Sons, NewDelhi, Sixth Edition.

S.S. Khanka (2000). *Entrepreneurial Development*, S. Chand & Company Ltd., New Delhi, Second Revised Edition.

S.K. Meti, "Employment Opportunities for Youth in Hitech Agriculture and Its Subsidiary Occupations", *Kisan World*, March 2005, pp. 55-56.

www.edindia.com

PART III

Performance Evaluation of Entrepreneurial Training Institutions

23

The Role of SISI in Promoting Entrepreneurship—With Special Reference to SISI, Mangalore

Mrs. H. Rashmi and Ms. Subraja

Introduction

Training programmes are expected to bring about economic and social changes in the entrepreneurs' behaviour. Training has to reiterate and vocalize the fact that good entrepreneurs are not born, but made. Training programmes are planned with a view to create risk takers, innovators, motivators, employers, visionaries, economic emancipators, etc. The society expects all these qualities to be interwoven in one person and training aims to develop individuals with the above characteristics. The economic good of the society very much depends upon such individuals. In the absence of such individuals, wants remain wants and resources remain resources. It is because of entrepreneurs that our society enjoys modern standards of living. An entrepreneur is a reformer. He reforms the society through his actions and creates demand for products, which are not in existence. Though he has to produce and sell what individuals require, his actions go beyond fulfilling demand requirements. As an innovator he is expected to produce things, which the people have not even dreamt of. He should, with his actions, convert savings into productive investments and create additional wealth. Besides capital formation, entrepreneurs owe a lot to the environment. They have to evaluate continuously their actions from the point of view of the environment and should undertake such actions, which would result in environmental improvement rather than its degradation. The poor and downtrodden consider him to be a philanthropist, who contributes a portion of his wealth for their economic well-being and look up to him for succour.

Research Methodology

The main objective of the study was to know about the various services rendered by SISI to promote entrepreneurship in the region of its operation. The primary data for the study on "The Role of Small Industries Service Institute (SISI) in Promoting Entrepreneurship—with special reference to SISI, Mangalore," was obtained by personally interviewing the concerned officials in the SISI at Mangalore. The secondary data required for the study was collected by referring to articles in journals and books.

Role of SISI, Mangalore in Promoting Entrepreneurship

Small-scale industries play a vital role in the fulfillment of socio-economic objectives, namely, employment generation, export promotion, reducing income inequalities etc. with a distinct advantage of low investment. Small industries service institute (SISI) Mangalore, is a branch institute of SISI Bangalore, which is a part of the national network under Small Industries Development Organization (SIDO), Ministry of Small Scale Industries (SSI) and Agro and Rural Industries (ARI). SIDO is an apex body and a nodal agency for formulating, co-ordinating and monitoring the policies for the development of small-scale industries in the country. Branch SISI Mangalore, has been set up by the Government of India to supplement the activities of State Government for the promotion and development of small-scale industries in the districts of Dakshina Kannada, Udupi and Coorg.

Services rendered by SISI, Mangalore

1. *Technical Consultancy Services*

Technical know-how about the process of production, quality testing and standardization of products, modernization and preparation of product design are services provided by SISI. Consultancy services are rendered by this institute in areas such as mechanical, metallurgy, glass and ceramics/minerals, electrical and electronics, chemical and allied subjects, food products and also assists entrepreneurs in product selection, choice of technology and selection of machineries and raw materials.

2. *Economic Information*

SISI collects and compiles statistical information regarding various aspects concerned with the establishment and development of small industries. Important aspects are demand and supply scenarios for different products, investment, raw-materials, industrial potential surveys of the district, and status report of different industries.

3. Supply of Project Profiles

Project profiles for various products containing details of technical and financial inputs needed in the process of establishing and running of manufacturing and servicing units are prepared or updated on a regular basis. These are disseminated to entrepreneurs interested in setting up small-scale industries and service activities. Project profiles are also available for Prime Minister's Rozgar Yojana (PMRY) applicants.

4. Marketing Services

Branch SISI assists small-scale units for enlistment under single point registration programme under National Small Industries Corporation (NSIC) for supply of stores to Government department.

5. Training Activities

Training activities are provided by this institute for the benefit of prospective entrepreneurs through:

(a) Chemical laboratory – courses include training on

- *(i)* Detergent and allied products
- *(ii)* Cosmetics
- *(iii)* Screen printing
- *(iv)* Fruit and vegetable preservation (preparation of jam, pickle, squash, syrup etc.)

(b) Common facility workshop – which includes

- *(i)* Machinist and turner trade.
- *(ii)* Training programme in programming and machining of CNC turning center.

In addition to the technical training programme demonstration is also provided in the chemical laboratory for items, namely, detergents and allied products, cosmetics, chalk, crayons and candles.

6. Management Development Programmes (MDPs)

Branch SISI, Mangalore conducts need based management development programmes for the benefit of middle and higher managers of small-scale units in areas like export, packaging and quality management.

7. Modernization

In-plant studies are conducted by Branch SISI, Mangalore, aimed at identifying areas for improvement and diversification in SISI on the special request of SSI entrepreneurs.

8. Activities for women Empowerment

EDP and counselling services are rendered to women from this region.

9. Support to State Government

(a) Capacity assessment of SSI units for producing raw-materials is being done jointly with District Industries Centre (DIC).
(b) Feasibility comment is provided to Karnataka State Small Industries Development Corporation (KSSIDC) for allotment of sheds/plots in their industrial estates.

10. Motivation Campaign

A motivation campaign is organized by this institute at educational institutions like ITI, Polytechnic, Engineering colleges and in rural areas to create awareness among the educated unemployed, regarding government policies and facilities available for self-employment and thereby motivate them to start their own venture.

Meaning of Entrepreneurship Development Programme (EDP)

EDP is designed to help a person in strengthening and fulfilling his entrepreneurial motive and in acquiring skills and capabilities necessary for playing his entrepreneurial role effectively.

Towards this end, it is necessary to promote his understanding of motives, motivation pattern and its impact on behaviour. A programme which seeks to do this can qualify to be called a programmer. This has to be stressed here, because there are a number of programmes which aim at providing informational or managerial inputs or focus on preparation of a project. Although all these inputs are required by a new entrepreneur, a programme not touching entrepreneurial motivation and behaviour cannot be called an EDP.

Though EDP has been recognized as an effective human resource development tool, many a times there are very many expectations from a single programme, like removing unemployment, promoting small scale industries, developing industrially underdeveloped regions, etc.

EDP is primarily meant for developing those first-generation entrepreneurs, who on their own cannot become successful entrepreneurs. It covers three major variables. Local, target group, and enterprise (entrepreneurial activities). Any of these can become the focus or starting point for initiating and implementing an EDP. An EDP by itself, therefore aims at achieving the specific objectives of the programmes and therefore cannot create any magical result. It is a continuous process of training and motivating prospective entrepreneurs to set up profitable enterprises.

Objectives of EDPs

The important objectives of EDPs are:

1. To develop and strengthen their entrepreneurial ability.
2. To analyze environmental set up relating to small industry and small business.
3. To select a product.
4. To formulate a project proposal for the product.
5. To understand the process and procedure involved in setting up a small enterprise.
6. To know the sources of help and support available for starting a small-scale industry.
7. To acquire the necessary managerial skills required to run a small enterprise.
8. To know the pros and cons of becoming an entrepreneur.

Phases of EDPs

An Entrepreneurship Development Programme consists of the following three phases:

1. Pre – Training Phase

The activities and preparations required to launch the training programme come under this phase. This phase accordingly, includes the following:

1. *Notification of the programme:* SISI, Mangalore, sends the details of the EDP to Directorate of Audio and Visual Publicity, New Delhi (DAVP) which publishes the same in

National and Regional dailies as specified by SISI Mangalore. Press release and notification through radio is also given by SISI Mangalore.

2. *Receipt of application and selection of candidates for the EDP:* Interested candidates have to apply in the given format to SISI Mangalore. For government sponsored EDPs, the selection criteria is specified. The age of male candidates applying for the programme should be in the range of 18-35 years and for female candidates it is 18-45 years. For both categories, the education requirement is a pass class in 8th standard. The minimum number of candidates required to conduct an EDP is 20. The fees payable for an EDP of one month duration is Rs. 250 (exclusive of lunch). Candidates belonging to SC/ST/PH get a concession of 50 per cent on the fees payable.
3. *Arrangement of infrastructure*: Necessary arrangements is made for conducting the EDP in a convenient location.
4. *Tie- up of guest faculty for training purposes:* Based on the content of the EDP, experts and faculty members are invited to take up sessions for the trainees.
5. *Finalization of training syllabus:* Based on the theme of the EDP and application forms received, the officials design the training syllabus.

2. *Training Phase*

Types of EDPs organized by SISI, Mangalore

The number of EDPs to be organized during a fiscal year depends on the funds allotted by the Government and the need and demand for a particular type of programme. It varies from State to State. During the fiscal year 2005-2006, SISI, Bangalore was sanctioned funds to organize 16 EDPs. It allotted 4 EDPs to Branch SISI, Mangalore. In case the SISI Branch realizes that there exists a need and demand for a particular type of EDP in its region of operation such programmes are organized with the help of NGOs and Self-Help Groups (SHGs).

Previously SISI, Mangalore used to conduct two types of EDPs. They are:

(a) *General EDPs:* In which trainees were given entrepreneurship inputs, managerial inputs and also inputs regarding financial support available from various institutions.

(b) *Managerial EDPs:* The trainees were imparted knowledge regarding techniques of managing small enterprises, problem solving techniques, book-keeping, working capital management and break-even analysis.

It was noticed by the officials at Branch SISI, Mangalore that the number of respondents for such EDPs gradually declined. The reason being, that they were aware of such theoretical concepts and found that it did not directly serve the purpose of starting an enterprise. Therefore the officials thought it necessary to restructure the content of EDPs organized previously.

At present the following types of EDPs are organized by the Branch SISI, Mangalore. They are:

(a) *Product oriented EDPs:* In these types of EDPs, trainees are given inputs regarding entrepreneurship and managerial aspects in addition to product demonstration. For example, manufacturing of simple chemicals and food based items.

(b) *Service oriented EDPs:* In these types of EDPs, some managerial and entrepreneurship inputs are given to the trainees. The areas covered under this type of EDP are T.V. repair and services, GSM mobile phone repair, Computer hardware and networking, Beautician courses and Desk Top Publishing (DTP). Since more emphasis is given to practical aspects trainees find these types of programmes as beneficial and interesting.

3. *Post–Training Phase (follow–up)*

The ultimate objective of the Entrepreneurship Development Programme is to prepare the participants to start their enterprises. Keeping this objective in mind, the officials at SISI, Mangalore try to keep in touch with the trainees. Guidance regarding various aspects of setting up an enterprise is provided by the officials. They review the project proposal prepared by the prospective entrepreneurs and give their expert comments and also help them to avail finance from banks.

Problems Faced by SISI Branch Mangalore

- *Mobilising Prospective Trainees:* The Branch Official finds it difficult to get the required number of candidates *i.e.* 20 people, to attend the training programme.
- *Long Duration:* The trainees find it difficult to stay on for a

training programme for a long period of time. They feel that a short training session emphasizing more on practical aspects is necessary.

- *Designing the programme:* The programme contents need to be designed, keeping in mind the needs and requirements of the target people. Making the programme an interesting and a fruitful one is a challenge to the officials.
- *Getting Faculty in Remote Places:* The Institute finds it difficult to get suitably qualified teaching staff in rural or remote places. Most of the faculty does not want to travel the long distance especially in Udupi and Kodagu areas.
- *Follow-Up:* Once training is over the trainees do not report back to the Institute to inform them about their employability status. The Institute has to be in touch with the trainees in order to ascertain such information which in turn will help them know the success rate of their training programmes.

Conclusion

SISI, Mangalore has been performing a number of functions in order to help the educated and unemployed youth gain self-employment. Some of them include providing training in various spheres; giving advice and helping entrepreneurs diversify into other areas of work. Such an Institute is very necessary in the Regions of Dakshina Kannada, Udupi and Coorg as these places are not industrially developed. If it continues in the same way and also modifies its course content to suit the ever changing needs of the business environment in future too, it can definitely make a huge difference in the lives of a lot of Indians.

REFERENCES

Desai Vasant (1992). *Dynamics of Entrepreneurial Development and Management,* Himalaya Publishing House, Mumbai, Fourth Edition 2005.

Hyderabad R.L. and Krishnamurthy B. "Impact of Training Programmes on Entrepreneurship Development: A Case Study", *SEDME,* Volume 29, December 2002, pp. 69-86.

Kaulgud Aruna (2003). *Entrepreneurship Management,* Vikas Publishing House, New Delhi.

Khanka S.S. (1999). *Entrepreneurial Development,* S.Chand & Co Limited, New Delhi.

Activity Brochure of Branch SISI, Mangalore.

24

Entrepreneurial Training Programmes of SISI—An Evaluation

Dr. P. Natarajan and Mrs. K. Thirumamagal

Introduction

Entrepreneurship development is one of the key factors in accelerating the economic development in India. Entrepreneurship in small-scale industries is well suited and a viable method to provide employment to be masses. It creates not only employment opportunities but also develops the infrastructure in the locality where the industry is located. Entrepreneurial success depends basically on the entrepreneurs ability in running unit. This requires effective entrepreneurial training. The largest extension training agency in the world concerned with small industry in the Central Small Industries Organisation (CSIO) of the Government of India. Attached to the Ministry of Industry, CSIO provides services through 43 Small Industries Service Institutes (SISIs). The operational performance of SISI has been measured in terms of number of Entrepreneurship Development Programme, Management Development Programme, Research and Consultancy Programme, Orientation Programme and CRR Scheme organised by SISI and how it measures entrepreneurship development. Hence, this chapter gives an outline about the training programme organised by SISI (Tamil Nadu Branch) for inculcating entrepreneurship during the last five years period (2001-05).

Entrepreneurial Development Programmes (EDPs)

SISI regularly conducts general and product specific EDPs for prospective entrepreneurs. TI programmes are conducted for 4 weeks in the trades of screen printing, manufacture of leather, chemical and allied products, electronics repair servicing of electronic and electrical appliances for setting up self–employment ventures by educated unemployed youth.

Table 24.1 exhibits that most of the candidates are very much interested to attend the EDP programmes on Herbal Products. In the year 2003-04, 1065 candidates were attended in EDP on Herbal Products. Table 24.1 shows that women are not as much interested in EDP the candidates who are attending ED programme are in increasing trend. Hence, EDP creates awareness to the people.

Table–24.1
EDPs Conducted by SISI–Chennai and its Branches During 2002-05

Sl.No.	Name of the Course	Total No. of Candidates				Total
		2001-02	2002-03	2003-04	2004-05	
1.	EDP on Herbal Products	247 (17.77)	255 (60)	1065 (88.38)	106 (18.79)	1426 (65)
2.	EDP (General)	497 (35.76)	147 (34.59)	73 (6.06)	229 (40.60)	449 (20.46)
3.	EDP (Women)	159 (11.44)	23 (5.41)	-	-	23 (1.05)
4.	EDP on Food Products	165 (11.87)	-	19 (1.58)	185 (32.80)	204 (9.30)
5.	Others					
	(a) EDP on Read more garments	98 (7.05)	-	30 (2.49)	-	30 (1.37)
	(b) EDP (Web designing)	141	-	18 (1.49)	-	18 (0.82)
	(c) Cell Phone Service		-	-	44 (7.80)	44 (2.01)
	Total	**1390**	**425**	**1205**	**564**	**2194**

Source: Annual Reports.

Management Development Programmes (MDPs)

MDPs are conducted for one week for industrial supervisors of small scale units. They are organised in the fields of marketing management, financial management, production management, material management, total cost management, total quality management, export management.

Ten MDP Training Courses were conducted during the year 2002-05 and 594 candidates were trained.

Table 24.2 exhibits that most of the candidates are very much interested to attend the management development programme on marketing management. In the year 2003-04, 126 candidates were attended in EDP on Marketing Management. The candidates who are attending MD Programmes are in increasing trend. MDP creates awareness to the people and motivate the managerial personnel to know about the latest managerial strategies and update them.

Entrepreneurship Education Programme

Creating awareness and orientation for college and university teachers on entrepreneurship has been one of the core areas. The institute will organise two faculty development programmes in entrepreneurship for college and university teachers.

Table–24.2
MDPs Conducted by SISI—Chennai and its Branches During 2002-05

Sl.No.	*Name of the Course*	*Total No. of Candidates*				*Total*
		2001-02	*2002-03*	*2003-04*	*2004-05*	
1.	Material Management	20 (3.7)	20 (15.04)	36 (13.33)	-	56 (9.43)
2.	Financial Management	68 (12.62)	26 (19.55)	-	42 (21.99)	68 (11.45)
3.	Personal Management	20 (3.71)	20 (15.04)	-	-	20 (3.37)
4.	Merchandising	74 (13.73)	27 (20.30)	-	47 (24.61)	74 (12.46)
5.	Communication Skills	20 (3.71)	20 (15.04)	-	-	20 (3.37)
6.	Sales and Marketing	100 (18.55)	20 (15.04)	28 (10.37)	-	48 (8.08)
7.	Export Documentation and Procedures	116 (21.52)	-	36 (13.33)	22 (11.52)	58 (9.76)

(Contd.)

Sl.No.	Name of the Course	Total No. of Candidates				Total
		2001-02	2002-03	2003-04	2004-05	
8.	Marketing Management	102 (18.92)	-	126 (46.67)	61 (31.94)	187 (31.48)
9.	Production Management in Garment Industries	-	-	44 (16.30)	-	44 (7.41)
10.	Tax law	19 (3.53)	-	-	19 (9.95)	19 (3.20)
Total		539	133	270	191	594

Source: Annual Reports.

In addition to this ten programmes for the students of college and universities will be organised during the financial year 2002-03. The institute has already organised five programmes for the students' community till November 2002.

Table-24.3
Entrepreneurship Education Programmes During the Year 2002-03

Type of Programmes	No. of Programmes	No. of Participants	Percentage
EAP for college and university students	3	98	52.69
EAP for Graduates and Post-graduates	2	88	47.31
Total	5	186	

Source: Annual Reports.

Training Programme Organized under Counselling Re-training and Re-deployment (CRR) Scheme

Counselling Re-training and Re-deployment Scheme is an activity piloted by the Department of Public Enterprise, Ministry of Heavy Industries, New Delhi for the benefit of employees rendered redundant as a result of modernization, technology, up-gradation and manpower restructuring in the Central Public Sector Enterprises (CPSEs). The objective of the scheme is to reorient the employees through short duration training programmes to enable them to adjust the new environment and adopt new avocations after their separation from PSEs.

The training programmes will equip them to engage themselves in income generating activities taking advantage of the available opportunities for self-employment. The programmes are offered at free cost and stipend is paid to the beneficiaries in order to participate in the programme eagerly.

Table-24.4
Training Programmes Organized Under CRR Scheme During 2001-05

Sl.No.	*Location*	*2001-02*	*2002-03*	*2003-04*	*2004-05*
1.	Chennai	108 (27.20)	116 (27.75)	110 (25.70)	120 (28.30)
2.	Trichy	98 (24.68)	84 (20.09)	97 (22.66)	86 (20.28)
3.	Coimbatore	86 (21.66)	98 (23.44)	96 (22.43)	60 (14.15)
4.	Ooty	59 (14.86)	63 (15.07)	55 (15.19)	75 (17.69)
5.	Salem	46 (11.57)	57 (13.64)	60 (14.02)	83 (19.57)
	Total	**397**	**418**	**428**	**424**

Source: Annual Reports.

Management Consultancy Services

SISI impart guidance in proper methods of industrial management, including cost reduction, financial management, production management, marketing and in the area of industrial engineering with a view to ensure intensive utilisation of resources. They provide and conduct complete integrated in–plant services as well as provide adhoc managerial advice on specific problems. They also provide special techno–managerial advice for cost reduction and quality improvement to export oriented small scale enterprises.

Training in Management and Entrepreneurship

SISIs devote considerable time and attention to the training of Managers and Entrepreneurs. Since this is of vital importance of the

Table–24.5
Research and Consultancy Projects During 2001-2005

National	*2001-02*		*2002-03*		*2003-04*		*2004-05*	
	No. of Programmes	*No. of Participants*	*No. of Programmes*	*No. of Participants*	*No. of Programmes*	*No. of Participants*	*No. of Programmes*	*No. of Participants*
Announced	24	462 (7.79)	11	168 (1.14)	20	200 (12.82)	31	368 (2.27)
Sponsored	50	1440 (24.28)	45	1567 (10.68)	30	450 (28.85)	75	2017 (12.42)
Outstation	35	994 (16.76)	199	10948 (74.61)	15	300 (19.23)	214	11248 (69.29)
International								
Announced	14	241 (4.06)	10	161 (1.09)	-	-	10	161 (0.99)
Sponsored	4	28 (0.47)	2	12 (0.08)	4	60 (3.85)	6	72 (0.44)
Educational								
PG Diploma	9	135 (2.28)	9	165 (1.12)	-	-	9	165 (1.02)
IT	30	516 (8.70)	7	72 (0.49)	15	150 (9.62)	22	222 (1.37)
IGNOV	6	541 (9.12)	6	482 (3.28)	-	-	6	482 (2.97)
Seminars and Workshops	37	1575 (26.55)	29	1099 (7.49)	20	400 (25.64)	49	1499 (9.23)
	209	5932	318	14674	104	1560	422	16234

Source: Annual Reports.

development of industry. Entrepreneurs and Industrialists also show considerable interest in this training.

Training of Workers, Foreman and Managers

Training of Workers

To train workers in other organisations all SISIs and extension centres from small industries in certain trades. The training may be of three to six months duration 8 hours per day. The training is given normal stipend.

The training is normally in machine shop practice tool and die making, fitter trade, heat treatment, welding electroplating, wood working, sheet metal work etc. The training provided is both theoretical and practical. Simple tests are conducted and certificates are awarded, the trainee attends atleast 80 per cent of the training sessions.

Training of Foreman

The SISI do not train foreman on an organised basis. Adhoc training is provided to supervisors mainly for testing lathes and other machine tools, reading blue prints. The training of foreman and supervisors has been attempted through open houses (Round table discussions) where a particular subject is introduced by a technical officer of the SISI and followed by a general discussions and demonstrations.

Table–24.6

Training Programmes and Number of Participants Conducted by SISI During the Year 2002-03

Sl. No.	*Programmes*	*No. of Programmes*		*No. of Participants*	
		2002	*2003*	*2002*	*2003*
1.	Promotion of New Entrepreneurs	37	15	1364 (73.81)	375 (43.35)
2.	Growth of Existing Entre-preneurship	-	1	-	25 (2.89)
3.	Creation of Environment for Entrepreneurship	5	1	136 (7.36)	25 (2.89)
4.	Education, Seminar and Workshop	5	12	186 (10.06)	300 (34.68)
5.	Information Technology	2	2	120 (6.49)	100 (11.56)
6.	Other	3	2	42 (2.27)	40 (4.62)
Total		**52**	**33**		

Source : Annual Reports.

Conclusion

Thus, Small Industries Service Institute, Tamil Nadu Branch as on institution committed to the development of small scale industries bridges the gap between the large scale buyer and the small scale supplier. SISI imparts training on various segments of entrepreneurial society and work for developing entrepreneurship at the grassroot level. Their training programmes are well scheduled as well as need based. Training skills imparted by them are very relevant and directly useful for application. However, awareness about SISI services are not created properly. They have to act as nodal agent along with District Industrial Centre and promote entrepreneurship in right prospective.

25

A Study of Entrepreneurial Training Programmes in Sivagangai and the Road Map for the Future

Mrs. T. Kalpana

Introduction

In agriculture dependent country like India wherein the gross domestic product from agriculture is the highest and the major population is dependent on agricultural related activities, the growth of the economy is slower. In case of a developed economy, it is *vice versa.*

The twenty first century being an era of electronics, the greatest focus has to be necessarily given for entrepreneurial development. The community-based occupation was even proposed as a part of curriculum in the olden days to develop inherited skills. It is needless to say that these traditional and olden skills are imparted through trainings using simple gadgets, equipments and machineries now-a-days, simple gadgets being used to replace the laborious but inherited skills. Hotels, grocery shops, washing of clothes, hair cutting saloons and milk business have taken a modern shape and have resurrected into catering services, departmental stores, dry cleaning business, beauty parlours and dairying respectively. The situation has come wherein anybody can be trained to do any job. Of late, the employment opportunity or self-employment opportunity has increased many folds because of this lucarativeness.

Many organizations are engaged in the business of training entrepreneurs. Both the Government of India and the State Government have also started imparting training for wide varied activities and have deviated from the earlier agenda of imparting training to farmers. In this changed scenario, entrepreneurial training needed an in-depth study with respect to its objectives, principles, methods, benefits and evaluation. In order to take the new generation successfully into the electronic era, changes in the entrepreneurial training programmes also needed a changed out look.

An attempt has been made to study the entrepreneurial training programmes conducted by various institutions in Sivagangai, the procedures adopted by them and the lacuna in the existing programmes so that a road map can be drawn for the future.

Entrepreneur

Entrepreneur is a person who discovers new ideas and business opportunities, brings together funds to establish a business, organizes and manages its operations in order to provide economic goods and services for the public. They have strong convictions, self-motivation, the will to grow and prosper tremendously and also the courage to go bankrupt if they fail in their venture. But in majority of cases they start with nothing but entrepreneurial ability and end with positive results.

Entrepreneurial Training

Beach observes, 'Training is the organized procedures by which people learn knowledge and/or skills or attitude for a definite purpose'.

The Manpower Services Commission's glossary of training terms defines training as a planned process to modify attitude, knowledge or skill behaviour through learning experience to achieve effective performance in an activity or range of activities.

Edward E. Scannel rightly observes, 'Training will not solve all problems. Not all the problems are training problems'.

Stanley says, 'The purpose of training is to improve the innate capabilities of entrepreneurs so that their efficiency and effectiveness on the job are increased'.

Objectives of Entrepreneurial Training

The entrepreneurial training programme shall be designed to subserve the following objectives. It should impart basic knowledge about the industry, product and production methods and should build the necessary skills of the entrepreneurs. It should assist the entrepreneurs to be more effective in his present profession by exposing him to least concept, techniques and information.

It should expose the entrepreneurs to the latest developments which directly or indirectly affect them and broaden the vision of them by providing suitable opportunities for an inter change of experiences within and outside the industry.

Moreover it should impart knowledge of marketing of goods. It should also prepare the entrepreneurs to shoulder responsibility or to switch on to the production of new products, if there is any diversification.

Objectives of the Study

The main objectives of the study are:

1. to find out the awareness of the unemployed youth about the availability of entrepreneurial training programmes in Sivagangai.
2. to study the role of Government agencies in disseminating knowledge about entrepreneurial training in Sivagangai.
3. to analyse the choice of selection of the ventures of the participants.
4. to evaluate the methods adopted by the instructors.
5. to find out the qualification and experience of the trainers.
6. to identify the problems in training and to offer suggestions for betterment.

Methodology of the Present Study

A survey was undertaken to study the system of functioning of the entrepreneurial training programmes offered in Sivagangai. The study was taken up during the month of October 2005. Not only the trainees but also the trainers of the Government Organisations like Centre for Entrepreneurship Development (CED) and Jan Shikshan Sansthan (JSS) and big Non-Governmental Organisations like Association for Sarva Seva Farms (ASEFA), Workers Association for Social Activities (WASA) and Integrated Rural Community Development Society (IRCDS) were interviewed to study the effective functioning of training centers. The survey was taken up by the using questionnaire. The prospective entrepreneurs were surveyed in the classrooms and outside the classrooms. The trained entrepreneurs were also interviewed in their working places. A total of 200 respondents were surveyed, out of them 25 per cent were trained entrepreneurs. Instructors of the training centers numbering 22 were also interviewed and data regarding their age, qualification, training undergone, experience, methodology adopted by them to train were collected.

Besides the survey of the prospective trainees, 100 unemployed and educated youth were also interviewed for their knowledge on the awareness of entrepreneurial training programmes. Those who were aware of the training programmes were again tested for their awareness on the method of selection for training. Simple percentage analysis was adopted for comparison.

Findings

1. *Awareness About the Entrepreneurial Training Programmes*

There was no clear awareness among the people about the conduct of the entrepreneurial training programmes, the opportunities and their scope.

Table–25.1
Awareness About the Conduct of Self-Employment Training Programmes

Education level	*Awareness about training*		*Awareness about the selection procedure*	
	Aware	*Not Aware*	*Aware*	*Not aware*
Matriculate	3	30	33	67
Secondary	12	22	25	75
Collegiate	17	16	23	77

Source: Primary data.

It is inferred from Table 25.1 that 68 per cent of the respondents had no knowledge about the availability of entrepreneurial training programmes. However literacy level had played a key role in the dissemination of awareness. About 50 per cent of the unemployed youth educated upto the level of college had some knowledge about the availability of entrepreneurial training programmes.

It can also be seen that while identifying the perspective entrepreneurs, no transparent procedures are laid down or the procedures laid down have not been given enough publicity. This could be gauged from the fact that irrespective of the educational levels, awareness of the selection criteria was not known to 75 per cent of the respondents.

2. Role of Various Government Agencies in Disseminating Knowledge About Entrepreneurial Training Programmes

It could be seen from the data given in Table 25.2 that out of the total of 200 respondents surveyed, only 20 per cent had the knowledge about the activities through CED. Awareness about the availability of entrepreneurial training programmes had reached through District Industries Centre, the State Government organization which was only a small proportion (14%). However out of the respondents, 57 per cent of them had come to know about the training programmes through the nationalized banks operating in their places. Friends of earlier beneficiaries had also been sources of information. Whereas the State Government should have played a key role in creating awareness about the conduct and utility of such programmes, the contribution is very meagre.

Table-25.2
Percentage Analysis for Various Variables

S.No	Variables	*Undergoing Training*		*Already Trained*		*Average*
		Number	*Per cent to total*	*Number*	*Per cent to total*	*of Per cent*
1.	*Sex*					
	Male	66	44	18	36	40
	Female	84	56	32	64	60
2.	*Age*					
	Below 20	36	24	18	36	30
	21–30	54	36	12	24	30
	31–40	36	24	10	20	22
	41–50	24	16	10	20	18
3.	*Qualification Level*					
	Matriculate	54	36	23	46	11
	Secondary	72	48	16	32	40
	Collegiate	24	16	11	22	19
4.	*Venture*					
	Service	42	28	11	22	25
	Business	78	52	26	52	52
	Manufacturing	30	20	13	26	23
5.	*Place of Business*					
	In Sivagangai	60	40	20	40	40
	Near Sivagangai	54	36	24	48	42

(Contd.)

S.No	Variables	Undergoing Training		Already Trained		Average
		Number	Per cent to total	Number	Per cent to total	of Per cent
	Far away	36	24	6	12	18
6.	*Proposed investment* Rs.					
	Up to 25000	78	52	28	56	54
	25001-50000	48	32	15	30	31
	50001-100000	24	16	7	14	15
7.	*Awareness of Training*					
	Friends	12	8	5	10	9
	DIC	18	12	8	16	14
	CED	30	20	10	20	20
	Bank	90	60	27	54	57
8.	Entrepreneurs by inheritance	30	20	6	12	16
	New entrepreneurs	120	80	44	88	84
9.	Free training	30	20	10	20	20
	Paid training	120	80	40	80	80

Source: Primary data.

3. Choice of Selection of Various Trades in the Entrepreneurial Training Programmes

Out of the prospective entrepreneurs, youth ranging between the age group of 20 to 30 were much interested in starting services like telephone booths with STD and FAX facilities, computer courses and job typing, xerox and domestic electric wiring and repairing and electronic shops and lending of chairs and vessels for functions. Those above the age of 30 were interested in business and marketing activities like grocery shops, household equipments, home appliances, vessels, cycle shops, coconut procurement and sales and ghee sales besides manufacturing activities like brick kilns, palm leaf products, coir making, shoes, chappals and leather bags making and vermi compost. Ladies were interested in textile business, tailoring, beauty parlours, dairying, basket making, soap, detergents, ink, candle manufacturing and cultivation of vegetables particularly mushroom.

It was also found that only 16 per cent of the respondents were interested in doing their community based occupation or traditional occupation whereas others were much confident in taking up new ventures.

Educational Qualifications of the Prospective Entrepreneurs

Out of the total respondents, nearly 90 per cent had completed schooling and the rest of them were graduates and post-graduates. It is a fact that the matriculate or those educated upto the level of higher secondary were more interested to take up new ventures rather that college level educated youth. It may be presumed that they may be interested in taking up white-collar jobs. This is a very important finding that can be used by the government in the framing of policies and guidelines and designing the various programmes.

Regarding tailoring course, out of the 20 trainees only 5 (25 per cent) of them own sewing machines. In the center there are 5 machines for 20 trainees. Each day they are trained for 2 hours. Inadequacy of machines at the center and non-availability at home was a hindrance for developing practical skill.

Payment *versus* Free Training Programmes

It was also observed that the respondents of paid training courses were more interested in gaining skill than the trainees attending at free of cost.

Methods of Entrepreneurial Training Programmes

Individual instruction, group instruction, lectures, demonstration, written instructions, management games, conference, practical assignments, role play, exposure training and market survey were the various methods followed to train the participants. To teach a complicated skill to a trainee individual instruction was given. To give general instruction to a group, doing similar type of work group instructions were given. The theory and practice to be followed by the trainees were communicated through lectures. It helped to clarify their doubts on the spot but practical knowledge was lacking whereas demonstration was more concerned with practical than theoretical aspects.

Written instructional method was found suitable where a future reference was to be made by the learners. It was found suitable where a standardized system was to be followed. *E.g.* Tailoring. Management games refreshed the skills of the participants. However conference method was frequently used thereby experts shared their ideas and brought to the notice of learners new ideas and techniques to increase production.

Among the methods adopted, the trainees gave more importance to exposure training, practical assignments and market survey which helped them to acquire practical knowledge. But this method of training was used only sparingly.

It was also found that the trainers made no follow-up after the completion of the training. The steps taken to evaluate the methods adopted and the knowledge and skill gained were also lacking.

It was also interesting to find that some of the trainees were proxies for the entrepreneurs and they attend the training in order to get an attendance certificate that enabled them to avail loan from the banks.

Success of any training programme lies in effective entrepreneurship ultimately enabling the entrepreneur to make his venture a profitable business. However, most of the entrepreneurs found it difficult to market their produce. So standardized training programmes should be given that can make them sustain the business or the government should come forward to help and guide in marketing the manufactured goods.

Qualification and Experience of the Trainers

Out of the 22 trainers of the selected training centers, only 14 were technically qualified and among them only 6 have some experience. The average age of the trainers was 28 and their average experience was only 8 months.

The frequent quitting and inadequate training affect the effective functioning of the training institutes.

Suggestions

The study paved way for the following suggestions and recommendations to be followed in future.

1. Government shall take enough steps to propagate the functioning of entrepreneurial training programmes by giving enough publicity. Since drop-outs from the schools is higher and only a portion of the students passing out of schools join the colleges, entrepreneurial training programmes shall be considered as a part of the co-curriculum in the school itself.

2. Follow-up measures need to be undertaken. For this, each trainee may be issued with a card where progress can be recorded from time-to-time. Project leaders can contact them by personal visit or ascertain the difficulties and follow up the requirements with the appropriate agencies.
3. The trainers should be of well qualified and properly trained. They should also be provided with refresher training as and when required. There should be no room for frequent quitting of the instructors.
4. Training should be of reasonably long duration so as to enable them to understand the theory and develop skills for managing the business accurately.
5. The level of training should be high. It must be comprehensive and the trainee should be familiar with the latest techniques in management. Mostly trainees feel bored with lectures. So the lectures should not only be informative but also interesting.
6. Any activity consuming the resources of the organization is evaluated to assess the returns on the investment. In that sense, training should also be evaluated in the pre, on-going and post-programme stages. The following rules should be followed for evaluation:
    - A specialist must do evaluation.
    - Evaluation specialist must be clear about the goals and purpose of evaluation.
    - Evaluation must be specific and continuous.
    - It must be based on objectives methods and standards.
    - It must provide the means and focus to the trainers to be able to appraise themselves, their practices and their products.
7. Since most of the unemployed youth are not aware of the entrepreneurial training and self-employment opportunities, the educational institutions should include this as a part of curriculum. In all affiliated colleges of Alagappa University, an Entrepreneurial Development Cell is functioning and 100 out-going students are given proper entrepreneurial training each year. The nodal officers of the cell have undergone proper training for a week.

Conclusion

The purpose of training will be served only if both the trainer and trainee are clear in the objectives of training and they work hard to achieve the objectives with the limited time span by planning properly.

REFERENCES

Dale S. Beach, *Personnel Management*, Mc Millan, New York, 19, pp. 401-78.

Less Donaldson Edward E. *Scannel. Human Resource Development*, Addition Wesley Publishing Company, Sydney, 1989, p. 30.

Lloyd, A. Stanley (ed.) *Guide to Training Needs and Assessment*, ICPE Training Series No.1, Yugoslavia, 1984, p. 9.

26

Improving the Competencies of the Members of Self-Help Groups: Need of the Hour

Dr. C. Natarajan Mr. S. Asok Kumar

Introduction

Over centuries, women in India have become a neglected lot. Though women enjoyed a pride of place in the earlier days, over time, they were suppressed and given an inferior status in rural society. They were not allowed to participate in decision-making and were not even given the right to express their opinion on matters concerning their betterment. They became overburdened with an overdose of children and gross undernourishment. They underwent many untold sufferings, both physical and mental and virtually had no role in shaping the society and their true potential remained unrecognized. The present economic, political and social realities of the day have further compelled women to take on additional role to ensure their own survival, their children and husbands. Although many families can only survive through the contributions made by women to the family income, women generally have little control over family income and expenditure decisions. As a rule, the men consider their wages as their own income and they give only a certain part to the women for family needs. Wages for agricultural work, even when paid to the women, are usually taken over and controlled by the household men. However, where the women have some control over the money they earn, they usually spend the bulk of it on the family's basic needs, especially food.

Statement of the Problem

The existing poverty reduction measures are unable to cope up with the increase in poverty levels due to rapid population growth and human and social factors. These social and economic barriers can be overcome, and the participation of women in the society and economy as equal partners is possible. Individual women are not able to stand up to and prevent discrimination. Hence it has been seen that if unity and cohesion are created between women of the same economic class, they are able to share experience, discuss solutions and implement them, which results in empowerment of women. A self-help group is an informal association of women, preferably belonging to the same economic classes who have come forward voluntarily to work for their own economic, social and democratic development. It provides the poor with the means of 'economic and social entitlements.' Self-help groups occupy a crucial role in the process of women-empowerment and have crossed several milestones with enduring results. Self-help group is conceived as a sustainable people's institution that provides the poor rural women with space and support necessary to take effective steps towards achieving greater control of their lives. It has played valuable role in reducing the vulnerability of the poor, through asset creation, income generation, provision of emergency assistance, and empowering women by giving them control over assets and increased self-esteem and knowledge. Though the success of self-help groups depends on several factors, mutual trust, competency level of the members and cordial relation among the members is the key to success and sustainability. They have successfully campaigned against female infanticide, child marriages, dowry menace and other atrocities against women. Husbands and in-laws respect lady-members better and they have a greater say in household affairs. Electricity, better roads, bus services, civic amenities etc., have been extended to their villages through group efforts.

Development in any walk of life has always depended on individual qualities. The phenomenon of change is a great challenge to the business and industry today is certainly going with increasing competitiveness something largely alien to the industrial sector in India till recent past. The average entrepreneur today is more qualified, enlightened and ambitious as compared to his counterpart a decade earlier. One important method to cope with this change is to develop a battery of competent of entrepreneurs. The survival of the business may be at stake if the organizations do not keep themselves fully alive to meet the emerging challenges, situations and demands of the society. Since self-help groups are a labour intensive industry, unless all the members are equipped thoroughly with the latest information relevant to the business, it would be difficult to ensure excellent customer services. In spite of so much contribution in the economy, these self-help groups are facing number of problems like finance, raw material, marketing, technology, dealing with government agencies etc. There are basically three strategies to match entrepreneurs with the requirements of the business. One strategy is to select the business according to their competency level. A second strategy is to re-design the business; the entrepreneurs are carrying out the activities within their capabilities. The third strategy is improving the competency level of entrepreneurs. To identify the answers to these and similar questions, an elaborate study is the need of the hour, and hence the researchers have made an attempt to study the competency level of the members of self-help groups in Salem District.

Objectives of the Study

The following are the objectives of the study:

1. To study the need and importance of the competency of self-help groups.
2. To study the competency level of the members of the self-help groups in Salem District.
3. To find out the incompetence areas of the members of the self-help groups in Salem District.
4. To offer appropriate measures to improve the competency level of the members of self-help groups in District.

Scope of the Study

In the present study, an attempt has been made to analyze the competency level of the members of self-help groups in Salem District. The scope of the study was confined to the members of the self-help groups only. The present study is an attempt to seek the members' opinion towards their capabilities in carrying out various entrepreneurial activities. The entrepreneurial functions are vast one; therefore more importantly the scope of the study was limited to the major entrepreneurial functions such as promotion of business, production functions, human resource functions, management of finance, marketing functions, legal aspects of business and public relations.

Research Design

This study is descriptive in nature based on survey method. The researchers had a discussion with the officials of the District Rural Develop Agency in Salem District. Based on the discussion, a questionnaire was prepared after going through some of the available literature on the topic. The adequate information contained in the questionnaire has been tested and the necessary changes were incorporated in the revised questionnaire in the light of the experience gained from the pre-test. A pre-test was conducted with 10 members of the self-help groups. By adopting the convenient sampling technique, 100 respondents were selected on the occasion of trade exhibition held at Salem during September 2005. The required data were collected from primary and secondary sources. The questionnaire method was employed for the collection of primary data. The secondary data was collected from the books, reports and periodicals. The questionnaire used in this study was constructed on 3-point scale (abundance, adequate and inadequate). The scores of the competency level of the members with the various entrepreneurial functions were ascertained and an analysis was made based on these scores only. The understanding of the competency level of the members would help to formulate policies for the development of future entrepreneurs of the nation. In order to study the competency level of the members, various statistical tools such as chi-square test, analysis of one-way variance and analysis of co-variance were employed. The chi-square test and analysis of one variance have been employed to study the association between the personal variables of the members of the self-help groups with their competency on the entrepreneurial activities. The co-variance has been employed to test the consistency in the competency level of the members of self-help groups.

Findings

1. There is no significant difference in the overall competency level of the members belonging to different age, educational standards and location status with the entrepreneurial activities.
2. The variations in the overall competency level was high among the members belongs to age group of 31-40; members have primary education and rural members on entrepreneurial activities.

3. There is no significant association between the competency level of the members belonging to different age, education and location status with marketing functions, production functions, human resource functions and legal aspects of business.
4. There is no significant relationship between the competency level of the members belonging to different age and education with management of finance, marketing functions and public relations functions. However, there is a significant relationship between the location status of the members and their competency level with management of finance, marketing functions and public relations.
5. The variation in the competency level of the members was high with respect to human resource functions and production functions.
6. More than 91 per cent of the members of the self-help groups were accepted that competencies are the most important one for the successful conduct of business and 51 per cent of the members' overall competency level with the entrepreneurial functions was adequate.
7. Ranging from 45 per cent to 50 per cent of the members' competency level with promotion of business, production function, human resource functions and public relations was high. Ranging from 51 per cent to 59 per cent of the members had adequate competency level on management of finance, marking functions and legal aspects of business.
8. Lack of update knowledge, lack of awareness about various incentive schemes, inadequate knowledge on competitors', inability to access the financial assistance and inadequate knowledge on the public relations were the incompetence areas of the members of the self-help groups in Salem District.

Suggestions

1. Thirty-nine per cent of the members of the self-help groups had incompetence on updating their knowledge and skills. The District Rural Development Agency shall take necessary efforts to update the knowledge of the members. Short-term orientation programmes and refresher courses can be conducted for the benefits of the members of self-help groups.
2. Majority of the respondents had lack of competency about

their competitors'. It is therefore suggested that number of entrepreneurial development programmes shall be conducted by the private as well as government agencies in order to adopt appropriate strategies under varied competitive circumstances.

3. Fifty-one per cent of the respondents were unable to avail financial assistance from various agencies due to their incompetence. It is therefore suggested that the financial intermediaries assisting self-help groups shall provide necessary guidelines to the members to avail such financial assistance. It will enable the members to impart knowledge on getting financial assistance at the right time.
4. Public relations are one of the major areas determining the reputation of any organization. More than 53 per cent of the members were not having adequate public relations skills. It is therefore suggested that the authorities shall conduct a special programme for the development of public relations skills of the members of the self-help groups in Salem District.

REFERENCES

Devi, L. 'Employment and Income Generation for Rural Women', *National Bank News Review*, Bombay, 1994, Vol.10, No. 2.

Puhazhendhi, V., Evaluation Study of Self-Help Groups in Tamil Nadu, *NABARD*, Mumbai, 2000.

Hegde, N.G., 'Development of Infrastructure for Rural Prosperity', Paper presented at the seminar on "Rural Prosperity on Agriculture" at NIRD, Hyderabad, 1999.

Puhazhendhi, V. and K.J.S. Satyasai., 'Micro Finance for Rural Poor: An Impact Evaluation, *NABARD*, Mumbai, 2000.

Pallavi Chavan, R. Ramkumar and P.Chavan. 'Micro Credit and Rural Poverty: An analysis of Empirical Evidence', *Economic and Political Weekly*, 2002, Vol. 37, No. 10.

Qazi, M. 'Self-Help Groups: A Novel Approach to Rural Development', *State Bank of India Monthly Review*, 1997, Vol. 36, No. 9.

Schuler, S.R., S.M. Hashemi and S.H. Badal, 'Men's Violence against Women in Rural Bangladesh', *An Oxfam Journal*, 1998, Vol. 8, No. 2.

Shylendra, H.S., 'Micro Finance and Self-Help Groups: A Study of the Experience of Two Leading NGOs in Gujarat, Research Paper, Institute of Rural Management, 1999, No. 16.

27

Factors Promoting New Entrepreneurs to Enter Industry

B. Rajasekaran

Introduction

The word 'Entrepreneur' first appeared in the French Language and was applied to leaders of military expeditions in 16th century. Then it was applied to other types of adventures, mainly civil engineering. Richard Cantillon, an Irishman living in France, was the first person to use the term 'entrepreneur' to refer to economic activities. He viewed the entrepreneur as 'a person who buys factors of production at certain prices and sell his products at uncertain prices in the future thereby bearing of non-insurable risk that may arise due to depressed demand for his products'.

The French economist J.B.Say defined an entrepreneur as one who performs the functions of rationally combining, coordinating and supervising various factors of production. F.H. Knight viewed that entrepreneurs are a specialised group of persons who bears risks and deal with uncertainty.

According to Noah Webster, entrepreneur is 'one who assumes the risk and management of business'. Schumpeter described an entrepreneur as 'an innovator, one who brings about change through introduction of new technological process or products'.

Thus, an entrepreneur refers to 'a person who bears the non-insurable risk, works under uncertainty, combines and manages the factors of production, innovates on all fronts on regular basis, functions as proprietary capitalist and is motivated by profits'.

Most of the authors consider entrepreneur as an individual and not a group. However, some authors consider entrepreneur as a group. In the opinion of A.H.Cole, 'entrepreneurship is the purposeful activity of an individual or a group of associated individuals, undertaken to initiate, maintain or aggrandize a profit by production or distribution of economic goods and services.

The entrepreneur is essence an institution, which comprises all the people, required to perform various functions. Peter Kilby has classified the functions of an entrepreneur into four groups as exchange relationship functions, political administration functions, management control functions and technology functions. According to him, the functions of an entrepreneur are:

1. Perceiving market opportunities
2. Gaining command over scarce resources
3. Purchasing inputs
4. Marketing of products
5. Responding to competition
6. Dealing with Government
7. Managing human relations in the company
8. Managing customer and supplier relations
9. Managing finances
10. Managing production
11. Industrial engineering
12. Upgrading process and product quality
13. Introducing new production techniques

To perform the above functions effectively, the entrepreneurs should be properly promoted and motivated. The desire to earn money is no doubt an important motivating force. However, entrepreneurs are motivated non-by profits alone.

This chapter presents the factors, which motivate the new entrepreneurs to start enterprises.

Factors Motivating Entrepreneurs

R.A. Sharma classified all the factors influencing the entrepreneurs into two types as follows:

1. Internal Factors

These included the following factors.

(a) *Desire to do something new:* Most of the persons desire to do the business something new. They do not like to do the different business; they would like to do the business differently.

(b) *Education:* Education plays an important role in business in general and in knowledge-based industry in particular. Education, Entrepreneurship and Development go hand in hand. The higher the level of education, the greater keenness of entrepreneurs to enter into business.

Technically or professionally qualified entrepreneurs considered educated qualification as the main promoting factor. Most of the technically qualified persons had established enterprises in the fields of their specialisation which shows that such entrepreneurs were promoted by their qualification or specialisation to undertaken the industrial activity.

(c) *Occupational background experience:* Business experience provides confidence to the entrepreneurs, which helps to reduce the element of uncertainty regarding demand of the product, technology, raw material, financial requirements competition, etc. Relationship between occupational experience of the entrepreneur and the nature of enterprise promoted suggests that occupational experience is an important motivating factor.

The unemployed persons may start their business with the occupational experience of their fathers. It seems that they are learning business skills by engaging themselves in their father's business and slowly developed confidence to start their own ventures.

(d) *Desire to work independently:* Desire to work independently in manufacturing line came out as another important motivating factor. An entrepreneur expressed a desire to have important share in the decision-making and control in the overall working of an organisation.

2. *External Factors*

These included the following factors.

(a) *Financial Assistance:* Among the external motivating factors, financial assistance from institutions and government emerged as the most significant factors. To provide financial assistance to entrepreneurs the government has set up a number of special financial institutions besides commercial banks like IFCI, ICICI, IDBI, EXIM Bank of India, UTI, LIC, GIC, NSIC, SIDBI, SIDCs, SIPCOT, TIIC, etc.

(b) *Attitude of the government to help new units*
(c) *Accommodation in industrial estates*
(d) *Purchase of machinery on hire purchase*
(e) *Financial assistance from non-government sources*
(f) *Encouragement from big business houses*
(g) *Availability of labour and raw materials*
(h) *Promising demand for the product*
(i) *Profit margin*
(j) *Unsound units available at cheap price*

After analysing the relative importance of the above factors, these may be concluded that a vast majority of the new entrepreneurial class was promoted to enter industry mainly because of three factors:

1. *Entrepreneurial Ambitions*

It includes the following. *(a)* To make money, *(b)* To continue family business, *(c)* To secure self-employment, *(d)* To fulfill the desire of self/parents, *(e)* To gain social prestige, *(f)* Making of a decent living, *(g)* desire to do something creative, and *(h)* To provide employment to others.

2. *Compelling Reasons*

It includes the following: *(a)* Unemployment problem, *(b)* Dissatisfaction with the job, *(c)* Make use of idle funds, and *(d)* Make use of technical/professional skills, etc.

3. *Facilitating Factors*

It includes the following: *(a)* Success stories of entrepreneurs, *(b)* Previous employment in the same line of activity, and *(c)* Influence of family members, etc.

Development of Entrepreneurship

The emergence and development of entrepreneurship is not a spontaneous one but a dependent phenomenon of some factors. These factors may influence the emergence of entrepreneurship positively or negatively. Positive influences constitute facilitative and conductive conditions for the emergence of entrepreneurship, whereas negative influences create inhibiting milieu to the emergence of entrepreneurship.

The following are the important factors affecting entrepreneurial growth:

Economic Factors

From the economic viewpoint, the factors, which promote the economic development, account for the emergence of entrepreneurship also. Some of the economic factors are:

(a) Capital

Capital is one of the most important prerequisites to establish an enterprise. Availability of capital facilitates the entrepreneur to bring together the land of one, machine of another and raw material of yet another to combine them to produce goods. The capital supply increases, entrepreneurship also increases.

(b) Labour

The quality rather quantity of labour is another factor, which influences the emergence of entrepreneurship. Adam Smith considered division of labour as an important element in economic development. According to him, division of labour which itself depends upon the size of the market leads to improvement in the productive capacities of labour due to an increase in the dexterity of labour.

(c) Raw Materials

The necessity of raw materials hardly needs any emphasis for establishing any industrial activity and, therefore, its influence in the emergence of entrepreneurship. In the absence of raw materials, neither any enterprise can be established nor can an entrepreneur be emerged.

(d) Market

The fact remains that the potential of the market constitutes the major determinant of probable rewards from entrepreneurial function. The size and composition of market both influence entrepreneurship in their own ways. Practically, monopoly in a particular product in a market becomes more influential for entrepreneurship than a competitive market. Thus, it appears that whether or not the market is expanding and the rate at which it is expanding are the most significant characteristics of the market for entrepreneurial emergence.

Non-economic Factors

The above economic factors may be necessary conditions, but they are not sufficient conditions for the appearance of entrepreneurship. It reveals that the influence of economic factors on entrepreneurial emergence largely depends upon the existence of non-economic factors *i.e.,* social and psychological factors in the society.

1. *Social Conditions*

(a) Legitimacy of Entrepreneurship

The proponents of non-economic factors give emphasis to the relevance of a system of norms and values within a socio-cultural setting for the emergence of entrepreneurship. Such system referred to as the 'legitimacy of entrepreneurship' in which the degree of approval or disapproval granted entrepreneurial behaviour influences its emergence and characteristics if it does emerge.

(b) Social Mobility

It involves the degree of mobility, both social and geographical, and the nature of mobility channels within a system. However, the social mobility is crucial for entrepreneurial emergence is not unanimous.

2. *Psychological Factors*

Many entrepreneurial theorists have propounded theories of entrepreneurship that concentrate specifically upon psychological factors. They are:

(a) Need Achievement

According to David McClelland, a constellation of personality characteristics which are indicative of high need achievement is the major determinant of entrepreneurship development. Therefore, if the average level of need achievement in a society is relatively high, one would expect relatively high amount of entrepreneurship in that society.

(b) Withdrawal of Status Respect

The following four types of events can produce status withdrawal:

1. The group may be displaced by force,
2. It may have its valued symbols denigrated,
3. It may drift into a situation of status inconsistency, and

4. It may not be accepted the expected status on migration in a new society.

Government Actions

The Government by its actions or failure to act also does influence both the economic and non-economic factors for entrepreneurship. Any interested Government in economic development can help, through its clearly expressed industrial policy, promote entrepreneurship in one-way or other. By creating basic facilities, utilities and services and by providing incentives and concessions, the Government can provide the prospective entrepreneurs a facilitative socio-economic setting. Such conducive setting minimizes the risks, which the entrepreneurs are to encounter. Thus, the supportive actions of the Government appear as the most conducive to the entrepreneurial growth.

Conclusion

Motivation is an inner spirit that activates and directs the behaviour of the entrepreneurs towards the goals. Many factors motivate and promote the new entrepreneurs to enter into the industry. At the same time, motivation can be developed through training and education. The entrepreneurship does not emerge and develop automatically and spontaneously. Its emergence and development depend upon the availability of certain factors also called 'supportive conditions'.

REFERENCES

Aruna Kaulgud (2003). *Entrepreneurship Management*, Vikas Publishing, New Delhi.

Gupta, C.B. and Srinivasan N.P. (2003). *Entrepreneurial Development*, Sultan Chand & Sons, New Delhi.

Peter F.Drucker, "The Discipline of Innovation" *Harvard Business Review*, August 2002, pp. 95-102.

James C. Collins & William C. Lazier (1992). *Beyond Entrepreneurship*, Prentice Hall, New Delhi.

28

Rural Development Programmes–A Boon for Diversified Entrepreneurial Activities

Dr. A. Sakunthalai and Mr. K. Ramakrishnan

Introduction

As long as women of India do not take part in public life there can be no salvation for the country.

– Mahatma Gandhi.

Women are a vital part of the Indian economy constituting one-third of the national labour force and a major contributor to the survival of the family. Despite progress in several key indicators a gender analysis of most social and economic data demonstrates that women in India continue to be relatively disadvantaged in matters of survival, health, nutrition, literacy and productivity. Two-third of all work is performed by women who constitute half the population but only share one-tenth of the income and one hundredth of the property (FAO, 1988).

As the patriarchial society pulls back the women to come to the forefront, they could not come out of the shackles of male dominance. Studies on women in agriculture conducted in India reveal that by and large women are found doing manual, low prestige, hazardous, arduous, monotonous, repetitive and time consuming jobs *viz.*, transplanting, picking, weeding, harvesting and processing. At the same time agricultural work is not free from hazards. In case of women, these get aggravated mainly due to prevalence of higher levels of malnutrition, anemia, parasitic infection, frequent child bearing, long hours of work and mishandling of agricultural tools and equipments.

In the words of Swaminathan (1988), despite women's importance to agricultural production, women face severe handicaps. They are in fact the largest group of landless labourers with little real security in case of family break-up, inheritance laws, land reforms and family customs discriminate against them. Agricultural development programmes are usually planned by men and aimed at men, mechanization to alleviate the burden of task that are traditionally men's responsibility leaving women's burden unrelieved or even increased. Extension workers, almost exclusively males, aim their advice at men, on men's activities and crops.

Even though, several theoretical concepts and indices to measure empowerment of women have been identified and proposed worldwide, a very few studies had been conducted empirically to measure *'women empowerment'*. In the present study, a pioneering attempt has been made to develop a scale to measure women empowerment and which was applied through case study analysis with the following specific concepts.

(i) The case study was conducted with a broad spectrum of highlighting the empowerment of women with a significant view of not only reformation and refining their life towards the egalitarian society but also into the direction of economic achievement of the country.

(ii) To know the efforts made by the out reach programmes to empower the women .

Brief Details

The pioneer attempt was made in Coimbatore district of Tamil Nadu State. There are 20 districts, out of which Coimbatore district was preferred to conduct the study because of the following specified reasons. The major women developmental programmes implemented in this district are: *(i)* Tamil Nadu Women in Agriculture (TANWA) *(ii)* Tamil Nadu Women Development Project (TNWDP) *(iii)* In this district, in general most of the farms are managed by the farm women and they are noted for their farm entrepreneurship. Out of 19 blocks of Coimbatore district, Thondamuthur block was selected based on the women beneficiaries and women developmental activities (EDP). Five revenue villages were selected randomly .Using random sample with probability proportion to size technique 110 samples were selected. The farm women selected for the case study were categorised as very low, low, medium, high and very high based on the Women

Empowerment Index (WEI) score. Being the successful case study the farm women were selected from the category of "high to very high" level of empowerment of the block, thus Tmt. Valliammal, W/o Perumal was selected as successful farm women of Thondamuthur block. The information collected from the case study analysis is presented below.

Mrs. Valliammal, W/o Perumal, aged 30, educated upto 8th standard lived with her husband aged 35, who is educated only upto 3rd standard. Her traditional occupation was farming. She belongs to tribal community; her family owned 1.5 acres of irrigated land which got irrigated from the river running through their area. Her village located near the Velliangry hills and comprised 50 numbers of families.

She expressed that, in the earlier days, there was no school, no facilities for drinking water, the houses without permanent roof which was just housed with teak leaves. There was no transport facilities, no communication facilities, and no medical facilities. They were handicapped in availing the basic infrastructure facilities. She was unaware of improved farm implements and technologies. Her village was totally detached from the nearby inhabitants. Their livelihoods were mostly depended on the minor forest products and consumption of only raw vegetables, roots, fruits, nuts and minor millets. She reared buffaloes for milk purpose, in addition to sheep and poultry which are for meat purpose.

Further, she explained about the introduction of an NGO called 'Centre for Soil Salinity Research' (CSSR) during 1996-97. Its consequent meeting in their village on "Environment and pollution free life" was the stepping stone for their village which forward them towards the modern civilization. Among the tribal people, Valliammal showed her interest toward the developmental activities. She voluntarily approached the officials of the NGO and collected information in connection with their empowerment. She had been selected as a leader of that tribal village by the officials because of her leadership quality and spontaneous active participation in all the meetings, demonstrations etc.

She told that the first meeting of the NGO taught about various scientific themes on 'how to be free from diseases and pollution' and 'how to keep the environment clean'.

During the year 1997-98, the village was adopted by another NGO called NERD (Non-Conventional Energy for Rural Development) which organised the programmes such as training on self-employment, income generating activities, cleanliness, how to be courage enough to face the problem, power of decision-making etc. She was imparted skills on tailoring, bag knitting, crop cultivation etc., for the empowerment of tribal community.

She described the changes that have taken place among them after undergoing the training programmes. The income generating activities helped them to earn some amount which contributed considerably to raise their family income.

During the year 1998-99, the tribal community was identified by the TANWA officials. They arranged all kinds of meetings, demonstrations, scientific way of crop cultivation, income generating activities. The officials of TANWA explained the ways and means for starting the self-employment. The tribal women narrated that the meetings conducted by the TANWA were highly useful for aware of new practices, improves her skill on modern technologies such as seed treatment with biofertilizers, Azospirillum, Rhizobium and Phosphobacteria. She explained that the TANWA officials paved a way for group activity. It helped them a lot to develop good qualities *viz.*, the way to move with others, adjustment with any social kind, how to be generous, human relations development, how to approach the financial institutions and about joint decision-making behaviour. These qualities improved her society in a desirable direction. The officials of TANWA also selected Mrs. Valliammal as a leader of a group of 16 members because of her distinguished involvement in the developmental activities. Her progressive nature helped others to avail the basic facilities.

In continuation of this, she approached the Block Development Officer (BDO) of Thondamuthur block and explained the situations existing in their households. She had a chance to meet the District Collector, Coimbatore with the support of the block development officials about the procedures to be followed to avail the facilities. Even though she was trained properly she could not avail those facilities because of her unawareness. The District Collector visited the village along with the development officials. The Collector encouraged the tribal community to be energetic in achieving all the basic attributes. He paved way for basic facilities, such as high school, medical facilities, drinking water, sanitation and constructed new cement walled tiled house replacing the mud with thatched roof and arranged for income earning activities such as tailoring and basket knitting. Besides this, with the help of extension officials of state agriculture department she could understand the technological bases of organic farming, preparation of EFYM, Panchakavya, vermicompost preparation etc.

With the support of District Collector her group was sanctioned Rs.1,00,000 to start self-employment activities. Further she was supplied one tractor with cultivator and trailer on free of cost so as to improve their farming. The Government supplied two cows in order to abolish the bonded labour as per the "Bonded Labour Abolition Act, 1976". The milk was supplied to the nearby milk society by engaging the unemployed men of their society which also facilitated men to get employment opportunity. To alleviate the hurdles in transport facilities of her village, she had decided to run auto rickshaw from Sadivayal to Kovai Kutralam (Tourism place). She discussed the same with the Collector of Coimbatore district and the society members to get the consent over it. In view of above efforts, the auto was sanctioned on subsidy basis. She was very prompt in repayment of the loan. She selected two girls from their community and trained them on auto rickshaw driving. Now two auto rickshaws are being operated from Sadivayal to Kovai Kutralam by charging Rs. 2 to 5 per head.

As a result of entrepreneurship training, she had taken effort to set up a business on marketing of forest products [Gooseberry, soapnut, kadukkai, tharbai grass, puchikai and jadhikai (nutmeg)] and marketed to Erode on cost basis.

Further more, she had shifted their cultivation method from paddy to marigold with Coleus as intercropping system due to water shortage which benefited them from the elephant damage and fetched higher income also. The heavy scented blooms were sent to a perfumery at Karamadai. She said that the advantage with marigold was the perfumery effect even in dried flowers. So wastage was minimal. To save input cost, some flowers were left out on the shrub itself so that she need not spent money on seeds. Otherwise she would spent nearly Rs. 600/ha.

The foothills of the Boluvampatti range also boasts of a lash forest, home to a variety of sweet-smelling flora. The Khadi and

Village Industries Commission (KVIC) had given 10 boxes with queen bees to tribal women on free of cost. She had been given training on the same.

She utilised the opportunity provided by the developmental departments. She had taken maximum efforts to bring economic revolution in her society in addition with social awareness and self-confidence. As an extraordinary sincere effort made by her was appreciated by the officials and appointed her as the President of Marudham Tribal Women's Federation (MTWF). It was an association of 18 tribal women self-help group (SHGs).Apart from these, she was also interested in the political activities, she said that, if opportunity would come she would participate and do better services for her society.

The uniqueness of this case of tribal woman for the success gained through Rural development programmes are:

- Courage
- Self-confidence
- Self-responsibility
- Better educational quality
- Good leadership quality
- Best organiser of group activity
- Good planner
- Voluntary and active participation in the developmental activities
- High entrepreneurship quality
- Positive attitude towards empowerment of women.

Conclusion

It could be concluded from the above case analysis that the establishment of unique qualities of the tribal women are due to the concerted effort taken by the rural developmental organisations. The aforesaid uniqueness is the evidence for her empowerment identified from the case analysis. These also derive support of the indicators developed for the empowerment of women.

Thus the results of the case analysis tangible for the various empowerment dimensions such as extension, social, economic, scientific, psychologic and political dimensions. Ultimately these empowerment dimensions contributed towards the 'high to very high' level of empowerment.

From the aforesaid case analysis, it could be derived that the developmental organisations which had objectively feminism should consider all the empowerment dimensions *viz.*, social, economic, extension, scientific, psychologic and political while formulating policy issues such rural developmental programmes would serve to achieve its ultimate goal in full-fledged manner.

REFERENCES

Nirmala Devi (2002). *Empowerment of Women in SAARC: A Selective Assessment.* Serials Publications, New Delhi, pp. 89-102.

Shanthasheela, M. (2002). *Performance Analysis of Elected Women Presidents in Village Panchayats.* Unpub. Ph. D. Thesis, TNAU, Coimbatore.

Shylashri, C. (2001). *Socio-economic Aspects of Women's Education – A Case Study of Bangalore.* Unpub. Ph. D. Thesis, Department of Economics, UAS, Bangalore.

Manjula, I. (2001). *Tribal Farm Families – A Critical Study.* Unpub. (M.Sc.Ag) Thesis, TNAU, Coimbatore.

29

Creating Entrepreneurial Awareness Among Rural Students

Prof. C. T. Sam Luther

"One cannot make decisions for the future. Decisions are commitments to actions in the present, and in the present only. But, actions in the present are also one and only way to make the future"

– Peter Drucker

Introduction

Entrepreneurship is a creative human act involving mobilisation of resources from one level of productive use to a higher level of use. It is a process by which the individual pursue opportunities without regard to resources currently controlled. It is an act of accepting the risk of starting and running a business.

Some of the many reasons people are willing to take the risks of starting the business are the following:

- Opportunity
- Better profit
- Independence
- Challenges

Attrition of Entrepreneurship

Can all succeed as an entrepreneur? People may learn about the managerial and leadership skills needed to run a firm. But, they may not have the personality to assume the risks, take the initiative, create the vision, and make others to follow their lead. Those traits are harder to learn or acquire. The following are such attributes to be nurtured and developed in one's life to become a successful entrepreneur.

- *Self-directed*: In order to be successful as an entrepreneur, one should be thoroughly comfortable and thoroughly self-disciplined. The success or failure depends upon one's own initiative and capabilities to manage and run a business even though he may be his own boss. Achieving leverage and the amplification of one's skills are the keystones to becoming a successful entrepreneur.
- *Self-nurturing*: The entrepreneur must believe in his ideas, even when no one else does, and must replenish his own enthusiasm. The one word that best characterises successful entrepreneurs is determination. When Walt Disney suggested the possibility of a full-length animated film, *Snow White*, the industry laughed. His personal commitment and enthusiasm caused the Bank of America to back his venture. The rest, as all of us know, is history.
- *Action-oriented*: Great business ideas are not enough. The most important thing is a burning desire to realise, actualise, and build one's dream into reality.
- *Highly energetic*: There is no substitute for hard work. He should always feel that it's his own business and he must be emotionally, mentally and physically able to work long and hard. Studies show that successful entrepreneurs usually devote more than 16 hours a day to the business.
- *Tolerant of uncertainty*: Successful entrepreneurs take only calculated risk. Still, they must be able to take more. Entrepreneurship is not for any one who is squeamish or bent on security.
- *Focus*: The prime factor that is attributed to most of the small businesses' failure is the lack of focus. Lack of focus is one of the common mistakes that cause start-ups to fail. Many entrepreneurs go in too many directions at once, and do not execute anything well. To focus means to concentrate attention on one '*big*' objective and move to achieve that objective.

Entrepreneurship in India

India needs entrepreneurs. It needs them for two reasons: to capitalise on new opportunities and to create wealth and new jobs. A recent McKinsey and Company-NASSOCOM report estimates that India needs at least 8,000 new businesses to achieve its target of building a $ 87 billion IT sector by 2008. Similarly, in the next 10 years, 110-

130 million Indian citizens will be searching for jobs, including 80-100 million looking for their first jobs; that are seven times Australia's population. This does not include disguised unemployment of over 50 per cent among the 230 million employed in rural India. Since traditional large employers – including the government and the old economy players – may find it difficult to sustain this level of employment in the future, it is entrepreneurs who will create these new jobs and opportunities.

Fortunately, today's knowledge-based economy is a fertile ground for entrepreneurs in India. Also, it has an extraordinary talent pool with virtually limitless potential to become entrepreneurs. India must, however, commit to creating the right environment to develop successful business builders.

Entrepreneurial Awareness Among Rural Students

Of course, it is true that the basic characteristics to start a business include drive, thinking ability, competence in human relations, communicative skills and technical knowledge. Unfortunately, these attributes are very poor among students who are hailing from the rural areas. *Mostly, the external factors such as economic, social, cultural and political factors dominate and subvert the internal factors of these students.*

'Entrepreneurs are born, not nurtured.' This saying is true in many Asian countries including India, wherein businesses are traditionally passed along the family line. So, even bright students of the rural mass have disdained entrepreneurship, instead choosing more respected or better chartered careers in public service, academia; and the medical, engineering and legal professions in few cases, and in many cases, just satisfied with little higher education especially the girl students. Even if few start their own business, mostly they are necessity-based entrepreneurship and not based on opportunity-based entrepreneurship.

Promoting Entrepreneurship at Education Institutions

In India, where over 300 million people are living below the poverty line, it is simply impossible for any government to provide means of livelihood for everyone, so also the case with the educated youth. The process of education addresses not necessarily to the immediate means of the learners to facilitate them to acquire jobs to make the ends meet, but it should be strategically oriented to help the society to empower itself to meet the future needs.

It is possible to encourage entrepreneurial behaviour within the context of the standard curriculum subjects, such as language and literature, mathematics, science, history, commerce and so on. But, quite unfortunate that the Indian education system is not providing such facilities and the universities are not incorporating a curriculum subject as compulsory. Though few disciplines have subject on entrepreneurship, they fail to reap the full potential due to multi-faceted problems associated with and inherent in the Indian education system, such as the quality of the subject handlers, marks-oriented evaluation, failure to link the curriculum to industry-interface, etc.

Entrepreneurs are to be created at the school/college level by imparting entrepreneurial motivation, skills, and vision so that they can seek the vast potential of resources in the midst of emerging challenges. Such situations surely demand for a continuous effort from the educational institutions, where the students are encouraged to come up with their entrepreneurial initiative. Entrepreneurial awareness camps, entrepreneurship development programmes, workshops and seminars are to be arranged on a continuous basis to find the potential students and if proper direction and motivation are given, chances of creating young entrepreneurs from the rural students are more.

Not every one is cut out to be an entrepreneur. The fact is that all kinds of people with all kinds of personalities have succeeded in starting small and large businesses. These are certain traits that seem to separate those who will be successful as entrepreneurs from those who may not be.

Keeping the above stated objective in mind, the researcher has conducted a one-day workshop to create entrepreneurship awareness among selected 80 undergraduate students of Nesamony Memorial Christian College, Marthandam and tried to evaluate the traits of the students which is narrated in the following paragraphs.

Objective of the Study

- To create entrepreneurship awareness among rural students by conducting an entrepreneurship training programme or workshop.
- To assess the students traits towards developing the entrepreneurial skills.

Methodology

Data collection

In order to obtain the data, a closed questionnaire model has been used by the researcher. The questionnaire had a set of twenty five questions about different traits of the students. Each question is provided with five options, *viz.* 'agree completely', 'mostly agree', 'partially agree', 'mostly disagree' and 'disagree completely' and points are awarded based on the degree of trait the student possesses.

Rating

The total points scored by each student is categorised as follows:

Points	*Category*
41-50	The entrepreneurial potential is great and the student can able to use the opportunity to use it.
31-40	This is close to high entrepreneurial range. If the other talents and resources are favourable, he can also be successful.
21-30	The score is in the transitional range. With some training offered, the student can probably develop the outlook for running his own business.
11-20	Things look pretty doubtful to become an entrepreneur. It would take considerable re-arranging of his life philosophy and behaviour to make it.
Below 10	Entrepreneurship is not really for him. Still, learning what it's all about won't hurt any thing.

Research Tools

Simple charts and Statistical sampling.

Data analysis and Interpretations

Table-29.1
Scoring at Different Levels

Category	*No. of students*
below 10	3
10-20	20
20-30	53
30-40	4
40-50	0
Total	80

The study conducted reveals the following:

- No student scored above 40 points,
- Only 4 students reached the level beyond 30,
- Of the total 80, 53 students are in the range of 20-30 level,
- 20 students are having the attributes in the range of 10-20, and
- 3 students scored less than 10.

Figure 29.1 : Scoring at Different Levels

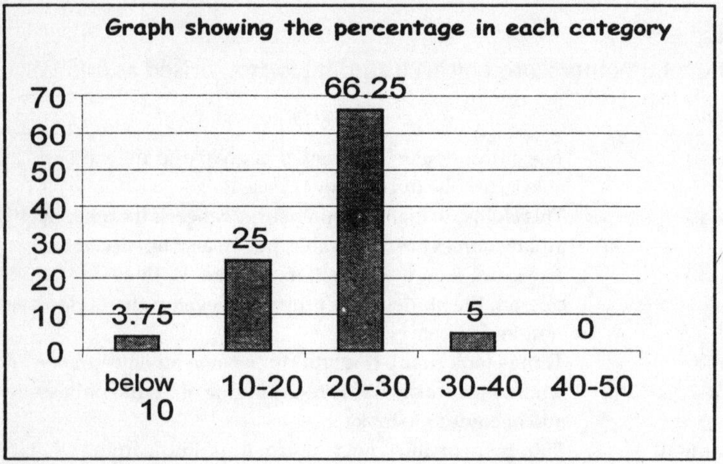

Sampling Test

If a student scores atleast 30 points, then he can be viewed that the entrepreneurship potential is high. So, we test whether the sample of 80 students can be drawn from a population with a mean score as 30 or not.

Null hypothesis H_0: $\mu = 30$

The alternative hypothesis is H_1: $\mu < 30$

So, we apply single-tailed test.

The test statistic is $z = \frac{(x - \mu)}{s/\sqrt{n}}$, where $\bar{x}$ is sample mean and s^2 is the sample variance.

The value of s is equal to 6.93, $\bar{x} = 19$ and $n = 80$.

Applying the × values, we get $z = -14.19$ and $/z/ = 14.19$ which is greater than 2.33 at 1 per cent level and $/z/$ is greater than 1.645 at 5 per cent level.

It is seen from the test that there is significant difference between the sample mean and the population mean, thus H_0 is rejected, that is the sample cannot be drawn from a population mean of 30.

Therefore, it is concluded that the students lack entrepreneurship qualities.

It is clear from the above analysis that the entrepreneurship awareness workshop has not created the desired results due to other external factors *viz.* social, political, economical and cultural. The study further reveals the following:

- More than 90 per cent of the students are hailing from backward and most backward regions.
- 87.5 per cent of the students' parents are farmers and coolies with poor education background.
- Of the 80 students, 36 students are girls, basically having poor enterprising qualities.
- The income level of the families of 86 per cent of the students is below 50000 rupees per annum.

Suggestions

1. It is true that all students cannot be made entrepreneurs. A well-designed value-based curriculum subject has to be evolved and imparted among the selected 'enterprising' students. They should be trained, instead of taught. Motivation is required than knowledge.
2. The attributes of and the requirements for entrepreneurship is highly complex and it is still by no means clear which of these attributes/requirements can be acquired or inherited. So, mere entrepreneurship education or awareness will not automatically create entrepreneurs. An entrepreneurship culture has to be developed among rural mass which is dominating more than 70 per cent of the population. An awareness should, not only be created among students, but also among the parents and the society. Studies reveal that though entrepreneurship education is well disbursed demographically in India, still there is a 70-30 per cent urban-rural imbalance exists. This urban-rural imbalance should be narrowed down by bringing the science and technological

developments to the rural villages, the benefits of which are at present enjoyed by a handful few, and an entrepreneurial climate has to be created in the villages. Unless, the full potential of developments reaches the poor mass in rural areas, opportunity-based entrepreneurs cannot be created in rural India.

3. Moreover, due to social rigidities, Indian women who represent half the population in India, especially rural girls, are denied the opportunities and discouraged to start their own business. It is estimated that, the self-employed women are as low as 5.2 per cent of the total self-employed persons in India. Further, women entrepreneurs in India accounted for less than 10 per cent of the total entrepreneurs. The girls who have innate talents and capabilities are also to be encouraged and motivated to start their own business.

Conclusion

The rapid pace of globalisation and the fast growth of Asian economies present tremendous opportunities and challenges for India. But, the wheels of India's bureaucracy still turn too slow for entrepreneurs. The educational system is not good at promoting entrepreneurial skills and attitudes. Indian institutes have not been as good as multinationals in R&D transfer, and India's physical infrastructure ranks lowest among the developing countries. Therefore, a well-designed strategy has to be evolved by the policy-makers, academicians and business leaders which has a blend of training the enterprising students as well as improvement of rural areas. Then only, India can attain the true potential of entrepreneurship. It would be worthwhile perhaps to conclude with the words of Rahul Bajaj, "*If we could have one entrepreneur in every family, India's economy would skyrocket.*"

REFERENCES

Understanding Business by Nickels and others.

The ICFAI Journal of Entrepreneurship Development, June 05 issue.

Entrepreneurial Development by S.S. Khanka.

www.bizmove.com.

Inspiring Future Entrepreneurs by Jennie Wong.

Entrepreneurship: Acquired or Inherited? by Jorn Axel Meyer.

30

Need for Entrepreneurial Development Programmes for the Youth

Dr. M. Ezhilarasan and Mrs. M. Selvalakshmi

Introduction

"An entrepreneur is someone who wants to add value to the economy by creating through leveraging his knowledge, his passion, his dreams and his desire. He is a catalyst for enormous change and can do so in a variety of different ways." —Ramesh Wadhwani, Aspect Development, i2 Corporation.

They are the ones who dare to dream the dreams, and then are foolish enough to try to make those dreams come true. Researchers distinguish an entrepreneur from a bread-winning business person based on his/her desire and propensity for growth.

Silicon Valley's most successful new immigrant entrepreneurs had been from countries like India and China. Sabhir Bhatia of Hotmail, Vinod Dham of Intel, Desh Deshpande of Cascade Communication and K.B. Chandrasekhar of Exodus are some who have created their footprints of success in Silicon Valley. The reasons could be multiple ranging from their educational background, middle class phenomenon, and lack of pressures or immediate reason to return to their home to their tremendous ambition.

Youth Potential for Entrepreneurship

Seven out of ten high school students say they want to start their own business according to a Gallup poll study done in conjunction with the Ewing Marion Kauffman Foundation. The dream of many high school students is to become self-employed. Results of a US Department of Commerce study show that youths' strong interest in starting a business derives from the freedom associated with being your own boss.

The dilemma is that these students are not getting the kind of entrepreneurial training and focus they need.

Eighty-six per cent of the students surveyed rated themselves very poor to fair on their knowledge of entrepreneurship and business.

Eighty-five per cent indicated they believed it was important to receive entrepreneurship education.

Seventy-nine per cent said they wanted to know more and they would be willing to take more classes to get the information. This reveals the burning untapped potential in youth.

Assets of Youth

Youth can contribute to the society thorough their positive attributes like:

- *(a)* Energy, Enthusiasm, and Willingness and open mind to learn.
- *(b)* Response to high expectations.
- *(c)* Understanding of Technology systems.
- *(d)* Loyalty.
- *(e)* New ways of working and thinking.

All this and more make them more suitable and apt to be trained extensively for a successful and adventurous future as an entrepreneur.

Why Training is Required?

What do we do when our vehicle which was giving 100 km mileage at the time of purchase gives 60 kms per litre after 3 years of usage?

Do we fuel it more?
Buy a new one?
Avoid using the vehicle for long distances?

No, rather we give it to a mechanic to service the vehicle. That is where the vehicle is cleaned and fine-tuned for a better performance. So is the essence of training to an aspiring individual. Proper and systematic training can mould him by refining his ideas, lubricating his thoughts and work process and help him to improve his effectiveness and efficiency.

Queries to be Handled

The value such as selfless hard work without desire for self-promotion is a key attribute to achieve success. However as per the quote "Behind every creative man there is a friend, an associate, or a co-worker who helps the man of ability to survive the blows of fate," triggers are required to fuel the journey of Entrepreneurship.

Starters have problems in finding a suitable path to embark. This is because of the unanswered queries such as:

(a) What attributes will fuel the success?
(b) Is it hard work, timing, education, dedication or is it plain luck?
(c) How to establish a start up?
(d) How to germinate ideas?
(e) What are the first few steps to build one's empire?
(f) How to build and lead teams?
(g) Where will the money come from?
(h) What are the pathways of people who have achieved success?
(i) What is the road block one might encounter?
(j) What sacrifices should one make to create a worthwhile history?

Answer to such questions with adequate examples will no doubt serve as a guiding light in their path. It will give them a sense of direction and intuition to see where the big opportunities are and how to explore them.

Core Areas for Entrepreneurial Training

Young people need to be trained in some certain areas to ensure their long term success in the competitive world.

The competencies they need to acquire are:

(a) To identify, organize, plan and allocate resources.
(b) To work with others.
(c) To acquire and use information.
(d) To understand complex inter-relationships.
(e) To work with a variety of technologies.

The core skills they need to be trained are:

(a) To read, write, and perform arithmetic and mathematical operations.
(b) To listen and speak.
(c) To think creatively, make decisions, solve problems, visualize, know how to learn and reason.

(*d*) To display responsibility, self-esteem, sociability, self-management, integrity and honesty.

What is of key importance now is to identify a more interesting learning project and an innovative way to teach technical skills to the budding entrepreneurs.

Training Methodology

Entrepreneurial training has over three decades of history in our country. The topics of importance were:

(*a*) Achievement motivation.
(*b*) Information or support environment.
(*c*) Business opportunity identification.
(*d*) Business plan preparation.
(*e*) Managerial function.

Technology today is more a driver of business strategy than a tool to implement the strategy. Internet has created seemingly unlimited opportunity for new businesses. Bearing this in mind, technology has to be incorporated in the training modules.

"The true power of growing any enterprise is 5 per cent technology and 95 per cent psychology" – Hatim Tyabji, Chairman and CEO (1986-1998), Verifone.

Entrepreneurial training should therefore focus on generating awareness, developing attributes and providing the necessary pathways. Delegation is critical for growth. Therefore, developing relevant attitude of delegation becomes important. Half-baked efforts in generating awareness could lead to differences and difficulties in building the right attitude.

In its efforts to foster and support entrepreneurship, The Indus Entrepreneurs (TIE) functions with three objectives, networking, mentoring entrepreneurs and integrating with main stream society. The firm ensures that the *Gurus* are willing and able to give the time and energy necessary to make their disciples successful. Their prime role is to bridge the gap between financial, marketing, technical, legal and networking strengths of the youth. Thus an effective way to channel the energies and ideas of the younger professional apprentices has to be worked out.

Conclusion

"Give a man a fish - You feed him for a day; Teach a man to fish - You feed him for his life".

Young people from disadvantaged backgrounds may face several impediments in achieving their dreams. 'Nuts and bolts' of the entrepreneurial world should be known and adequate insight has to be given on the innovative and successful management skills utilized by them which would enable them to move mountains. The brain power of the visionaries has to be mustered to facilitate their amazing achievements as entrepreneurs.

REFERENCES

Donald L. Sexton and Upton N. Bowman (1991). *Entrepreneurship: Creativity and Growth*, New York: Macmillan.

Gurmeet Maroola, *The Entrepreneurial Connection-East Meets West in the Silicon Valley*, Tata McGraw Hill.

K.V.S.M.Krishna. Bridging the Gap: Conceptual Paradigms and Training for Entrepreneurial Development, *The Journal of Entrepreneurship*, Vol. 12, No.1, January-June 2003, pp. 90-116.

http://www.edtecinc.com
www.neighborhoodnetworks.org

31

Training for Unemployed Educated Youth Under PMRY Scheme

Mr. R. Ayyamperumal

Introduction

Prime Minister's Rozgar Yojana was launched on 2nd October 1993 to assist educated unemployed youth to set up self-employment ventures. The scheme targeted for setting up of nearly 7 lakh enterprises and consequent employment generation to more than one million educated unemployed youth in the last four years of the 8th Five Year Plan. Initially, the scheme was implemented only in the urban areas of the country. Since 1994-95, it is in operation in both urban as well as rural areas. The scheme continued in the 9th Five Year Plan with the plan target of 11.00 lakh beneficiaries with annual target of 2.20 lakh beneficiaries. The PMRY is continuing in the 10th Five Year Plan also with the plan target of 11.00 lakh beneficiaries.

Common Minimum Programme (CMP) of the UPA Government envisages creation of additional employment opportunities in the rural non-farm sector. Accordingly, the target for the year 2004-05 and 2005-06 under the Yojana has been enhanced from 2.20 lakh beneficiaries to 2.50 lakh beneficiaries per annum.

Objective of PMRY

The PMRY aimed to provide employment to more than a million persons by setting up of 7 lakhs micro enterprises by the educated unemployed youth during the last four years of VIII Five Year Plan *i.e.* 1993-94 to 1996-97. The Scheme has been continuing in the X Five Year Plan. It relates to the setting up of the self-employment ventures in all economically viable projects (except direct agricultural operations). The Scheme also seeks to associate reputed non-governmental organisations in implementation of PMRY Scheme especially in the selection, training of entrepreneurs and preparation of project profiles.

Target Group/Eligibility

1. Age

(i) 18 to 35 years for all educated unemployed.
(ii) 18 to 40 for all educated unemployed in North-East States, Himachal Pradesh, Uttaranchal and J & K.
(iii) 18 to 45 years for Scheduled Castes/Scheduled Tribes, Ex-servicemen, Physically Disabled and Women.

2. Educational Qualification

VIII pass. Preference will be given to those who have been trained for any trade in Government recognized/approved institutions for duration of at least six months.

3. Family Income

Neither the income of the beneficiary along with the spouse nor the income of parents of the beneficiaries shall exceed Rs. 40,000/- per annum.

4. Residence

Permanent resident of the area for at least 3 years. (Relaxed for married men in Meghalaya and for married women in rest of the country. For married men in Meghalaya and for married women in rest of the country, the residency criteria apply to the spouse or in-laws.)

5. Defaulter

Should not be a defaulter to any nationalized bank/financial institution/cooperative bank. Further, a person already assisted under other subsidy, linked Government schemes would not be eligible under this scheme.

6. Activities Covered

All economically viable activities including agriculture and allied activities but excluding direct agricultural operations like raising crop, purchase of manure etc.

7. Project Cost

Rs.1.00 lakh for business sector. Rs. 2.00 lakh for other activities, loan to be of composite nature. If two or more eligible persons join together in a partnership, project upto Rs.10.00 lakh are covered. Assistance shall be limited to individual admissibility.

8. Subsidy and Margin Money

Subsidy will be limited to 15 per cent of the project cost subject to ceiling of Rs. 7,500 per entrepreneur. Banks will be allowed to take margin money from the entrepreneur varying from 5 per cent to 16.25 per cent of the project cost so as to make the total of the subsidy and the margin money equal to 20 per cent of the project cost.

9. Collateral

No collateral for units in industry sector with project cost upto Rs. 2.00 lakh (the loan ceiling under the PMRY). For partnership projects under Industry Sector, the exemption limit for abstention of collateral security will be Rs. 5.00 lakh per borrower account. For units in service and business sector no collateral for project up to Rs. 1.00 lakh. Exemption from collateral in case of partnership project will also be limited to an amount of Rs. 1.00 lakh per person participating in the project.

10. Rate of Interest and Repayment

Normal rate of interest shall be charged. Repayment schedule may range between 3 to 7 years after an initial moratorium as may be prescribed.

11. Reservation

Preference should be given to weaker sections including women. The scheme envisages 22.5 per cent reservation for SC/ST and 27 per cent for Other Backward Classes (OBCs). In case SC/ST/OBC candidates are not available, States/UTs Government will be competent to consider other categories of candidates under PMRY.

12. Training

Each entrepreneur whose loan is sanctioned is provided training as per details given below:

(*i*) For industry sector: Duration: 15-20 working days.
Stipend: Rs. 300/- } Per beneficiary
Training expenditure: Rs. 700/- } Per beneficiary

(ii)	For service and business sector:	Duration: 7-10 working days. Stipend: Rs. 150/- Training expenditure: Rs. 350/-	Per beneficiary

13. Implementing Agency

The District Industry Centres and Directorate of Industries are mainly responsible for implementation of the Scheme along with the banks.

Objectives

(a) *General Objective:* To Study About the Training Given to the Unemployed Educated Youth Under PMRY Scheme.

(b) *Specific Objective:* To Study the impact/effectiveness on training based on Age, Sex, Education and Experience.

Research Methodology

(a) *Research Type:* The research is descriptive in nature.

(b) *Nature of Data:* The data collected is primary in nature.

(c) *Tool for Data Collection:* The data were collected by Interview Schedule.

(d) *Sample Size:* For the purpose of research the sample taken is 67 from SUN Computers, Virudhunagar—all the members of two PMRY training Programme in this year.

(e) *Sample Unit:* The respondents are the Educated youth undergoing training to get Loan under PMRY Scheme.

(f) *Method of Data Analysis:* The Collected data were analyzed using Percentage method and Bi-Variate Tables.

(g) *Sampling Technique:* Convenience Sampling.

Analysis and Interpretation

Table–31.1
Age and Confidence Level in Finance

Age	*Total*	*Highly Improved*	*%*	*Improved*	*%*	*Not Improved*	*%*
25 to 30	28	3	10.71	22	78.57	3	10.71
30 to 35	15	1	6.67	14	93.33	0	0
Above 35	4	0	0	4	100	0	0
18-25	20	5	25	13	65	2	10

From Table 31.1 we can infer that in the age group Above 35-100 per cent, 30-35 – 93.33 per cent of the respondent's confidence level in Finance has improved.

Table–31.2

Age and Confidence Level in Marketing

Age	*Total*	*Highly Improved*	%	*Improved*	%	*Not Improved*	%
25 to 30	28	8	28.57	20	71.42	0	0
30 to 35	15	6	40	9	60	0	0
Above 35	4	0	0	4	100	0	0
18-25	20	5	25	13	65	2	10

From Table 31.2 we can infer that in the age group Above 35-100 per cent of the respondent's confidence level in marketing have Improved.10 per cent in the age group 18-25 have said Not Improved.

Table–31.3

Age and Exposure in Marketing

Age	*Total*	*Not Good*	%	*Good*	%	*Very Good*	%
25 to 30	28	0	0	15	53.57	13	46.43
30 to 35	15	0	0	8	53.33	7	46.67
Above 35	4	0	0	3	75	1	25
18-25	20	0	0	13	65	7	35

From Table 31.3 we can infer that in all age group none of the respondent's exposure to marketing in Not Good.

Table-31.4

Age and Level of Understanding Finance Topics

Age	*Total*	*Good*	%	*Not Good*	%	*Very Good*	%
25 to 30	28	21	75	0	0	7	25
30 to 35	15	8	53.55	3	20	4	26.45
Above 35	4	1	25	2	50	1	25
18-25	20	12	60	0	0	8	40

From Table 31.4 we can infer that in the age group 25 to 30 – 75 per cent of the respondent's level of understanding is Good. In the age group 30 to 35 – 20 per cent, Above 35 – 50 per cent respondent's level of understanding Finance topic is Not Good.

Table-31.5

Age and Reason for Attending this Programme

Age	*Total*	*Certificate*	*%*	*Loan*	*%*	*Others*	*%*	*Training*	*%*
25 to 30	28	14	50	8	28.57	2	7.14	4	14.28
30 to 35	15	7	46.66	7	46.66	1	6.67	0	0
Above 35	4	1	25	1	25	2	50	0	0
18-25	20	8	40	5	25	1	5	6	30

From Table 31.5 we can infer the reason for attending PMRY under 18 to 25 years 40 per cent attend for Certificate and 14.28 per cent for Training, 25 to 30 years 50 per cent attend for certificate, 30 to 35 years 46.66 per cent respondents attend for Certificate and Loan, Above 35 years 50 per cent attend due to other reasons (for Husband).None in the age Above 30 attend for training.

Table-31.6

Age and Opinion Regarding the Timing of the Programme

Age	*Total*	*Yes*	*%*	*No*	*%*
25 to 30	28	24	85.71	4	14.29
30 to 35	15	10	66.66	5	33.37
Above 35	4	3	75	1	25
18 - 25	20	17	85	3	15

From Table 31.6 we can infer the opinion regarding the timing, 30 to 35 years 33.37 per cent, Above 35 – 25 per cent of respondents say it is Not Comfortable.

Table-31.7

Education and Confidence in Marketing

Education	*Total*	*Highly Improved*	*%*	*Improved*	*%*	*Not Improved*	*%*
Degree	14	6	42.85	8	57.15	0	0
Diploma	10	1	10	9	90	0	0
High School	7	4	57.14	3	42.86	0	0

(Contd.)

Education	Total	Highly Improved	%	Improved	%	Not Improved	%
Hr.Sec.School	30	8	26.67	22	73.33	0	0
Less than 8	4	0	0	4	100	0	0
PG	2	0	0	0	0	2	100

From Table 31.7 we can infer the confidence level in marketing, 100 per cent improved in Less than 8th standard, Higher Secondary School 73.33 per cent say Improved, High School 57.14 per cent say Highly Improved, Diploma 90 per cent say Improved, Degree 57.15 say Improved, PG 100 per cent say Not Improved.

Table-31.8
Education and Exposure in Marketing

Education	Total	Not Good	%	Good	%	Very Good	%
Degree	14	0	0	8	57.14	6	42.86
Diploma	10	0	0	7	70	3	30
High School	7	0	0	5	71.43	2	28.57
Hr. Sec. School	30	0	0	14	46.67	16	53.33
Less than 8	4	0	0	3	75	1	25
PG	2	0	0	2	100	0	0

From Table 31.8 we can infer Exposure given in Marketing, A majority of 100 per cent in PG say Good, 53.33 per cent in Higher Secondary School say Very Good, none said not Good.

Table-31.9
Education and Level of Understanding Finance

Education	Total	Good	%	Not Good	%	Very Good	%
Degree	14	3	21.43	0	0	11	78.57
Diploma	10	7	70	0	0	3	30
High School	7	6	85.71	0	0	1	14.29
Hr. Sec. School	30	25	83.33	2	6.67	3	10
Less than 8	4	1	25	3	75	0	0
PG	2	0	0	0	0	2	100

From Table 31.9 we can infer the level of understanding Finance Topics, 100 per cent in PG say Very Good; 75 per cent in less than 8th Standard say Not Good.

Table–31.10
Education and Reason for Attending the Programme

Education	*Total*	*Certi-ficate*	*%*	*Loan*	*%*	*Others*	*%*	*Training*	*%*
Degree	14	8	57.14	4	28.57	0	0	2	14.29
Diploma	10	6	60	2	20	2	20	0	0
High School	7	4	57.14	3	12.86	0	0	0	0
Hr. Sec. School	30	11	36.67	8	26.67	3	10	8	26.66
Less than 8	4	1	25	2	50	1	25	0	0
PG	2	0	0	2	100	0	0	0	0

From Table 31.10 we can infer the reason for attending PMRY programme, 100 per cent of PG attend, 50 per cent of Less than 8th attend for Loan; 57.14 per cent in Degree and Diploma, 60 per cent in High School education attend for Certificate.

Table–31.11
Education and Sufficiency of Training (Overall)

Education	*Total*	*Highly*	*%*	*Not*	*%*	*Suffi-cient*	*%*	*Very*	*%*	*Not at all*	*%*
Degree	14	1	7.14	0	0	12	85.72	1	7.14	0	0
Diploma	10	1	10	0	0	8	80	1	10	0	0
High School	7	0	0	0	0	7	100	0	0	0	0
Hr.Sec.School	30	6	20	2	6.67	18	60	4	13.13	0	0
Less than 8	4	0	0	0	0	4	100	0	0	0	0
PG	2	0	0	2	100	0	0	0	0	0	0

From Table 31.11 we can infer the Over all sufficiency of training, A majority of 100 per cent in High School and Hr. Sec. School, 80 per cent in Diploma, 85.72 per cent in Degree say sufficient; 100 per cent in PG say Not Sufficient; None say Not at all sufficient.

From Table 31.12 we can infer the reason for attending the programme, a majority 63.63 per cent in 2-4 years, 72.72 per cent in 4-6

Table-31.12

Experience and Reason for Attending the Program

Work Exp.	*Total*	*Certi-ficate*	*%*	*Loan*	*%*	*Others*	*%*	*Training*	*%*
2-4	11	7	63.63	2	18.18	2	18.18	0	0
4-6	11	8	72.72	3	27.28	0	0	0	0
Less than 2 Yrs.	21	10	47.62	8	38.10	2	9.52	1	4.76
More than 6 Yrs.	6	3	50	3	50	0	0	0	0
No Experience	18	2	11.11	5	27.78	2	11.11	9	50

years, 47.62 per cent in Less than a Year join for Certificate; 50 per cent in more than 6 years join for Loan and Certificate; 50 per cent with No Exp. Join for Training.

Table-31.13

Experience and Sufficiency of Training (Overall)

Work Exp.	*Total*	*Highly*	*%*	*Not*	*%*	*Sufficient*	*%*	*Very*	*%*
2-4	11	0	0	1	9.10	7	63.63	3	27.28
4-6	11	0	0	1	9.10	9	81.80	1	9.10
less than 2 Yrs.	21	1	4.76	0	0	20	95.24	0	0
More than 6 Yrs.	6	1	16.67	0	0	5	83.33	0	0
No Experience	18	6	33.33	2	11.11	8	44.45	2	11.11

From Table 31.13 we can infer the Overall sufficiency of Training, 9.10 per cent with 2-4 and 4-6 yrs say Not Sufficient; 11.11 per cent with No Experience say Not Sufficient.

Table-31.14

Sex and Sufficiency of Training (Overall)

Sex	*Total*	*Highly Sufficient*	*%*	*Not Sufficient*	*%*	*Sufficient*	*%*	*Very Sufficient*	*%*
Female	28	4	14.29	0	0	23	82.14	1	3.57
Male	39	4	10.26	4	10.26	26	66.66	5	12.82

From Table 31.14 we can infer the Overall Sufficiency of Training, 10.26 per cent of male said Not Sufficient; none said Not Sufficient.

Table-31.15
Sex and Confidence in Marketing

Sex	*Total*	*Highly Improved*	*%*	*Improved*	*%*	*Not Improved*	*%*
Female	28	10	35.71	18	64.29	0	0
Male	39	9	23.08	28	71.79	2	5.13

From Table 31.15 we can infer the Confidence in Marketing, 5.13 per cent (2) Male say Not Improved.

Table–31.16
Sex and Suitability of Marketing Examples

Sex	*Total*	*Not Always Suitable*	*%*	*Suitable*	*%*	*Very Suitable*	*%*
Female	28	1	3.57	8	28.57	19	67.86
Male	39	2	5.13	24	61.54	13	33.33

From Table 31.16 we can infer the suitability of marketing examples, 1 male and 2 female say Not Always Suitable.

Table–31.17
Sex and Reason for Attending this Programme

Sex	*Total*	*Certificate*	*%*	*Loan*	*%*	*Others*	*%*	*Training*	*%*
Female	28	9	32.14	9	32.14	4	14.29	6	21.43
Male	39	21	53.85	12	30.76	2	5.13	4	10.26

From Table 31.17 we can infer the reason for joining the programme, 32.14 per cent of Male join for Loan and Certificate; 53.85 per cent Female join for Certificate; 21.43 per cent Female for Training.

Table–31.18
Sex and Timing Suitability

Sex	*Total*	*Yes*	*%*	*No*	*%*
Female	28	25	89.29	3	10.71
Male	39	29	74.36	10	25.64

From Table 31.18 we can infer the Suitability of Timing, 25.64 per cent Male and 10.71 per cent of Female say Not Suitable.

Table–31.19
Sex and Understanding of Finance Topics

Sex	*Total*	*Good*	*%*	*Not Good*	*%*	*Very Good*	*%*
Female	28	14	50	5	17.86	9	32.14
Male	39	28	71.79	0	0	11	28.21

From Table 31.19 we can infer the Understanding of Finance Topics, 17.86 per cent Female say Not Good.

Findings

Based on Age

1. In the age group Above 35 – 100 per cent, 30-35 – 93.33 per cent of the respondent's confidence level in Finance has improved.
2. In the age group Above 35 – 100 per cent of the respondent's confidence level in marketing have Improved. 10 per cent in the age group 18-25 have said Not Improved.
3. The main reason for joining is Certificate and Loan.
4. Their Exposure and Confidence level in marketing have improved. Except 18-25 years.
5. Between the age 25-35 they say the Timing is not comfortable.

Based on Education

1. The Confidence level for PG respondents have Not Improved.
2. None have said that the exposure given in Marketing topics is Not Good.
3. 75 per cent (3) in less than 8th Standard say Not Good in understanding Finance topics.
4. 100 per cent of PG attend, 50 per cent of Less than 8th attend for Loan.
5. 100 per cent (2) of PG say that the Overall training is Not Sufficient.

Based on Experience

1. Reason for attending the programme, a majority 63.63 per cent in 2-4 years, 72.72 per cent in 4-6 years, 47.62 per cent in Less than a Year join for Certificate; 50 per cent in more than 6 years join for Loan and Certificate; 50 per cent with No Experience Join for Training.

2. The Overall Sufficiency of Training, 9.10 per cent with 2-4 and 4-6 years say Not Sufficient;11.11 per cent with No Experience say Not Sufficient.

Based on Sex

1. Overall sufficiency of training, 10.26 per cent of male say Not Sufficient.
2. 5.13 per cent (2) Male say that the Confidence in Marketing has Not Improved.
3. 32.14 per cent of Male join for Loan and Certificate; 53.85 per cent Female join for Certificate; 21.43 per cent Female for Training.
4. 25.64 per cent Male and 10.71 per cent of Female opinion regarding Timing as Not Suitable due to their own business, Already employed, House Work.
5. In the Understanding of Finance Topics, 17.86 per cent Female say Not Good.

Others

1. Respondents have suggested to include topics like Project Appraisal, Project Feasibility and to give exposure to various range of projects.
2. 83.33 per cent (10 out of 12) respondents say Highly Sufficient; None say Not Sufficient regarding the Practical Training given and its sufficiency.

Conclusion

As per the government effort for self-employment of the unemployed educated youth, the training programme is serving its purpose by building confidence in becoming an entrepreneur. As per the PMRY Scheme the training is given and some have suggested including certain topics. In my study I was found that around 15 per cent of the respondents join this programme for practical training in the area like DTP, Stitching, Cooking and visits to factories making Candles, Bathi etc., The training programme at Virudhunagar is successful and at least 75 persons are benefited every year. The main draw back is in getting loan from banks who insist on collateral security, so few entrepreneurs are killed in the seed and if supported after proper project appraisal they would be a ***BEAUTIFUL ROSE***.

REFERENCES

http://ari.nic.in/pmrydetail.htm

http://megindustry.nic.in/citizen2.htm

http://www.smallindustryindia.com/schemes/pmry.html

http://www.smallindustryindia.com/schemes/wenterpre.htm

Index